COLLECTED T

B. B. ██████.
London '97

C.H. SISSON

Collected Translations

CARCANET

First published in 1996 by
Carcanet Press Limited
402-406 Corn Exchange Buildings
Manchester M4 3BY

A CIP catalogue record for this book
is available from the British Library.
ISBN 1 85754 292 4

The publisher acknowledges financial assistance
from the Arts Council of England.

Set in 10pt Palatino by Bryan Williamson, Frome
Printed and bound in England by SRP Ltd, Exeter

Contents

Preface

This is a miscellaneous volume. A translator can, at best, offer no more than an approach to a poem in a foreign language – one which does not preclude others, above all the essential one of reading, or at least fishing in, the original text. This volume contains, interspersed in it, adaptations as well as what would generally be thought of as translations, and there is a respectable history of such practices in past centuries. One's perception of English verse can only be sharpened by excursions into other poetries, and the great masters of European literature, ancient and modern, must have first place in this. The English poet of the twentieth century is in a great succession, and all these popularisations of 'creativity' and 'self-expression' which barely deign a backward glance are no help either to the reader or the writer of poetry.

It may safely be asserted that there never was a poet who was not profoundly affected by poetry, not in the sense merely of having been open to identifiable influences, some of them perhaps superficial, but in the sense of finding that he belonged to a far-spreading company which, for all its individual diversity, shares some modes of perception which compel the linkage with words and rhythms which lie close to the heart of every language. The affinity between poets even of very different experience is no doubt part of the reason which was driven so many, through long centuries, to attempt translation, particularly of those masters who have profoundly affected all the literatures of Europe, to say nothing of variously motivated snatches at contemporaries and near contemporaries in other languages.

This general presentation of a well-known literary phenomenon is of course in some sense an apology for my own performance as a poet. My first wholly adult poem was written on a troopship in 1943: my first verse translations were done in an army camp perhaps eighteen months later. These translations were my *Versions and Perversions of Heine*, in which some of the perversions unmistakably reflect my life at the time. My next major attempt at verse translation came in 1964-5, and was – at first – of odd bits of Catullus and, finally, of the whole of his extant work. Catullus is a model of clarity and directness, and my interest in him was consonant with what I hoped was the drift of my own work – by which I do not implicate our respective subject-matters, though the verses I wrote by way of Preface and Valediction show that I felt some affinities even there.

A new epoch in my life as a translator – as indeed generally – began when I escaped from a busy and time-devouring office. As before, my prey was work with which I had had an acquaintance for many years. The *Ars Poetica* was my first victim, and the version I produced bears witness – some might say, too emphatically – to what I saw as the basic identity of the problems of the poet in Augustan Rome and in the London of our own day. It was followed by Lucretius's *De Rerum Natura*, which I had long been aware of: the Roman poet's openness of mind had not been rendered out of date by the scientific advances of modern times. After a chance diversion with *Some Tales of La Fontaine*, I returned to what is almost certainly the most fundamental poem, for the twentieth century, of all the European succession – *The Divine Comedy* of Dante, whose lucidity is exemplary for our own century, full as that is of shallow and extended talk. This was followed, several years later, by the *Aeneid* of Virgil, mostly neglected since my schooldays, though more or less immediately after the Catullus I had done a rhymed version of the *Eclogues* and variations on one or two themes from the *Aeneid* itself.

That does not complete the list of my long translations, which have included three plays of Racine, the *Song of Roland*, and a play of Plautus, and all these works have been interspersed with – on the whole unrelated, and never directly related – poems of my own. In all these longer works is writ large what appears in the shorter translations in this volume – an irresistible, or at any rate unresisted attempt to get close to the work of foreign poets and to understand what they were saying, in their different times and places, in ways which make sense here and now. My reading and writing of poetry have always been closely allied. I seek communication with the masters of other places and times, and I try to say what I have to say in such a manner that it may be apprehensible by those who have access to more or less of the poetic continuum themselves.

All the translator's prefaces I have written for my long translations present in some form more or less of the view I am trying to put here. The volume of miscellaneous pieces now before the reader is, naturally, not the fruit of any continuous process of design, but it represents a series of moments, spread out over more than half a century, when my casual browsing over poets ancient or modern reached a point of affinity – or perhaps I should more modestly say, of subjective interest – such that more or less of what the poet was saying found its way into my note-book, in such verse as was within my reach at the time.

My own verse has been profoundly affected by the interests and aspirations indicated by my choice of matter to translate, and what I have been able to do, and such understanding as I have been able to achieve of the nature of poetry, has depended in no small degree on my non-resistance, over the decades, to the temptations of translation. No one, certainly, will be the more ignorant, or the worse poet, for such non-resistance.

VERSIONS AND PERVERSIONS
OF HEINE

Warning

Verletze nicht durch kalten Ton

Do not injure with a sneer
The youth, however shy and odd,
Who comes to you and asks for help
For he may be the Son of God.

And you may see him once again,
The light around his head ablaze;
Then, when he judges and condemns,
Your eye will not withstand his gaze.

Silesian Weavers

In düstern Auge keine Träne

Not a tear in their dark eyes
They sit weaving, and one cries –
Germany, we weave your shroud;
We're weaving it with curses loud.
    We weave, we weave.

A curse for God, to whom we told
Our pain in hunger and in cold:
But he did nothing; heavenly love
Loved best, it seems, to put us off.
    We weave, we weave.

And curse the king; the idle sot
Though touched, could not improve our lot.
He taxed us, treated us like dung
And in the end he had us hung.
    We weave, we weave.

A curse upon the lying name
Of fatherland: it brought us shame;
Rot in the guts and in the head
But never brought us peace or bread.
    We weave, we weave.

We weave till we are worn away,
Weaving your grave-sheet, night and day.
Germany, we weave your shroud
With bitter heart and curses loud.
    We weave, we weave.

In October, 1849

Gelegt hat sich der starke Wind

The wind's no longer blowing wild:
All is still as still can be.
Germania, God bless the child,
Is once more playing round the Christmas-tree.

We are content: the hearth-fire burns
And every higher wish deceives.
The swallow, that loves peace, returns
And builds once more beneath the eaves.

Peacefully sleep both wood and stream
With the soft moonlight over all.
Occasionally a shot rings out, a scream –
They've put a friend of yours against the wall.

Perhaps they found him, with a gun,
A bit uncertain what to say.
(Not all have got the wit to run
As Horace did, and throw their arms away.)

Another bang! And this time, possibly,
It's crackers at a Goethe celebration.
It's nice to know that we are free
To enjoy at least this form of consolation.

And Liszt pops up again: how nice to see
This hero with us once again.
We thought him dead in Hungary
But, though a hero, he has not been slain.

4

Franz is alive, and in old age
Will tell his family, never bored
To hear of grandpa's martial rage
'And thus did my heroic sword.'

When I hear of Hungary
My heart swells till my skin's too small.
My hot blood rages like the sea;
The name sounds like a trumpet-call.

And when I hear about the wrong
We did them: how, against all odds
They fought, I hear once more the song
Formerly called the twilight of the gods.

Though the new song may be without
A hero, still it is the same:
The fighting and the final rout;
All that is altered is the name.

The same results from the same passion –
The flags fly bravely, but of course
The hero, in the usual fashion
At last's defeated by mere witless force.

This time the ox has made a pact
With the dumb bear, to get your blood.
But courage, Magyar: by this act
You suffer, but we too eat mud.

Plain wild beasts fought you till you broke.
It was a battle, and you lost;
But we have fallen beneath the yoke
Of wolves and swine, to our enduring cost.

Swine, wolves, and sneaking dogs: I can
Scarcely endure the victor's stink.
But quiet, poet: you're a man
But you are sick; rest now, and save your ink.

Ich mache jetzt mein Testament

For months I have been feeling ill;
I now sit down and make my will.
Suffering such torment and such wrong
It's queer I have survived so long.

Louisa, you revolting flirt you
I leave you, as a prize for virtue
Twelve old shirts, a hundred fleas
And thirty thousand blasphemies.

And you, whose taste for good advice
Reached the proportions of a vice,
Take this advice on my behalf:
Marry a cow and get a calf.

What lusty fellow shall inherit
My faith and deep religious spirit?
Give it tax-free to Mr Gandhi
Or anyone who finds it handy.

Official promises and hopes
– A bubble made with beauty soaps –
I leave that fidei defensor
Who calls himself the unit censor.

The deeds that I have never done
By which our freedom should be won
I leave the heroes of the nation
With a good cure for constipation.

Item, I leave those two or three
Who cared for human liberty
A pair of ear-plugs each, or more, in
Case they wake themselves with snoring.

I leave the guardians of our morals
This and the other side the Urals
A colt revolver (but not loaded)
Disused, the barrel well corroded.

Lastly, if any legatee
Rudely declines his legacy,
Send it on, bristling with priorities,
To the British military authorities.

Moriturus

Erstorben ist in meiner Brust

In my etiolated head
As in my body, joy is dead.
Hatred of evil, the pretence
Of freedom and the very sense
Of others' needs as of my own
Have gone, and left my spirits stone.

The curtain falls, the end has come;
The German public hurries home.
They are not fools: they drink their wine
And eat their sausage and feel fine.
Oh! he was right, that noble spook

Who spat it out in Homer's book:
The smallest living Philistine
That ambles up and down the Rhine
Is happier far than I, the hero dread,
Great Pelides, hero indeed, but dead.

Es gibt zwei Sorten Ratten

There are two sorts of rat
The hungry and the fat.
The full and fat sort stay at home:
The hungry are inclined to roam.

They wander many thousand miles
And never stop between the whiles
They go right on and never stop
No sort of water holds them back.

They climb up all the mountains and
Swim any river in the land
And if some choke or die of drink
The others simply let them sink.

Rats, with their ill-bred perseverance
Present an impolite appearance:
They wear such proletarian hats
And looks as sinister as rats.

These bolshie rats, it's very odd,
Have no idea at all of God:
They don't baptise their progeny
Their wives are common property.

The sensual and degraded beast
Does nothing else but drink and feast,
Preferring binges, on the whole
To care of his immortal soul.

Further, these wild, free-thinking rats
Do not fear hell, or even cats;
Having no worldly goods, or few
Want to share out the world anew.

Reader, these wandering rats, I fear,
Just now, are coming very near:
It frightens me to hear them squealing!
Really the beasts are most unfeeling!

We're lost! ten thousand of them wait
For us outside the city gate.
The mayor and fathers of the city
Are at a loss: a dreadful pity!

Abandon your important airs
Not peals of bells, or even prayers

Or special powers and regulations
Or bombs and guns will save the nations.

You won't convince rats they are free
By parliamentary oratory.
You don't catch rats with syllogisms
With soph- or any other isms.

The hungry belly, you will find
Is different from the well-fed mind:
It gloats for hours upon roast beef
But likes your arguments quite brief.

For fish and chips and cake and jelly
Satisfy the public belly
Better than a Mirabeau
Or any talker since Cicero.

Wir Burgermeister und Senat

We elders, governors of the city,
Touched with a swollen head, or pity,
Wishing to better your condition
Instruct you in complete submission.

It's foreigners and such-like weeds
Mainly, of course, who sow the seeds
Of disaffection: such irrationals
Thank God, are rarely British nationals.

And in the main they're atheist,
For anyone who shakes his fist
At God, will with his earthly double
Quite quickly find himself in trouble.

Whether you're Christian or a Jew
Obey your God and policeman too:
Say your prayers and do not mock
And be in bed by eight o'clock.

And any meeting, without fail,
Break up at once or go to gaol.
Let no one in the streets at night
Be seen about without a light.

All firearms will be kept in store
Locked up behind the guard-room door
And every dangerous munition
Will be preserved in like condition.

Anyone reasoning a lot
Will expeditiously be shot
And reasonable dumb insolence
Will also be a grave offence.

Have trust in the authorities
Who always, always, try to please:
They will protect and save the nation –
You hold your tongue and know your station.

Die Briten zeigten sich sehr rüde

The British took a certain pride,
Brutal perhaps, in regicide.
King Charles's sleep was somewhat light
In Whitehall on that fatal night.
Before his window sang the clown:
He heard the scaffold hammered down.

The French were scarcely more polite
For they – one cannot but reproach
Then for this dreadful oversight –
Forgot to send the royal coach
For Louis, when they took his head:
They sent a taxi round instead.

And then poor Marie Antoinette,
When her turn came, what did she get?
A farm cart and, as maid of honour,

A working chap to wait upon her.
The widow Capet scowled and bit
Her heavy Hapsburg underlip.

The French and British, unlike us,
Of course, are very barbarous.
Even as terrorists we show
Ourselves as kindly, dumb and slow,
We have, for the monarchic notion
A pious and absurd devotion.

And there will be a frightful stir
When we behead our Emperor.
We shall lay carpets for his feet
And, through the flagged, respectful street
In an expensive limousine
Conduct him to the guillotine.

Und die Husaren lieb ich sehr

I love all kinds of soldier lads
Impartially. I'm very
Kind to them all, whether they wear
A bush-hat or a beret.

I love the chaps in armoured cars
Also the chaps in tanks,
Recruits and blokes with service in
Captains and Other Ranks.

The infantry I love, and love
Also the R.A.C.,
And I've slept many a pleasant night
With the artillery.

I love the Germans and the French
The Flemish and Walloons
I love the human being in
The patriotic coons.

It's all one what a man believes:
The Christian or Confucian
Is welcome to my bed if he's
Of vigorous constitution.

Philosophy and country are
Just articles of dress.
Away with them! I like to feel
The bare man on me press.

I'm human, and to human-kind
I'm anxious to give pleasure:
Those who have cash can pay at once
The rest can pay at leisure.

I've put out flowers before my tent
I wear my best apparel:
To add to these attractions I
Am tapping a new barrel.

Der Nachtwind durch die Luken pfeift

The night-wind whistles through the cracks
And blows about the attic:
The wretched couple in the bed
Look skinny and asthmatic.

One of these wretched people cries
'Oh, darling, put your arm
Around me, please, and kiss me too
For kissing keeps me warm.'

The other wretch replies: 'My dear
When I look in your eyes
I'm apt to think we have no cares –
Which isn't very wise.'

They kissed each other quite a lot:
They hugged each other, cried

And even laughed and sang and then
Apparently they died.

For when next day the P.A.C.
Official called, he said
(The panel doctor quite agreed)
That both of them were dead.

The doctor said he thought the cold
Combined, of course, with hunger
Sufficiently explained the fact
That they had lived no longer.

He added: 'When the frost sets in
The poor should put on woolly
Garments and eat good food: they don't
Appreciate that fully.'

Crapülinski und Waschlapski

Crapülinski and Waschlapski
Fought for freedom: They were Poles.
To the wicked Reds and Nazis
They opposed their Polish souls.

They fought bravely, after which they
Went to Paris, which was grand.
Living wasn't much less pleasant
Than dying for the Fatherland.

Like Achilles and Patroclus,
David and his Jonathan,
These two exiles loved each other
Kissed and cried 'Kochan! Kochan!'

Neither would betray the other;
They were two exalted souls.
After all were they not Polish,
Out of Poland, briefly, Poles?

13

Living in the same apartment
Sleeping in the self-same bed,
Scratching the same flea and sharing
Everything they thought and said.

Lunched and dined in the same café,
And so tender were they either
Could not bear the other paying
So the bill was paid by neither.

And the same good Henrietta
Washed for both. That is to say
Once a month she called upon them,
Took their dirty clothes away.

For they really did have linen,
Two shirts each (though full of holes) –
After all were they not Polish,
Absolutely true-blue Poles?

Now they're sitting by the fireside,
Heave a comfortable sigh
While outside, in snow and darkness
Trains and buses rattle by.

An enormous bowl of punch
(But without – this is most weird –
Sugar, lemon or hot water)
Has already disappeared.

The effect of the raw spirit
Is to bring tears to their eyes.
Overcome, poor Crapülinski
To his mate Waschlapski cries:

'If I only had in Paris
My fur coat and warm pyjamas,
Articles which now adorn the
Heroes of the German armies!'

Then Waschlapski answers him:
'Loyal fellow, how you dote

On the Polish fatherland,
Warm pyjamas and fur coat!

'Poland is not lost, dear comrade,
For our wives bear children still.
Our young spinsters too are fruitful –
Bear heroic brats at will.

'Heroes like the hero Sobski
Like Schelminski and Umotski
Roguavitch and Schubioski
And the hero Idiotski.'

from Germany: A Winter's Tale

Canto I: Im traurigen Monat November war's

When I set out for Germany
– How well I now remember –
The wind blew till the trees were bare;
It was in mid-November.

And when I crossed the frontier I
Was moved, I could not keep
My heart from beating heavily
And I began to weep.

And when I heard the German tongue
I felt absurdly pleased:
My heart beat patriotically
But in due course was eased.

Outside the carriage window stood
Seraphs with concertinas
Displaying soulful sentiments
In howls like a hyena's.

They sang the usual sort of stuff
All love and sacrifice:

15

The moral was that after death
Everything would be nice.

Such phrases as 'this vale of tears'
Occurred with frequency:
The good would be rewarded by
The Best Society.

They sang the usual pitiable
Song of renunciation
With which our noble leaders soothe
The idiotic nation.

I know these songs were written by
Old gents who like a skinful.
The sort that, as they drink their wine,
Declare that drinking's sinful.

I will invent a better song:
The general line is this –
Give every man on earth a chance
Of genuine heavenly bliss.

Why not be happy here on earth
And, as a start, ensure
That lazy bellies do not eat
What working hands procure?

There's bread enough for all on earth
Enlightenment and pleasure
With girls and lollipops and art
To fill our copious leisure.

Yes, lollipops for everyone,
And here! In others words
Heaven we can safely relegate
To God and the dicky-birds.

And, if we grow wings after death
And feel divinely frisky
We'll blow in on you one fine day
And you can give us whiskey.

A new song and a better song
In this, you will agree.
We might arrange the fun to last
For all eternity.

The virgin Europe is engaged
To freedom; and what bliss is
Ours when we see the lady swoon
Beneath his film-star kisses!

If they forgot to ask the church
To bless them when they bedded
It doesn't change the fact that they
Are well and truly wedded.

I celebrate their marriage and
I drink their health in oceans
Of third-class wine; and pray for them
In my devout devotions.

Since I arrived in Germany
I cannot get enough
Music and song and beer and girls.
– Yes, chum, I'm getting tough.

Canto II: Während die Kleine von Himmelslust

Now while the seraphs sang their songs
Of love and heavenly peace
My baggage was inspected by
The customs and the police.

They turned my cases upside down;
They had to make quite sure
I hadn't any whiskey or
Forbidden literature.

Poor idiots, looking in my case,
You're hopelessly misled:

17

The contraband you're looking for
I carry in my head.

I have there many articles
Which, I am bound to state,
It is your job as patriots
To tax or confiscate.

I also carry other things
That you would think your pigeon –
The principles and blue-prints of
A curious new religion.

My head is full, I warn you,
Of the most disgraceful books,
And if I chose to take them out
You would not like their looks.

For, in the Devil's library
There are not books more beastly:
Some of them are as dangerous as
The works of J.B. Priestley.

A fellow-passenger remarked,
Watching the police with pride,
'These gentlemen ensured that we
Were fully unified.

'They give us outward unity
Under their manly grip;
Spiritual unity we get,
Of course, from censorship.

'Identity of thought we get
From that fine institution –
Which gives us an unshakeable,
If stupid, constitution.'

Epilogue

Unser Grab erwärmt der Ruhm

The dead are comforted by fame.
Fools do a lot for a good name.
The sort of comfort that I like
Is that of any mangy tyke.
I like to feel a woman's lips
And like still more to feel her hips.
I like the warmth that comes from beer
Better than a posthumous tear.
If I can drink and eat my grub
In any dirty back-street pub
Among the common thieves and punks
The half-wits and the hopeless drunks;
If I can breathe and shuffle round
Even though snivelling and unsound
I'm better off than Thetis' son
Because, when all is said and done,
Was he not right, great Pelides?
The beggar counting out his fleas
Is in a less unpleasing fix
Than any ghost beside the Styx
Than even that world-famous ghost
That Homer celebrated most.

MISCELLANEOUS PIECES FROM SEVERAL CENTURIES

Augelletto selvaggio per stagione

At the right time a bird will sometimes sing
The sweetest verses in the proper way.
Another will sing loudly, and I not hear him,
For to sing loudly is not everything.
But, when the tune is soft and sweet I say
That is what makes a song; there is the art.
Few have it, there are many who pretend;
They make up all kinds of verses which are
Nothing or less than nothing in the end.
Yet we are to suppose that the world is so full
Of masters that there is no room for disciples.

attributed to St Peter Damian (1007-72)

Quis est hic

Who is this
Who beats at the door
Breaking the sleep of night,
Calling me, O
Beautiful virgin
my sister, my wife
My splendid diamond
Get out of bed quickly
To let me in
Sweetest.

I am
The great king's son,
Eldest and youngest,
Who, out of heaven
Have come to these shadows

To liberate
Prisoners' souls
I have supported death
And many injuries.

Soon I
Have left my bed
Run to draw the latch
So that for my lover
The whole house is open
And my mind sees most plainly
Whom it desires

But he
Had gone away already
Left the door
What could I
Miserable, what could I do?
Weeping,
Following the youth
Whose hands
Created man.

The city guards
Have found me, questioned me
Stripped off my clothes
Given me another cloak
Sung me
A song I did not know
It is by this
I come to the king's palace.

A Variation on Eustache Deschamps
(1340-1410)

You who live in this brilliant world today
And live in blazing strength and confidence,
Have you forgotten death, so trusting sense?
Those who preceded you have gone away,

Dust true to dust, false only to pretence,
You who live in this brilliant world today,
Have you forgotten death, so trusting sense?

Think of it now, for you will soon be grey,
And cold before you spend your life's last pence;
Your end will be in naked indigence.
You who live in this brilliant world today
And live in blazing strength and confidence,
Have you forgotten death, so trusting sense?

Two XV Century Songs

Della la riviére sont

Beyond the river there are
Three girls, all charming;
Beyond the river they are:
Then jump up and are away.

I lost, sitting here,
I lost, sitting here,
A cap, it was my friend's:
A cap, it was my friend's.

'And you have it' –
'And you're a liar' –
'Who has it then?' –
'We do not know.'

Beyond the river there are
Three girls, all charming;
Beyond the river they are;
Then jump up and are away.

Gentilz gallans de France

'Gentle soldiers of France,
Going to the wars,
Be so kind, I beg of you,
Say hullo to my friend.'

'How shall I say hullo?
I shall not recognize him.'
'That is easy to do,
For he is armed in white.

A white cross he has on,
His spurs are gilt,
And at the tip of his lance,
A point of silver gilt.'

'Then weep no more, my lovely,
For he has passed away;
He died in Brittany,
The Bretons killed him.

I saw his grave made
At the edge of a meadow;
I saw them sing for him,
Four monks, there were.

Antoine Héroet (1492-1568)

Epitaph on Louise de Savoie*

No, it is not I, passing traveller,
This bejewelled body you see lying here
Dead, as it is, awaiting burial,
It is a piece of nature, that is all.
It is not I, this body that lies dead,
Nor was I ever such as here is laid;

* Louise de Savoie (1477-1531) was the mother of Francois I and of Marguerite de Navarre.

What provokes tears and makes the passer sigh
Was mine indeed, but yet was never I.
It's true indeed that sixty years ago
God sent me in this flesh, so different now,
To govern and direct it as it grew,
Moved, and was seen by others as by you.
This body was a thing that I possessed,
Conducting it as seemed to me the best
In that condition to which I was called,
Whether well or ill he knows, the Father of all.
God is my judge and he will deal justly;
Leave it to him to pass judgement upon me.
If I found ways out of danger, and made
The country safe and criminals afraid,
If Frenchmen in the end could thank me for
Their France delivered from incessant war,
And if by treaty, promise and alliance,
Convention, ransom and deliverance,
A woman in a short time could release
Christendom from whatever threatened peace;
If you have seen me use my wits to reign,
The fact of my success at least is plain,
But your knowledge, tainted by human weakness,
Ignores the rights and wrongs of my success,
Which nobody can know unless he has
Turned back and found himself as once he was,
I mean so far as understanding goes,
A thing available only to those
Whose souls are purged of shadows, and who find
The love of God, and with it their whole mind,
As a man may if he will only glance
At his own limits and his ignorance.
O traveller, if this death touches you,
Consider first how small a part you knew;
You do not know whether to laugh or cry,
Whether to hope to live or wish to die
When you see anything that happens here,
Because the worst may give no cause for fear.
If you will pity me, like the multitude,
I will explain why, though the Beatitude
Blesses the meek, my soul has yet allowed
These honours which seem fittest for the proud.

When I ordered my body to make ready
To set out on its inevitable journey,
As my mind understood that it was stained
By earthly things, and laden and restrained,
Just so my body, by long conversation
Had acquired something of my own complexion
And wanted to make an immortal Woman
Because my soul and nature so began.
But seeing the body growing old and shrinking,
Its age and diminution set it thinking
It could not last for ever, so it said
It would take on another life instead.
So was it granted, since, for its descent,
Not only a son but a daughter had been sent.
The one is your king, who by his victories
Has won such glory from his enemies
That his misfortunes, both future and past
Are in heaven as on earth quite effaced.
You will think it strange, perhaps, from his mother,
Such praise as never was given to another,
And that I know what future stars decide
For his virtue, and for three sons besides.
Know only that, as long as they shall reign,
Our memory and our story will remain;
If they bring any benefit, it will
If not be I, at least be mine still.
That is the good which comes by the cupidity
Our body has for immortality.
Peace, traveller, there is nothing to deplore,
Now that you know what you did not know before.
For all the honours of which your hearts are full,
And all you pities and regrets are null
To me, in my new habitation here,
And if I want them I can have them there.
Have done with weeping, make an end of it,
And do for me whatever seems most fit.
You will find my daughter loved by her brother
And all who would do honour to her mother;
You will see her continuing to weep,
Mourning for what she could not always keep,
So that, without a word from me she might
Lose the good name that should be hers by right.

Tell her that human tears are wasted breath
And often hurt a soul after death,
That it is I, through you, who tell her this
And that the news comes from a heavenly place.
It is not this alone that will shake here
She of herself will turn towards her maker,
Reasoning of faith, the soul, and what is natural,
What comes to one by chance and what is fatal?
Take care, if she excuses her complaining,
She does not trick you with her reasoning.
She will say, I am sure, that, as we know,
The body has its passions here below,
That every woman has them, and the best
Cannot achieve mastery of the flesh
Unless their strongest passion may control
The earthly body and so govern all;
She will say further that no one offends
Custom or nature who will mourn her friends.
And that if she is weeping for her mother
The passion is so bitter that no other
Can take its place, and so in these sad days,
She offends God the less in other ways.
Then, traveller, it behoves you to be quick
To set the truth against her rhetoric,
And tell her that to a soul which has to wait
Imprisoned here, though it be desperate,
Is not allowed an exit, come what may,
Unless God wills it and appoints a day.
Meanwhile it must be ready till it hears
Its master's call, which it must promptly answer.
And as a man who kills himself to free
A soul God has not set at liberty
Not only sins damnably, but any man
Is criminal also, who abets his plan,
So when God claims his creature it must go.
As all but vitiated souls must know,
For only such as value heaven less
Than they love the world, will refuse blessedness,
And only minds guilty of ignorance
Withhold consent from such deliverance.
This is your message, there's no more to say.
So, traveller, if you please, go on your way.

Epitaph on Marguerite de Navarre

If death is only the separation
Of soul and body, and what we know
About God is acquired by elevation
Of spirit, leaving the body here below,
For Marguerite there can be no difference
Between death and life but that, life past,
She has acquired an unimpeded sense
Of what she wanted and now has at last.

A Dialogue with Maurice Scève (1511-64)

SCÈVE

Free was I in the April of my years,
Without a care, for in that adolescence
The eye did not yet know the force of tears
But saw itself surprised by a sweet presence
Which by its true exalted excellence
Astonished so my senses and my mind
That love pierced me with arrows of such a kind
As took away both liberty and breath:
And, as on that, so to this day I find
In her beauty is both my life, and death.

CRITIC

'Amaritude': the word was quickly lost
And yet remains, as if beauty should say:
'I defy you to say that all is past
Of what touched you in a now distant day.'
And what girl passes who does not portray
The faithful image of your young desire?
As underneath the ashes lies the fire,
So in her voice, her walk, and in her eyes,
Under the shield of ordinary attire,
Ignore it as you will, nakedness lies.

Louise Labé (1526-66)

Tant que mes yeus pourront larmes espandre

So long as my eyes can shed tears
At the past happiness I had with you,
And while my voice still finds strength enough,
Despite sobs and sighs, for me to be heard;

So long as my hand can still touch the strings
Of my sweet lute, to sing of your graces;
And while my mind is content to guess
At your thoughts, and they are still everything,

I shall have no wish to die yet.
But, when my eyes are no longer wet,
My voice cracks, and my hand loses its power

And my voice can no more in this mortal life
Give any sign that love is what it is for,
I shall beg Death to put out my light.

Estienne Jodelle (1532-73)

J'ayme le verd laurier

I love green laurel neither winter nor ice
Spoil the greenness of, for it always wins,
The emblem of eternity, prefiguring
What neither time nor death can change or efface.

I love also holly's evergreen surface
And its thorny leaves with their sharp jabbing;
I love ivy too with its amorous twining
Which holds an oak or a wall in its tight embrace.

31

I love all these three, the green of which resembles
The immortal thoughts day and night assembled
Within me, of you I idolise and adore:

But my wounds and prickings and the knot which ties me
Are greener and sharper and cling to me more
Than the green laurel, the holly or the ivy.

Catherine des Roches (d.1587)

Quenouille, mon soucy, je vous promets et jure

Distaff, my chore, I promise and I swear
To love you always and never to change
Your domestic honour for one more strange,
Wandering incessantly, soon no more there.

You at my side, my lot is far more fair
Than if paper and ink saw fit to arrange
Themselves around me; for you sooner estrange
A wrong and make it easier to bear.

Distaff, my darling, still I do not mean
For all my love of this domestic scene
To give up all the credit I have when

I write occasionally: for then I say
How valuable my cares are every day,
Holding at once the spindle and the pen.

Toutes les herbes croissent

Now all the grasses grow,
And all the flowers show;
Your love alone, in May,
Decreases night and day.

And now in every valley
The streams sound musically;
Your love alone, in May,
Still freezes night and day.

Sweet are the little flowers,
And sweet the grassy hours;
Your love alone, in May,
Is bitter night and day.

Now all the fields are green,
And make a hopeful scene;
Your love alone, in May,
Saddens me night and day.

The wind is sweet, and dies
Sweetly in sweetest sighs;
Your love alone, in May,
Is bitter night and day.

Everywhere laughter fills
The meadows and the hills;
In love, alone, in May,
I weep, both night and day.

Jean-Baptiste Chassignet (1570-1635)

Four Sonnets

1 *La viellesse arrivée on est recompensé*

When old age enters we are well repaid
For the excesses of our youth; from one
Hearing, and from another strength, has gone.
The fittest stumble, by their eyes betrayed.

Our senses, each in turn, begin to fade,
Except the sense of desolation:
Disease grows stronger as the time goes on.
What a poor coffinful the corpse has made!

There is no part of us inhuman Fate
Does not mark as its own before due date,
Knowing that we grow weaker all the way.

Enough, everything dies in us but vice
Which, subject to a greedy avarice,
Living on death, grows younger every day.

2 *Faisons mourir en nous notre concupiscence*

Make sure you stifle your concupiscence,
Tearing the world's temptations from your heart,
But choosing your own moment to depart
Is something for which you are without God's licence.

The Christian leaves his earthly residence
When his due time is up: to flee in fear
From this pained body before the time is here
Offends the God to whom we owe obedience.

You must not hate your days too much, nor yet
Love them too much, for always there is set,
For one and the other, an appointed day.

God has determined that we are to fight
Here in the body till he sends the night:
The chief commands, the soldier must obey.

3 *O grande, émerveillable estrange affection*

O great, amazing, strange affection
Of our Redeemer, whose avenging death
Not only saves our souls while we have breath
But saves the body for resurrection.

Formerly corruptible, in incorruption
It will live again; although sown in weakness,
It will rise again in vigour and in prowess
To live in glory, rescued from confusion.

Made in an animal body, it lives again
In a spiritual body, not serving men
But for the Lord, glorifying his name.

So life is alive and death itself dies
Because the second Adam bought this prize
And it was for this vivification he came.

4 *Qu'est-ce que d'estre mort? – que n'estre plus au monde.*

What is it to be dead? Not to be here.
Before you came here, were you ever in pain?
And those not born at all need not complain.
Death is not, more than sleep, a thing to fear.

Not all the troubled waves of all our ills
Can change the luck of one asleep or dead;
Asleep or dead, there is nothing to be said
Once sleep or death have exercised their skills.

Life is what tortures us, and it is death
Drags us from danger when it stops our breath,
And we speak ill of it only through envy.

Only accuse the time before we were born
Of all the cuts and pricks by which we are torn,
And I will say death is worse than life will be.

Jean-Baptise Chassignet

Ode sur la fragilité de la vie humaine

Quant le jour favorable

When the friendly light
Escapes below the ground
And so the fearful night
Brings shadows all around,
When dark mists everywhere
Make the world seem less fair;

Chaos a thousand-fold,
Replete with fear and terror,
Shadows, alarms untold,
In silence and in error
Make of our earthly room
The image of the tomb.

So tardy age at last,
Hostile to everything,
Takes from a broken past
Of cheerless suffering
The long calamity
Of sick humanity.

There is no hope at all
For one of those who go,
When death puts out its call,
To the deep world below:
It could not be too late
To enter this sad state.

What purpose can there be
In hastening the end;
We can only agree,
Because we all depend
Upon a rule of law
Without mistake or flaw.

The hour we first see light
Calls us at once to death;
Our growth brings on the night,
The first brings the last breath;
From first to the last day
Time carries all away.

It flies, and when it flies,
Cannot come back again,
As a stream never tries
To hold its course, but when
Its waters move, they flow
The way the first must go.

And every mortal thing
Which happens on these boards
Is managed by the pulling
Of less than certain cords:
Even what matters most
Can make no higher boast.

The limits of his days
Are set for everyone,
And yet merit has ways
Of saving what is done
For all eternity
By acting generously.

After the westering sun
Has run its course, no trace
Of shade for anyone
Remains in any place:
There is no shadow here
If light does not appear.

Below earth's blackness we
Must go, and he who goes
Is lost from memory
When death, with his heavy blows
Drives soul from body where
It is gaoled in despair.

The body's fragile glory
We set such store upon,
Decayed and transitory,
Is in an instant gone
When the eternal soul
Leaves it, it has no role.

One may compose and trade;
Another, breaking free,
Faces a cannonade,
But all its vanity:
And few indeed are those
Who find desired repose.

Until fate at the last
Laughs as our purpose fades,
And cuts us from our past
To drift among the shades,
Making of no effect
All that we could expect.

Nobody can resist:
The shot is accurate,
No one is ever missed;
It comes, early or late,
According to the will
Destiny must fulfil.

Everything that you do,
And all your idle ways,
Your laughing, silence too,
Weeping or talking days.
You go your way, and yet
The limits still are set.

Though men may differently
Their different days expend,
The same death finally
Undoes them in the end,
Always, after day's light
Follows the self-same night.

Yet that which we call death
Is nothing we can know;
So quickly ends our breath,
We hardly feel it go.
Why do we fear so much
So light and brief a touch?

It brings shame on us all
That men of character
Should feel a pain so small
As a great matter –
Men whose sole pleasure is
In their excesses.

Happy indeed is he
On whom the blazing sun
Never looked. And happy
Also is anyone
No sooner born to light
Than overcome by night.

For, from our mother's womb,
We still are born with pain
And, living still in gloom,
We leave in tears again
The fruit of all this fuss,
Those who come after us.

The little child, who cries
At his nativity,
Shows that his future lies
In such infirmity,
Puny, weak and afraid,
A body that will fade.

Unable on its own
To eat or yet to drink
To recognise the known,
Or to know what to think,
He chops and changes goods
As his mother her moods.

My brother is decay
And my sister is death,
My parents worm and clay,
The grave that draws no breath
Is the last resting-place
Of our imprisoned race.

Once in his coffin man
Changes into a worm;
The next stage in the plan
Is dust, and yet the term
Of dust is once again
Earth, which composes men.

It is the vile, hard earth
Which forms man's heavy frame,
And what its matter's worth,
The earth is worth the same,
And when his life is done
The earth and he are one.

But when it first begins,
Soul, prompt, alive and warm,
Bows itself as it wins
Its way up, though the form
Which holds it on the road
Remains a heavy load.

So while the tongue of fire
Rises towards the sky,
The mere scrapings of mire
Sink, to show what must die:
So soul and body find
They are not of one kind.

Great-minded father, see
How, drawn towards the vaults
Of high sublimity,
You leave this place of faults
And all earthly resort
To seek a heavenly port.

This world indeed is such
As to hold in defiance
A mind that held so much
Of doctrine and of science,
For, far-back, centuries
Show no such prodigies.

When Dawn lets down her hair
Each day, the brilliant sun
Takes on a red colour,
And when the day is done
It shows itself once more
Red, as it was before.

But, at the very top
Of its shining ascent,
The colour seems to drop
As if the whitening meant
The sun soars as on wings
Above all earthly things.

As if, far from the dirt
Of this round edifice,
In heaven you can assert
Truly, whatever is,
With that mind which, below,
Laboured to find things so.

Mocking the treacherous wiles
Of hated traitors, who
Sell their country with smiles
And trade in its law too,
A law which you observed.
Always, and never swerved.

But yet the ways of fate
Are that the irreligious
Are not taken till late,
While, and the more to grieve us,
Those who are wise and just
Must earlier come to dust.

So, my dear father, rest
And rest on happily:
The serpent who likes best
To rouse malignancy
Will always do most harm
To those he can alarm.

Francesco Petrarca (1304-74)

O aspettata in ciel beata e bella

Whom heaven awaits, blessed and lovely soul,
Clothed, and not burdened as we others are
By our humanity, as you make your way;
So that henceforth the road may be less hard,
O you obedient handmaid whom God chose
That you may cross to His kingdom today
In this vessel so newly under way,
Turning its back upon this blind land
To steer to a better port
With a delightful western wind for comfort:
Which, through this dark valley where without end
We weep for our own and for Adam's fault,
Will lead you, set free from our old burden,
Till soon at hand
Is the true east towards which you are turned.

Stanzas. Consolation to M. Du Perrier

Your grief, Du Perrier, cannot be confined
    And the sad language
A father's love suggests to your mind
    Will only increase its rage.

Your daughter's calamity, going down to the tomb
    The way all must go,
Is it some labyrinth in whose inky gloom
    Your reason cannot follow?

I know the delights her childhood gave
    And I know it is unfit
For a friend to insult your pain, and to behave
    As if it helped for him to scorn it.

But she was of the world, in which the loveliest things
    Must suffer the worst fate,
And, a rose, she has lived like a rose for a morning
    And found noon too late.

And then, even supposing that she might,
    Your prayer answered, in the end
Have lived to years in which her hair grew white,
    What would have happened?

Do you think that, when she was older, heaven
    Would have welcomed her more?
Or that she would have felt herself less riven
    By worms under the church floor?

No, no, my Du Perrier, for as soon as Death
    Takes the soul from the body
Age vanishes on this side with the breath,
    Not bearing the dead company...

Death has rigours like no others here,
    We oppose her in vain:

She is so cruel as to stop her ears
   And leaves us to our pain.

The poor man in his hut, under the thatch,
   Finds her laws compelling,
And the guard at the Louvre, however he may watch,
   Cannot save our kings.

To murmur against her and lose patience
   Cannot be best:
To will what God wills is the only science
   Which will give us rest.

           Nicolas Boileau (1636-1711)

L'Art Poétique
A Shorter Boileau

Boileau says authors should not hastily
Proclaim that what they write is poetry.
The gift is given only to a few,
Depending on their genes and how they grew.
You are the prisoner of the man you are:
The self-selected never travel far.

So you who feel inspired, and sure you can
Be famous as a literary man,
Don't think that only geniuses write verse:
In most, it is a sign of something worse.
Before you take the bait, take pains to find
What kind of work best suits your brilliant mind.

Nature has many gifts and likes to share
Them out to authors, one here and one there.
Consider what she's given you, before
You decide what it is intended for.
See what you can do well, and stick to that,
For if you try too hard, you will fall flat,
Or worse, may have immediate success
Because you make a fashionable mess.

If that is what you want, of course go on:
Your chance of writing poetry is gone,
But still, the name is used by many who
Have no more sense of poetry than you.
And, frankly, it would cause me no surprise
If you should win a competition prize:
It was for such as you that it was meant:
But poetry is something different.

Jean de la Fontaine (1621-95)

Fables XI, 9

The Mice and the Tawny Owl

Never say to people, Listen:
This is witty, or, Here is a strange thing.
Do you suppose that other men
Will think as you do and not think it boring?
Yet this is something quite exceptional:
Quite unbelievable I'd say, and so may you!
Yet every word of my account is true.

Someone had an old pine-tree, about to fall,
An owl's palace, the dark and gloomy hide-out
Of that bird which can tell when Death's about.
In a hollow trunk, which time had gnawed away,
There lived, with other lodgers, small and big,
A lot of footless mice, as fat as pigs.
The bird set them on heaps of corn, then operated
On every one of them, and so they waited
Upon his pleasure; the bird was reasoning.
In his time he had hunted mice, but seeing
The first he took escape, he took this measure
To ensure the rest could be consumed at leisure.
Their legs cut off, their patience much increased,
And he could choose his time to have a feast,
One one day, and the rest the day after.

To eat them all at once would be absurd,
He thought, bad for the health of any bird.
Such foresight is not something for our laughter:
He went so far as bringing all
The food they needed for survival.
Would a Cartesian still have seen
The owl as an elaborate machine?
A watch, perhaps, which had a spring
Advising him to keep his birds well penned?
If that's not reasoning,
Then reason does not fit means to our ends.
His argument was short and clear:
This lot, when captured, won't stay here;
They must be eaten as they're caught.
All! But impossible! So I must feed them
So as to have them there when I most need them.
Keep them here somehow! That's a thought!
But how? Take off their feet? That's best.
Enough to make a human being proud.
What else could Aristotle and his crowd,
With their philosophy, suggest?

Andreas Gryphius (1616-64)

Thoughts on the Churchyard and the Resting-Places of the Dead

for Kurt Ostberg

1

Where am I now? Is this the ground
In which humility may flower?
Is there refreshment to be found
For those who knew in busier hours
The heat and burden of the day?
And bore the frost of bitter nights
And in the midst of hurts and slights
Took up their share of care and pain?

2

Where am I? Here are the narrow plots
Which hide within their pregnant wombs
What has been sown there by the God
Who can wake corpses from their tombs.
Where some see splendour, I see fear.
Not for me the Hesperides
Or Babylonian luxuries;
I see the best of gardens here.

3

Although here no seductive scent
Streams from the jasmin and the rose,
Although no tulips here present
Their brilliant military shows,
Though here no cultivated land
Grows pomegranates or such-like fruit
It bears here what I long for but
What the world does not understand.

4

O School, in which the best instruction
Is given to us mortal men!
No pages full of false deductions
And no delusive apophthegms.
While I have passed in vanity
The wasted treasures of my time
The hours spent here instead define
The straight way to eternity.

5

O School, which utterly appals
Those whom the world regards as clever,
Which those for whom repute is all
Or money all, regard with terror.
O School which terrifies the mind
That knows the lot and has no conscience!

O School which offers no emollients
To cut-throats claiming to be kind.

6

O School, which puts men in a sweat
And makes their hair stand upon end
When they are near the judgement seat
But nearer their lascivious friends.
O School, which makes a man's knees knock
And his limbs tremble, cold as ice,
Because with all money can buy
He knows his mind is closed to God.

7

I go to school with you and long
To fathom where true wisdom lies.
Examine me! There's nothing wrong,
You will find, with my ears or eyes.
What Socrates once taught me, now
Is nothing, and the Stagirite
Has quite collapsed. There is no light
In Greek philosophy I know.

8

Who is there now that will explain
The subject that I want to master?
Set out the principles and main
Conclusions that I should hold fast to?
Or can I here and on my own
Sit down and work the answers out
That will put paid to every doubt
That troubles me? No, not alone.

9

What's happening? Is the ground I stand on
Reeling? And is that roar the trees?

Is the earth tearing its mouth open
So as to let the roots get free?
Do I hear dry bones rattling? Say,
Do I hear clamorous human voices?
Is that the south wind getting boisterous?
Or heavy stones, rolling away?

10

I stand and stare. A bitter cold
Freezes my veins, my heart, my lungs.
From my brow streams of sweat have sprung.
I am glued where the ground still holds.
The whole field has become a grave
And all the coffins are revealed.
What dust, brick, plaster once concealed
Is open now and plain as day.

11

O last but still uncertain house!
The refuge into which we creep
Whenever the clock tells the hour
And the rose pales upon our cheek.
That palace, which the world once gave,
Swearing that it would last for ever,
That same world, once our life is over
Destroys to assail us in the grave.

12

You for example were wrapped up
In tin and you perhaps in copper.
And you perhaps once had a flood
Of liquid lead to line your coffin.
You were rich, no expense was spared;
This one, now that I think of it
Had gold and marble in his pit.
Then how is it I find you bare?

13

Ah, greed and fury have not scrupled
To open up the grave's dark night,
And what I sought in pain and trouble
Lies patent in the deathly light.
Ah, lifeless men, no robber's hand
Would have intruded on your rest
Had you seen proper to entrust
Your bones in plain boards to the sand.

14

For even cedars shrink at last,
The rotten pine-boards go to nothing
And the oak's strength is quickly past,
The grave is her grave, no escaping.
Why do you value the light fir?
The joints will always crack and split.
The narrow box will go to bits
However hard you caulk and hammer.

15

God help me. Coffins open wide,
I see the bodies in them move.
The army of the once alive
Begins to exercise anew.
I find myself surrounded by
A host death has deprived of power,
A spectacle which forces showers
Of burning tears from my blank eyes.

16

O spectacle which makes the world
And what the world most values, stink.
I feel my arrogance desert me,
My courage and my folly sink.
Are these the men who ruled our land,
Defied it, knocked it, held on tight,

Who sharpened daggers, swords and pikes
And held it down with bloody hands?

17

Are these the men who mollified
The Father's heart with sighs and prayers?
Who, though distressed and mortified
Dared face his anger with their cares?
Who bewailed nothing but their faults
Though money and possessions vanished,
Though anguish left the body famished,
The oppressed spirit nipped and gnawed.

18

Are these the men who put aside
All trace of decency and shame,
Who brought from hell into the daylight
Abominations without name?
Who piled up crime on crime, who slit
Throats for fun, poisoning the world
Until the hour when they were hurled
With thunder and lightning into the pit.

19

Are these the men who were not stained
By pleasure in their pleasant youth,
Whose young minds were early inflamed
By passionate desire for truth?
Those who now sing before the Lamb
The joyful song not many know
And walk in garments white as snow
In endless peace before I AM.

20

Are these those who once strutted round
In purple, silk and gold, and these

Those who crept by on humbler ground
In hunger, nakedness, disease?
And these those whom envy so roused
They begrudged others even breath?
Whom no land could contain? In death,
In what packed quarters are they housed?

21

Where are the miracles of grace,
Beauties who captured souls by storm?
Of their delights I see no trace,
Only some ghastly heads, deformed.
Where are those whose store of knowledge
Astounded everyone? Who were
Honoured as great philosophers?
Time has demolished the whole college.

22

Now for the most part all I find
Is bones from which the flesh has slipped,
Skulls with no cover of any kind,
Faces without noses or lips,
Heads missing skin or maybe ears,
The brow and cheeks have gone to nothing
And where the lips should be hanging
Only a tooth or two appears.

23

The bones that once made up the spine
And neck, still somehow hang together
But nothing now keeps them in line,
The ribs stick out and they will never
Again hold heart and lungs close pressed;
The chest's as empty as can be,
The contents eaten, similarly
The double pleasure of the breasts.

24

What use now for the shoulder-blades?
The arms have now lost all their strength.
What served the man in all his trades,
The hand that had the management
Of tools and achieved mastery
Of sea, land, air and dared such feats
Of heroism, is in pieces,
Deprived of all activity.

25

The belly empty, hip and shin
And foot are nothing now but bones,
Hollow, misshapen, yellowy green,
Broken and dry like shards or stones.
In thousand-shaped deformities
Deformity is recognised.
Here every quality's disguised,
Young, old, poor, noble, lovely, wise.

26

And these are they against whom time
Has fully carried out its sentence;
There is no trace of flesh or slime
Mortality could take from them.
Far more repulsive are those here
Who wrestle still with putrefaction,
On whom decay pursues its action,
Those who were with us till last year.

27

The pretty ringlets fall away,
The plaits begin to come apart.
Where the moist flesh still has its say,
About the temples, movement starts.
And the unseeing eyes begin
To be unstable, as the worms

Inside the head hatch out and stir,
Wrinkle the nose and break the skin.

28

The lovely cheeks crumple and shrink,
The chin and tongue and teeth show white.
Upon the coral lips black ink
Spreads blots which put colour to flight.
The forehead splits, the snowy throat
Becomes earth-coloured, as if the sun
Which shone above it, had begun
To melt the frost and the soil showed.

29

What whisper comes out through the wind-pipe?
What is that hissing in the breasts?
It seems to me that I hear vipers
Whistling their music with the rest.
What an intolerable vapour
Rises into the frightened air
Made heavy by the poison there!
So is it by the Avernian lake.

30

So steams the marsh of Camarina,
So smoke the yellow dragons' dens.
The tortures of the Japanese
Do no worse to half-strangled men
Than the plague striking from the mist
Which rises from the popping corpses
Bathed in sweet oils not long before
And incense brought from lands far distant.

31

Filth from the guts breaks through the skin
Where the maggots have bitten through.

I see the guts dissolving in
Pus, blood and water. It makes me spew.
The mildewed flesh that time has left
Is gobbled by a snaky mob
Of bluish worms which do the job
As if they revelled in the mess.

32

What is the use of aloes now?
They cannot keep beauty in shape.
What about myrrh? It has no power
To stop the youthful limbs from ageing.
Is what came out of Palestine
Asphalt or flesh? There is no knowing.
We cannot tell, of all these bones,
Which went with which in former times.

33

What use now is a splendid dress
Embroidered with a golden thread?
And is not all this silk now pointless,
Embellishing the banished dead?
See how the purple loses colour
And all that work becomes unpicked,
How quickly patterns are unfixed
Which once cost hands so much endeavour.

34

You dead! Ah, what I learn from you!
What I am, what I shall become,
A little dust that the wind blew
Is all I carry to the tomb.
How long will my body persist?
How soon shall I conclude my years?
Say good-bye to those left here
And go where time does not exist?

35

Shall I be able to prepare
Thoughtfully for the long journey?
Or shall I have no time to spare
When I am called whence none returns?
Do not be sudden, Lord of Life,
Or send for me without warning!
But be with me on that last morning,
Protector, guide, my Way, my Light.

36

Where shall I leave my lifeless body,
Entrust it to the final grave?
How many, thinking to make ready,
Have their tombs built, but yet in vain!
How many lie in unknown sand?
Who can guess how chance may fall?
How many has the ocean rolled
To throw up in an unknown land?

37

It does not matter very much
Whether I'm married or lie alone,
Lord, so long as I may touch
Your garment, pleading at your throne.
I see the appointed hour like some
Tremendous prelude with great crashes
Of thunder and great lightning flashes,
And soon eternity will come.

38

When, amidst prodigies and trumpets,
We hear God's final battle-cry
Echoing through every land in triumph
Announcing death itself must die,
When marble, copper, metal, stone
And Pharaohs' tombs from their long night

Deliver to the air the light
And re-invigorated bones;

39

When the sea gives up its dead
Casting up thousands on the shore
From its deep gulfs and tangled weed
The bodies that the Judge has sent for,
When what the north wind blew off course,
What tigers ate up in Morocco
Or flames devoured in Persia,
What rivers that were sown with corpses;

40

What the Brazilian cannibals
Ate, wilder than their own wild beasts,
And those whom appetite for gold
Buried beyond hope of release;
When what Vesuvius overwhelmed
With burning ash and blazing sparks,
What Ætna buried beyond help
Or Hekla spat at in the dark;

41

When what time winnows in the air
Will suddenly be whole again;
Prisoners, however deep they are
In dungeons, will become free men
To see the Son of the Most High
Come in glory and put to shame
His foes, and in his Father's name
Sit where all causes will be tried.

42

Now hear how the Judge will pronounce
His principal and final sentence,

He who himself was judged here once
And bore it for me with all patience,
Who gives new light from heaven above:
How he makes earth dissolve, and breaks
The heavens asunder! Here stand and quake
The Jesus-haters, the Jesus-lovers.

43

Those whom I see here now without
Distinguishing one from the other
I shall see (as I cannot doubt)
Plunged into joy or sorrow, either
Into joy more than sense can know
Or sorrow such as none felt before,
Into delight for evermore
Or everlasting loss and sorrow.

44

Joys that the world cannot contain,
Sorrow before which Hell will reel,
Pleasure that destroys all pain,
Sorrows none here could bear to feel,
Pleasures that will drown all cries,
A sorrow that is pure despair,
Bliss which leaves no place for care,
Sorrow so keen it never dies.

45

Then I shall see you in your skins,
Free from corruption, with full veins;
All that before was hidden in
The grave, will be alive again.
I'll see you, but how different!
Transfigured some, O what delight!
Others disfigured, terrifying!
Joy! I shall shout, and then lament.

46

I'll see you shine with more brilliance
Than would be in ten thousand suns.
I'll see you and avert my glance
From those who have no consolation,
See some more beautiful than beauty,
Some uglier than ugliness,
Some finding comfort, some the darkness
Pregnant with ghosts and devilry.

47

Many the world called good and great
God's sentence designates as lost.
Many spat on and reprobate
Are chosen for the heavenly host.
Never mind how the marble reads,
Epitaphs may be pitched too high.
Corpses however cannot lie
Nor this Court ever be deceived.

48

The corpse shows that you must decline
In rottenness and stink to dust,
That nothing in the world's too fine
To go to ashes when it must,
That though we are not equal here
In death there is equality.
Go and prepare your case and be
Wide awake when the Judge appears.

49

He alone knows how to distinguish
In the confusion death has brought
Who will depart to endless anguish,
Who find the peace that they have sought.
He ensures that no single speck
Of dust from bodies shall escape him.

Air, wind and water keep from him
Nothing, in spite of time and death.

50

You dead! Ah, what I learn from you!
What I was, what I then shall be!
What is eternal, what is true!
No more the world shall trouble me.
Oh you who lie there, teach me so
To stand, that when I end my days
And take leave of the world, I may
Leave Death, and find Life where I go.

Andreas Gryphius

Sonnet

Wir sindt doch nuhmer gantz/ja mehr den gantz verheret!

We are utterly lost, and more than utterly.
Impudent armies, nations, frantic trumpets,
The sword that feeds on blood, cannon like thunder
Have consumed all our stores, our sweat, our industry.

The prison is in flames, the church is upside-down,
The council-chamber in fear, the strong are cut to pieces,
The girls publicly raped, and around all we see is
Fire, plague, murder, death. Here, between wall and town,

There, between trench and sandbag, runs blood, always fresh
        blood,
For eighteen years now, our rivers have been in flood
With corpses, pushed forward inch by inch.

I say nothing of what is stronger than death,
You, Strasbourg, know it, famine, and that with breath
The soul is torn out of many and many.

Conlie Ditch

Puisque de nouveau, vous faites la Bretagne

Who levied us in the black month – November –
    And parked us there like cattle
To leave in the mud, in the blacker month – December –
    Our sheepskins and our own skins.

Who was it left us there, empty, without hope?
    We had not even despair.
Looking at one another, as if we were looking for France...
    Comical, unless you feared us.

– Soldiers if that's what you call us... a soldier is someone
    Made to forget the taste of bread?
We were about to beg; they sent us to grass instead
    And we did graze, in the end.

Please can we have? – something to put in our mouths!
    Half heroes and half beasts!
... Or something here: a heart or some cartridges
    – They have left us pity.

Charity: we got it at last. – May they get their reward,
    Those beatified drunken Uhlans
Who fed us at last with a stray bullet...
    And pleasantries, like the odd penny.

We were survivors on a raft. – Poverty. –
    We collapsed before the horizon.
Our confused eyes looked out to a country...
    And a cry came out: Treason!

– Treason!... it is war. Who is there for us to shout to?
    We have no need. Why betrayed?
I have seen some among us, in their mother country,
    Dying of home-sickness.

– How sadly it went away, our sweet life!
    A sigh that smelt of remorse
Because we could not press a wafer on our lips,
    A dog's death between our teeth!

– A great lout came our way, propped up by two gendarmes
    – He did not know what was happening –
Wine all over his face, except what was tears or sweat,
    With a *biniou* under his arm.

He sat down in the snow and said: I like sometimes
    To play a tune; leave me alone.
Two days later, with his bag-pipes
    We buried him. – Why?

Why? Tell them, you Fourth of September gang!
    Twenty thousand of us would like to know.
Civilians ordering victories as you sit on your arses,
    Tyrants who keep your distance, feeble.

– Your turn to speak – and words are light enough.
    Disgrace is a whore... She went by.
Those whose green feet are sticking out of the earth there
    Have nothing to say... too outspoken for you perhaps.

– Ha! Bordeaux's a fine place, don't you think so?
    Still in France too, isn't it?
Your *garde mobile* were warm enough there
    Marking time under your windows.

The resurrection of our gaiter-straps is too far
    Away for you to think about it.
Your names are on the placards everywhere, O masters!
    Shame can bite no deeper.

– Politicians! They did well to feel themselves indisposed.
    The fancy-dress gang, with tin swords.
Some of them even got up and turned out on parade
    With the Punch-and-Judy.

'Morale was excellent.' These princes all had princesses
    Tied up in their sleeping-bags.

Long dresses go well with polished boots
	And valour needs love.

Enough! There was no need to call us with bugles;
	We just had to get the hay in.
We: who happened to have remained simple, in our way,
	Soldiers, Catholics, Bretons.

All those who died gaping at the battle
	A verminous collection with no name
Showing respect to the first superior who came our way
	Telling us where we belonged.

All right: to the humane killer! We were a scabby lot
	To keep the Prussians happy
And, seeing us grovelling under their rifle-butts,
	The French shouted: Good dogs!

In at the death! Brought back alive! The missing
	– God knows how many. There is enough contempt;
Driven, dragging our feet, eaten by shame
	We went home to spit on the hearth.

– So, Conlie ditch, water that is not drunk
	By our young impoverished blood
Until the grain shoots, and there has been time to forget
	Our bodies, rotting there.

The flesh clotted upon our ragged shirts
	– A bit of a dung-hill, you might say.
– Do not eat this bread, mothers and young girls!
	The ergot of death is in the rye.

THE REGRETS
OF JOACHIM DU BELLAY

(1525-60)

To the Reader

I offer you this little book,
Sweet and bitter, take a look
And take a grain of salt with either,
That will give you the right flavour.
If you like that, it suits your palate,
I invite you, come and have it;
If it doesn't, stay away,
It is not compulsory.

To his Book

Book (and please don't think that I am jealous),
You are off to the king's court without me.
I only wish I had been as lucky,
To see what you see would have been marvellous!
If anybody there is polite to you,
Wish him all the best when he is at home:
But if some clever customer raises his eyebrows,
Wish him my troubles, I can spare him a few.
Wish him the pleasures of prolonged travel
And a distant view of his home, and all the while
May his heart be on those fields where he is not:
Hope that he grows old in a life of servitude,
And that all he gets in the end is ingratitude,
And while he is absent somebody whips the lot.

1

I will not bother with the secrets of nature
Nor ask what makes the universe go on as it does,
Nor do I propose to explore the depths of the seas
Or draw a plan of the celestial architecture.
I don't paint my pictures in such bright colours,
Don't go looking for that in my verse.
Starting from what happens, for better or worse,
I take a pen to write, and the rest follows.
I grumble if I have something to grumble about,
Joke or, if I have secrets, tell them out loud
As if my poems were very discreet secretaries.
I don't doll them up to look smart in public
Or disguise them with grand names to make them look big
But regard them as no more than records or commentaries.

2

A wiser man than I (Paschal) will meditate
With Hesiod upon the two-topped hill
And, so that everybody will think well
Of him, splash in the waters of Pegasus naked.
As for me, I think nothing of making a line longer
By snipping a bit off my brains, nor of making a rhyme
By sand-papering my wits until they shine,
Banging the table or biting my nails for a song.
So my idea (Paschal) is to compose
Pieces of prose in rhyme, or rhyme in prose
Without expecting to be crowned with laurels for that.
It may be that some who think themselves skilful
And imagine those things can be done by any fool
Will find, when they try to imitate, the result is flat.

3

Before I was so much exercised
By all the bad luck which has come my way,
I used to operate poetically
No one had more inspiration than I.
Now these divine sources are closed to me
And I have troubles instead to keep me going,

I have developed a skill appropriate
To one who knows what it is to be in need.
That is why, my lord, having missed the path
Which Ronsard followed to Parnassus and back,
I walk around in the ordinary dirt:
Lacking the heart, the strength and the mere breath
To follow, like him, with difficulty and sweat
The uneasy up-hill which leads to virtue.

4

I'm not going to pore over exemplary Greeks
Or try to re-produce an Horatian outline,
Still less to imitate Petrarch, and be sublime
Or sound like Ronsard when it is my own grief.
Those who are the true Apollan poets
Will have no difficulty in writing more grandly:
I, working up a more commonplace anger
Do not pretend to meddle with such secrets.
I shall be satisfied with simply writing
Whatever my disquiet suggests I might
Without looking for more serious subjects.
So in this book it is not my objective
To imitate those who imagine they will live
For ever because their works are respected.

5

Those who are in love will write about love,
Heroes will write about their reputations,
Those at the centre of things will give explanations,
Distinguished people will tell us where we get off.
Those who love the arts will be inexhaustible,
Those who are virtuous will let us know they are,
Those who love wine will tell us they've drunk some more,
Those with nothing to do will invent fables.
Those who enjoy slandering will slander away
While the jokers find more harmless ways to annoy,
Those who have shown courage will boast about it,
Those who are pleased with themselves will tell us why,
The flatterers will improve on their flattery,
I have no luck and shall grumble about that.

6

And where is my contempt of fortune now?
Where is that heart which is above adversity?
That noble desire for immortality?
And that gift ordinary people are without?
Where are those pleasures which on a dark night
The Muses used to afford me, when in all freedom,
On the green carpet beside a secluded stream
I took them dancing in the moon-light?
Now Fortune is the only mistress I have
And my heart, which used to be its own master,
Is subject to a thousand annoying griefs.
Posterity is now my least concern,
My burning desire to write no longer burns
And the Muses, as if strangers now, escape me.

7

In the days when my writings were read at court
And the king's sister, the incomparable Margaret,
Doing me more honour than I merited,
Cast a favourable eye on what I wrote
The movements of my mind lifted me to the skies
On wings untouched by time or by death,
And the learned ladies who inhabit Parnassus
Kindled my ardour with the divine fire.
Now I am silent, as one sees the prophetess
When she loses the god by whom she was possessed
Suddenly lose inspiration and voice.
Who is not pleased to have a Prince command him?
The arts feed upon honour, and the Muse wants
A public to strut before, and the King's service.

8

Do not be surprised, Ronsard, you who are half of me
If France does not read your Du Bellay now
And if, in the Italian air, he has not learned how
To breathe in the fire of Italy.
The sacred light that comes from your lady's eyes
And, not less sacred, the favour of the Prince,

Yours and mine, that, Ronsard, is worth something
And warms you up to your superb lines.
But I, with the rays of my sun blotted out,
How should I feel warmth as you do,
Near as you are to the divine flame?
The sunny hillsides are covered with tendrils,
But from the extreme north there comes still
Nothing but cold, cold and snow and rain.

9

France, mother of arts, mother of arms and laws,
You gave me suck from your abundant breast:
Now like a lamb crying for what is lost
I fill the rocks and forests with my call.
If at one time you admitted I was yours,
Why are you silent now, why are you cruel?
France, oh France, answer me mercifully!
But the echo only brings back my own words.
I am left to wander among hungry wolves,
Winter approaches, I feel its breath is cold
– It rasps, and sends a shiver down my back.
Your other lambs are not without pasture,
They fear no wolves, nor wind, they are secure
Yet I am not the worst of the flock.

10

It is not the proud banks of this Tuscan river,
It is not the Latin air nor the Palatine hill
Which makes me talk Latin, not at all,
Ronsard, nor makes for any change whatever.
It is the boredom of three years and more,
Nailed like a Prometheus to the Aventine;
It is cruel hope, in this miserable time,
Not the compulsion of love, which holds me here.
If in exile, Ronsard, Ovid could change his language
For a barbarous tongue, there being no one at hand
Who could follow what he said, who can blame me
For a more civilized change? Nobody, for your French
To which you have given a Greek or Latin elegance
Is, in this Latin place, understood by nobody.

71

11

Although people at large have nothing to do with poetry,
Although it is not a way of getting rich,
Although soldiers need not carry it with their kit
And to the ambitious it is merely silly:
Although important people think it funny
And those who are clever keep away from it,
Although Du Bellay is sufficient witness
To prove it is not a skill that is valued highly:
Though writing for nothing seems idiotic to courtiers,
Though workmen don't expect payment from sonneteers,
And although following the Muse is the way to be poor,
Yet I don't feel tempted to give up
Because writing poems is my only comfort
And the Muse has given me six years writing and more.

12

Given all the business that I have to do,
Given the cares which worry me all day
And given all the subjects I have for complaint,
You are amazed to find I write poems.
They call them songs, Magny, I call them tears,
Rather I sing all right, but blubbering
And sing to charm my tears as much as anything:
Nothing could give me reason to sing oftener.
So workmen sing who do not like their job
Or ploughmen when the furrows are too long
Or travellers who cannot get back home,
So young men who have trouble with their girls
Or sailors when the oars are hard to pull
Or prisoners desperate to be out of prison.

13

Now I forgive the delicious lunacy
Which made me use up all my best years
Without my work bringing any advantage other
Than the pleasure of a long delinquency.
Now I forgive this agreeable exertion
Because it alone puts all my cares to sleep,

And because it alone offers me hope
And quiet in the middle of the storm.
If verses have been the folly of my youth
In my old age at least they will have some use,
They were my madness, they will be my reason,
They were my wound, they will be my Achilles,
They were my poison, they will cure my ills
– The only cure there is, nothing else will please.

14

If I am worried by my creditors
Poetry banishes thoughts of them at once:
And if a job I asked for is badly done
I put up with it, Boucher, and write some more.
If anyone loses his temper with me
I sick my heart out all over my poems:
And if work makes me too tired to go on
A few verses soon make the work seem easy.
Poetry soon drives away idleness,
Poetry does not make me love liberty less
But sings for me the things I dare not say.
So if I get so many benefits,
Need you ask, Boucher, what is the good of it
And what I get by writing poetry?

15

Panjas, you know what my amusements are?
Thinking how to save money, watching the expenses
From day to day, so as somehow to content
Scores of creditors without having funds for half.
I come and go and have no time to lose,
Make up to bankers and arrange for loans.
When I've got rid of one, someone else comes,
I don't get through a quarter of what I hope to.
One worries me with accounts, a letter, a note,
Another tells me, Tomorrow the cardinals meet,
One makes my head ache with his facts and chatter,
One has objections, one moans, murmurs or shouts.
With all this trouble, Panjas, can you make out
How I write poetry, or why it matters?

16

While Magny works for his great Avanson,
Panjas for his cardinal and I for mine,
All three of us here are wasting our time
With the delights of hoping to get on;
You meanwhile make your addresses to Kings,
Praising Henri, the paragon of the age,
Honouring yourself and him, while he repays
With honour the honour you do him in your songs.
We meanwhile are spending our best years
On the unfamiliar banks of a foreign river
Where our luck makes us write these doleful poems
Like a trio of swans about to die,
Sitting upon the new grass side by side,
Far away from the lake that is their home.

17

After wandering long enough on the bank
Where so many poor devils stand and lament,
You have reached the further shore everyone wants,
Out of the way of poverty and its pains.
The rest of us meanwhile, still on this side
Stretch out our hands in vain, we lack the penny
You have to offer to the ferryman
For only those who pay get near his boat.
So you enjoy a life of blessed leisure,
Over there with the educated lovers
Deep in a wood you lose yourself with your lady:
You take a long draught of forgetfulness,
Think no more of your past, nor yet of us
Still waiting on the quay or still labouring.

18

Morel, you don't know what I'm doing here
– Not making love or anything like that:
I look after my master, to be exact
His whole establishment is my affair.
Good God! you say, it is a miracle
To see Du Bellay mixed up with such things,

Not only that, but writing verse in Latin!
Why, wolves and sheep get on about as well.
It is like this, Morel, there is poetry
To keep me going, nothing else is needed
And nothing else can make me give it up.
You will reply: If I were you, my lad,
I think I'd put that old horse out to grass
Before it gets worse and its wind gives out.

19

While you say your Cassandra is divine
And praise the King as the heir of Hector
And that Montmorency as our French Nestor,
While Henry shows you favour all the time:
I walk alone beside the Latin river,
Regretting France, regretting a whole crowd
Of old friends, the best fortune I had,
And my house in Anjou, where I lived.
I regret the woods and the fields of corn,
The vineyards, gardens and the green meadows
Through which my river runs: there is nothing here
But the heaps of stones of which they are so proud
Among which I am supposed to live on hope
– And the more I think of that the less there is there.

20

Happy the man whose death brings him fame
And happier he whose immortality
Does not begin only with posterity
But before death has taken him away.
You, Ronsard, enjoy while you are alive
The immortal honour you have so well earned:
There is recognition of your virtues
– A rare thing in a world so full of envy.
Courage, my Ronsard, you have won through,
The King is on your side, and speaks for you,
You wear triumphal laurels while you're here
And so thick are the crowds that gather round
They are like the spirits of the underworld
Gathering round Orpheus while he holds his lyre.

21

Count, who never took account of greatness,
Your Du Bellay is finished, like a tree-stump
Lying across a stream with the roots torn up
And no more life apart from a few green leaves.
If I write sometimes, I am not inspired
But write simply to say what I feel
With the first words that come, for good or ill,
I am cold, that is reflected in my style.
You Aristotelian followers of nature,
Whose art is not simply a matter of portraiture,
Imitate the best works of Greece and Rome.
I aspire to no such masterpieces
And, compared with your pictures my sketches
Are no more than Janet's beside Michelangelo's.

22

Now more than ever I must love the Muse,
Whether I write in French, or the Roman language,
Because an enlightened Prince is at hand
To give judgement in favour of literature.
For that reason your sacred vocation
Will not now be an unrewarded exercise,
And the *Franciade* that you have promised
Will have no excuse for being late.
Meanwhile, Ronsard, without hope of riches,
But to console myself, I shall do my best
To keep up with your now wearied flights.
Not everyone has deserved to receive,
Like you, from a King's liberality,
A gilded bow or a lyre with a mitre.

23

Do we always have to read about love?
Cupid the exacting god, Venus on Mount Ida?
Must Mars always be cluttered with Aphrodite?
Can't we have Ronsard without all that stuff?
Must people go on for ever about sex
And tell us all their experiences?

76

Must we always be hearing about Orestes,
And Roland only as an erotic subject?
Meanwhile your Francus hoists his sails in vain,
Holds the tiller, looks up at Charles's Wain
As if ready to go off where he ought to be:
He has a fair wind, he is well equipped
But he is stuck there at Troy with his ship,
Can't you persuade him, Ronsard, to put to sea?

24

How lucky you are, Baïf, and more than lucky
Not to be following the blind goddess
Who raises hopes and lands us in a mess,
But the blind boy whose business is with love!
You, Baïf, do not feel the rigour of a master
Who scowls at you: but the gentle severity
Of a beautiful, courteous and good-humoured lady
Who makes you languish indeed, but not too fast.
Meanwhile, far away from the eyes of my Prince,
I grow old, luckless, in a distant province
To avoid poverty, but do not avoid
Regrets, exasperations, work, worries,
Belated repentance for ridiculous hopes,
And responsibility, always at my side.

25

Unlucky the year, the month, the day, the hour
And unlucky the hope that flattered me
When, to come here, I left my own country,
France, and my own Anjou it hurts to remember.
Truly that bird was a bird of ill omen
And my heart gave me warning at the time
That there were malignant influences in the sky
And Mars was in conjunction with Saturn.
A hundred times I was warned not to leave
But still fate pulled away at my sleeve,
And if desire had not blinded my reason
Would it not have been enough to hold me back
When, on my own doorstep, by more than ill luck
I fell and twisted my ankle as I was leaving?

26

Anyone who is planning a long voyage
Should listen to one who has already travelled that way
And, having suffered from the wind and waves,
Come out wet and dripping, but alive,
So you will believe me, Ronsard, although you are wiser
And, I believe, a year or two older,
Because I have sailed this sea before you
And my ship has already arrived here.
Therefore I warn you that the Roman sea
Is full of shoals and runs dangerously,
Hiding a thousand perils, and that here often
Deceived by the sirens' delusive singing
You fall against Scylla to avoid Charybdis
Unless you know how to sail whatever the wind.

27

It is not ambition nor the love of gain
Which made me give up family and home
To see the Alps and their eternal snows
Or to seek my fortune in this dangerous way.
Of the unpretentious honour which does not wither
And the true virtue which alone is immortal
I have had all I need and more than all
And do not need to call on the gods for more.
Honourable servitude, or simply my duty
Compelled me to cross the Alps from France to Italy
And to stay three years in this foreign land
Where I languish now. And duty likewise
Could make me change France for the ultimate islands,
Or change heaven for hell, if it comes to that.

28

When I said good-bye to you, to come here,
You said to me, Lahaye, I remember well:
Remember how you are now, Du Bellay
And be the same when you come back from there.
And I am coming back as I went out:
Except for a regret which eats my heart,

Wrinkles my brow and has given me grey hairs
And collects all my thoughts into a frown.
This regret which so gnaws and scrapes at me
Is not for any crime, my hands are clean,
It is for having stayed here for three years:
For having been kidded by a fatuous hope
Which, in order to find poverty here,
Made me abandon France, I am such a fool.

29

I hate a young man who stays at home
And never goes out, except for holidays,
Hugging his house as if he were afraid
Like a wild creature, or like a man in prison.
But neither do I like an old man
Who is for ever travelling here and there,
Not so much light of foot as weak in the head,
And stops no longer than a courier can.
The one does nothing but look after himself,
The other hasn't a moment's peace till the end,
Always in dangerous places day and night:
The one is happy to be rich and a fool,
The other behaves as if he were destitute
And acquires a knowledge which brings him no delight.

30

To live under a foreign sky, Bailleul,
For years on end, to put up with travelling
Half round the world as if looking for something,
Or gape contentedly where the sky is blue:
To put family affections out of one's mind,
Or even your girl-friend, if it comes to that,
Or the place you were brought up in, which no one forgets;
To push on with no thought of what's left behind:
These are the marks of a man of stone, of a bear
Or of one who had a tigress for a mother,
Inhuman, you might say. Yet even animals
– Wild ones – go back to their holes or dens
While the domestic kind think of their friends
And always want to get back home if they can.

31

Happy the Ulysses who gets back home,
The Jason who conquers the golden fleece,
They can be full of reason and experience
And impress the relatives who did not go!
But when shall I see my little village,
With its smoking chimneys, at what time of year
Shall I see my not magnificent house which is more
To me than a province, though that may sound silly?
The little place built by my ancestors
Pleases me more than Roman palaces,
And all this marble is nothing to my slate:
I prefer my Loire to the Latin Tiber
And my little Liré to the Palatine,
And the soft air of Anjou to this climate.

32

I will master the secrets of philosophy,
Of mathematics and of medicine as well,
Become a legal expert and – who can tell? –
Perhaps even aspire to theology:
For recreation painting and playing the lute,
With a little fencing and dancing. So I used to say
And boasted I would learn all that one day,
The change from France to Italy would do it.
But where does talking get you? I have come so far
For a fortune in boredom, wrinkles and grey hair
And to waste my best years in travelling.
So the sailor who sets out to look for gold
May find that in the end he has in the hold
Not a pile of ingots but a few herrings.

33

Morel, what do you think I should do?
Should I stay on in this benighted land
Or should I take another look at France
As soon as the spring sunshine has melted the snow?
If I stay in Rome it will be to waste my time
Imagining that things will come right here,

And if I look for security elsewhere
All the work I have done will go for nothing.
But have I to live like that in vain hope?
Or have I to waste three years and give it up?
I'll stick it out. No, I will turn my back on it.
No, I will stay, if that is what you advise.
Anyway, Morel, say something, you decide,
For I am in two minds what to tell my feet.

34

As a sailor who knows what a storm can do
To a man battered by it on the high seas,
Having once rowed his own vessel to safety
When shipwreck seemed to be inescapable,
Once in port watches without a trace of fear
The waves, and the wind lashing up the foam,
And someone else in danger of going down
Stretching his hands in vain to the shore:
So you, Morel, stand on the harbour front,
Look at the sea, and watch with great content
While it is drawn into a thousand whirlpools:
You see it tossed up as far as the sky
And in the middle of it all your friend Du Bellay
Sitting at the tiller in a ship full of holes.

35

Dillier, the ship that has been long at sea
Is, in the end, laid snugly up in port,
And the ox which has drawn furrows for so long
Has his yoke taken off him finally:
The old horse in the end is turned loose
Before it is broken-winded and cracks up,
And its old rider finds he has had enough
And turns away from war to quietude:
But I, who till now have known nothing but trouble,
The trouble and distress of hopes that bring nothing
But disappointments, cares, regrets, annoyances,
Am growing old by inches beside the Tiber,
And I cannot hope, even if I get a prize,
Ever to get away from these endless labours.

36

Since I deserted my natural habitat
To come here to this crooked Roman stream,
The sun has three times moved to the extremes
Of its summer and winter courses, and moved back.
But so great is my longing to return
The siege of Troy seems short in comparison,
And such my desire to see Paris again
The changes in the sky themselves slow down:
So slow the movement seems, and so careworn,
So heavy and dejected, that cold Capricorn
Does not shorten my days, nor does Cancer my nights,
That is how long time is for me, Morel,
Far from France and away from you as well,
And how nature draws out all but my delights.

37

Not long ago I had no more to do
Than to be what I am and to ask no more;
To live on what the family had before,
Contented with my pen and with my books.
But it did not please the gods to continue
The liberty of my youth, or to allow me
To live so free of labour and anxiety
And I had not even ambition as an excuse.
It did not please the gods that in old age
I should know the pleasure of having my own place,
Living at home and envying no one:
Instead, they decreed I should pass my time abroad,
Lose my independence and stay locked up,
Turned to winter too soon, my best years gone.

38

O happy in the man who can spend his life
Among his own kind: and who, without pretence,
Without fear, without envy, and in full content
Reigns peacefully at his own poor fireside.
The wretched trouble of acquiring more
Does not tyrannise over his affections,

His highest desire, a desire without passion,
Extends only to what his father had before him.
He does not bother with other people's affairs,
His main hope is for what is already there,
He is his own master in all that he does.
He does not waste what he has abroad,
He does not risk his life for a foreign cause,
And he does not want to be richer than he is.

39

I love liberty, but I am a servant,
I don't like servile manners, but must have them,
I do not like pretence, but I pretend,
I like straightforwardness, but I am learning:
Property bores me but I work for avarice,
I do not care for honours, but must act as if I do,
I like to keep my word, my employer says no,
I look for decency and find only vice:
I look for peace, and find something else,
For pleasure, and I do not get it myself,
I don't like argument although on the right side:
I am not fit, and yet I have to travel,
I am born for poetry, but my job is to manage,
Am I not, Morel, the unluckiest man alive?

40

Only a little sea lay between Ulysses
And Ithaca, his home; the cloud-capped Apennines
And all the snowy mountains of Savoy
Keep me from France, captive in Italy:
My native place is rich, while his was poor,
I am no wizard, he was full of tricks
And he had those at home who watched his interests
But no one ever considers what mine are:
While Pallas guided him, I steer by chance,
He could take any strain, I falter at once,
And in the end he brought his ship to port,
I have no certainty of getting back,
He could stop those who hated him in their tracks,
My enemies fear nothing of the sort.

41

So fate thought that my troubles were too few
For me to become hateful to myself,
And took away the friend I loved so well,
Without whom my own life is nothing too.
Eternal darkness has consumed your light
Without my following you among the shades?
You who loved me more than your happy state
And whose happiness I loved more than my life.
Alas, old friend, must I no longer be
Your twin, as you were surely twin to me?
For we were more than brothers, you and I.
Accept these tears as pledges of my friendship,
These verses which will carry the memory of it
As far as may be into eternity.

42

Now, my dear Vineus, take a look at me,
Do you know anyone in such a mess?
I cannot be even the man I was,
Having let youth escape so idiotically.
I remain poor, and eaten out by care,
My days are miserable, my nights still more so
With what I didn't do and what I must do!
If I were a satirist – I wish I were –
I'd attack others and not feel a thing,
My pen would run freely, I'd not be wondering
What my superiors would have to say.
I tell you, Vineus, the only true superior
Is he who is not in duty bound to please
And can write as he will from day to day.

43

Thieving and fraud are hardly in my line,
Religion I have taken as it was taught,
I have done nothing contrary to law,
Incurred neither imprisonment or fine:
I have always given my master faithful service
And helped my friends, but only properly,

I think that nobody can fairly say
That I have ever done him a bad turn.
I am like that: yet somehow, Vineus
If I had been unfriendly and rebellious
Misfortune could not well have bitten deeper:
But I have this comfort, people say
I should not have been treated in this way
And that I am good enough to have done better.

44

If having spent one's youth without crime,
Not having made the family rich by cheating,
Not having played with homicide or treason,
Not having ever cut corners too fine,
Not having broken any promises
Should make one happy in one's later years,
If I keep my head I should do well in future
And have an old age full of happiness.
So never mind present adversity,
No need to ask the gods to make me happy
Unless you count going on being patient.
O gods, if you care about us at all,
Give me that gift at least, I hope you will,
And hope for your pity and my innocence.

45

Stepmother nature (and you are a step-mother
Or you would have borne me happier and wiser)
Why did you not make me, shall we say, less supine,
Able to act as reasonably as others?
I see two roads, the wrong and the right,
I know which is the better, and I choose
Infallibly the one I should refuse,
To follow a vain hope which looks delightful.
Does that do any good? No, not the least!
I spend my last ounce of energy
To get the wrong result and more trouble.
It is the stranger benefits by my service.
I wear myself out in fatuous exercises
And get the blame for other people's muddles.

46

If by hard work and sweat, and being reliable,
By humble slavery and exorbitant patience,
Using up body, money, mind and conscience
Without regard to one's own profit or pride,
If not by badgering people to give one
Senior appointments or any other prizes,
One ought to get rich, then I should think I
Shall do well in the end, with all I have done.
But if pilfering is the way to make progress,
Lying, flattery and deceiving the boss,
And doing worse than that, as happens often,
I have to admit I have been sowing in the desert
Or thought sieving water was rather clever,
And am, Vineus, an unprofitable servant.

47

If ever your heart was touched by pity,
Seeing your friend so pointlessly tormented,
Or if your eyes ever knew what it meant
To be goaded to tears by real misery,
Consider my pain which is not artificial
As these verses and my directness are not:
And if you are not incited to weep a lot,
At least do not burst out laughing at this rigmarole.
So, my dear Vineus, I hope you may never
Feel the disappointment felt by the deserving
When they are defrauded of the fruits of their labours:
So may your king cast a favourable eye
On you and you not be taken in entirely
By promises, as the cleverest sometimes are.

48

Happy is he who is not compelled to hide
The thoughts which truth forces him to think,
And whose respect for dignity and rank
Does not compel his pen to compliance!
Why do I feel this knot strangle my liberty
When the complaint I want to make is perfectly just?

And why cannot my mind become accustomed
To not feeling pain, or not expressing its agony?
I am put to that torture, and I dare not cry out,
People see me suffer, and I do not see how
I can ask for pity. Oh, a common trouble!
The fire that cannot get out is desperate,
The pain in the bones has the hardest bite,
No grief so great, as that which must be dumb.

49

If after forty years of good service
The one I serve has given, here and there,
Expending his best energies everywhere
In affairs that were worth the exercise,
He finds himself the object of envy and malice
From a foreigner who strains every nerve to harm him
And who, without respect for God or for anything,
Marshals against his worthiness, ignorance and vice,
Why should I worry, I who do not count,
If, because someone perhaps envies my chances,
I do not find things done to my liking?
I console myself, therefore, and seeing my excellent master
Sinking in the same sea where I am in danger,
I am pleased to be swept out on the same tide.

50

Let us go out, Dilliers, and make way for envy,
And keep out of the way of this civil disorder
Since there cowards and rascals come to the fore
And the better part is the one chosen least frequently.
Let us go where it is worth going and where chance takes us,
Even if that means Scythia or the source of the Nile,
And send ourselves into eternal exile
Rather than foul ourselves with all this fuss.
Get on your feet then, and before the conqueror
Makes us a butt for common mockery
Let us steal a march on him and banish merit.
Do you not remember the banished Roman,
Turned out because his own people were inhuman,
Who settled among the barbarians and found credit?

51

Mauny, let us take a liking to bad luck
For no one can be sure of having good
And the bad is always a little hopeful
– Since fortune changes all the time, it must be.
The wise helmsman is always doubtful of Neptune,
Knowing that good weather never lasts long:
And isn't it better to smile when the wind is too strong
Rather than to fear the sea may be importunate?
Good fortune always deceives us all,
Bad fortune makes us all a little more careful,
The former debilitates, the latter is strengthening:
The one looks encouraging, but is false,
The other distinguishes our friends from the other sort
And even enables us to know our own failings.

52

If tears were a cure for unhappiness
And crying could stop one being sad,
Tears would be worth whatever money one had
And nothing on earth would fetch a better price.
But in fact crying has no value at all,
Because whether you don't bother yourself with it
Or whether you lament day and night.
The grief whatever it is will run its course.
The heart sends this vapour to the brain
And the brain, through the eyes, sends it down again,
But the evil is not distilled out through the eyes.
Then what is the use of all this blubbering?
It is like pouring on oil to stop something burning,
And you simply lose your sleep and lose your appetite.

53

Let us live, Gordes, live and never mind
What the old people say, but enjoy ourselves:
Let us live, for life is sweet and short as well,
For kings as for the rest of humankind.
The light goes out each night, comes back each day,
And seasons go by as seasons go by,

But when a man has lost this amiable light,
Death makes him sleep for all eternity.
Shall we therefore live the life of beasts?
No, but with our heads held high, at least
Sometimes taste all the sweetness of pleasure.
Only a fool would always give up
The certainty of pleasure for a doubtful hope,
And always go against his own desire.

54

They call you Rascal but it's only a name,
And, to tell the truth, you are a philosopher:
If you were eating your brains out to make sure
Of avoiding poverty, would your face be the same?
The one who is really rich and lives happily
Is the man who, keeping his distance from both extremes,
Limits his wishes and is not over-keen,
For the true way to be rich is live easily.
Come on then, you Rascal, and while our master,
With his mind as usual on public disasters,
Worries himself about other people's affairs,
Go out there by the vine and prepare a salad:
Before you get another we may be dead.
Today is the time to live, and the place is here.

55

Montigné, you know all about the law:
If one of the gods, who has most influence
Promised us both the peaceable enjoyment
Of the world's goods, swearing by Styx and all,
He has not fulfilled his promise very well
And we should take the case to Jupiter:
But if there's no appeal in the matter
Of fortune and what the Fates decide is final,
We will make no appeal, because we're not
More privileged than other men who are brought
To judgement and condemned in such a case:
But if annoyance got a court order
To turn all our indifference out of doors
We should resist whatever the law says.

56

Baïf, like me, you know adversity:
It doesn't always do to fight the storm,
One has to strike sail for fear of worse
And give way to the fury of the sea.
Still one must not, by pusillanimity,
Just be a victim: better to be brave
And wear a hopeful look upon your face,
Making a virtue of necessity.
So, without taking things too much to heart,
But helping ourselves out as best we can,
Let us resist misfortune. I declare
That in future, I am against Fortune;
If she doesn't like it, let her change her tune,
For I, Baïf, shall carry on the war.

57

While you pursue the hare across the flat,
The wild boar in the woods, the kite in the air
And, watching the saker and sparrow-hawk up there,
Take gentle exercise and have pleasant sport,
We the unlucky ones at the court of Rome
No longer, as in your days, hear them talk
Of laughter, parlour games, dances and balls,
But of blood and fire and inhuman slaughter.
Meanwhile, the only pleasure for your friend Gorde
And me, is to talk of your absence and deplore it,
Then read a book or write the odd poem.
Otherwise, all we have to occupy us,
Dugaut, is trouble and work, and to cheer us up
Nothing except laughing at Le Breton.

58

Le Breton is educated, and knows how
To write in French, in Tuscan, Greek and Latin,
His conversation is witty and humane,
He is good company, tells jokes by the hour:
His judgement is good, it doesn't take him long
To tell black and white apart; he writes very well

And can draft a letter that is readable,
Excels in everything and is never wrong:
Only he's lazy, and so afraid of his job
That if he had to go hungry for a month
It would not make him work for fifteen minutes.
He is so idle that I can truly say
That after the eight weeks since he came this way,
If I see his shadow, my energies diminish.

59

You never see me, Pierre, without saying
That I should study less, and make love instead,
And that it's all these books about my bed
Make my eyes dazzled and give me a headache.
But you don't understand: my indisposition
Does not come from too much reading or too long a stay here
But from having to attend to my office work all day:
That, Pierre my friend, is what I spend my time on.
So say no more about it, if you really want
To give me pleasure and not leave me disgruntled:
But instead, while you apply all your skill
To making my beard look smart, and cutting my hair,
To relieve my boredom, tell me what you have heard
About the Pope, and all the latest scandal.

60

Do not imagine the enclosed is about
The praises of the King, or the Guise's reputation,
Nor yet the lady of the Chastillons,
Or the temple that the great Montmorency built.
And don't expect to find Philosophy
Knitting her brow here, or to hear anything
About heaven, the devil or the stars, or involving
Fortune, or justice or mortality,
Certainly not about gold, it's too lofty a matter:
What you will find here is praise of a cat,
Which I send you herewith: my only present,
Take it therefore my lord, and please excuse
The fact that my modest music being no use
For the grand ball, a country dance is sent.

61

If I am near your heart I should be near your purse:
That is what one hears from a frank borrower
Who is generous with the money of others
And is himself bound for the workhouse, or worse.
But consider this: however abundant the spring
It can be exhausted, and the richest lender
Can find himself asking for a loan in the end,
From having too many dealings with those who have nothing.
Gordes, if you want to live happily as a Roman,
Speak fair to everybody but do not let your hand
Dip into your pocket for everyone you come across.
Fair words may win over even an enemy,
While you can lose a good friend by lending him money
And if you lose the money too, that's a double loss.

62

The wily Horace touches on every vice
His friends may have, sparing nobody,
And raising a laugh from the man on whom he seizes,
Appeals to his victim as well as to everyone else.
If therefore any clever person notices
That I attack with a smile, let him not imagine
That I only pretend friendship to those I pin-prick;
Anyone who thinks that will be surprised.
Satire, Dilliers, is a public model,
A sort of mirror in which the wise can tell
In what respects they are hideous or pleasing.
Let no one who reads me now or in the future
Be annoyed at my idea of humour
If he sees something of himself in what he reads.

63

Who is the man who would like us to believe
That he is a good friend? but who, when the wind changes
Finds the winning side more to his taste,
And he prefers those who have the means?
Who is the man who says he can manage the King?
– Or says it when he is in a foreign country

And far enough from the court: L'Estrange, maybe?
L'Estrange, between ourselves, who do you think it is?
Tell me, who is it that is so good at disguises
That among churchmen he passes for a military type
And among soldiers is more likely to pass as a priest?
I don't know his name: I know only that whoever
It may be, he is not a friend, not well in with his master,
Not worth anything to the army, and not a man you could trust.

64

Nature is often kind to bastards
And bastards are often people of energy,
Perhaps because they are begotten the more vigorously
There being more pleasure in it for the father.
Theseus who tamed Medusa, the untameable Hercules,
Bacchus who conquered India, and Castor and Pollux,
And all the other bastard gods who were so valiant once,
Make the whole problem, Bizet, more than life-size.
And how many bastards do we see nowadays
Doing better as poets, or soldiers, or in other ways
Than any legitimate offspring can hope to do?
These bastards are still of noble mind,
But there is one bastard, Bizet, as we now find,
Who could make one wonder about the others too.

65

You are not afraid of my furious pen,
Thinking I have nothing to say against you
Except the sort of vomit you treat me to,
Grinding your poisonous teeth like a hound of hell?
You think I know you only by reputation
And that when I have said you are unreliable,
That you insult people, that your actions are treasonable,
I shall have come to the end of my commination.
You think I can say nothing by way of revenge
But that you eat and drink and serve your own ends:
But I can say something a little more mordant.
What? That you go in for buggery? That you are an atheist?
Neither of those things. Perhaps some other vice?
The long and short of it is, you are a pedant.

66

Do not be surprised that he despises everybody,
Treats everyone with disdain, and admires himself,
Thinks everyone should write just as he tells them
– An Aristarchus, his own supreme authority.
Paschal, he is a pedant! disguise it as he may,
He will always be one. A pedant and a king
Have a lot in common, don't you think?
Something psychological, I would say.
The pedant sees his scholars as his subjects,
His classes are states, his ministers are his prefects,
His college is the entire works of government.
That is why the tyrant Dionysius,
Having been driven from his throne in Syracuse,
And unable to be a king, set up as a pedant.

67

Magny, I cannot stand someone who does nothing but praise,
Finds everything well done, is always delighted,
Approves what I get wrong as much as what is right,
As if I were so distinguished it is all the same.
But I dislike equally the nit-picker
Who finds fault equally with the good and the bad,
Who is always reading his own work, but looks tired
The moment he reads someone who may be better.
The over-praiser by his flattering nonsense
Stops me changing bad verses into decent ones,
And so by pleasing me stops pleasing anyone.
I hate the nit-picker because I cannot do
Anything to please him, and he disgusts me too
With all that he does himself and with all I have done.

68

I hate Florentines for their usurious avarice,
The crazy Sienese for their lack of judgement,
I hate the untruthfulness of the Genevan,
And the Venetian for his cunning malice:
I hate the Ferraran for I don't know what vice,
I hate the Lombards for not keeping their word,

The Nepolitan, whose vanity is absurd,
And the idle Roman for his lack of exercise:
I hate the surly English, the bragging Scotch,
Treacherous Burgundians, Frenchmen who talk too much,
Proud Spaniards, and Germans for their boozing,
Indeed, I hate some vice in every nation,
And I hate myself for my own imperfection,
But most of all I hate pedantic learning.

69

Why snap at me, like a starving dog,
As if Du Bellay couldn't defend himself?
Why insult me, have I treated you to insults,
Unless you count your having been in my thoughts?
You envious cur, what has set you against me,
When I am abroad? Do you imagine my vengeance
Won't reach you because you are in France?
It will, and with more than your sort of fury.
I omit your name, not to spoil my book,
Or to give you in future an important look:
You miserable devil, I won't do you that favour:
But, if you persevers in your abuse,
I'll send you from here, for your personal use,
A poisonous snake or a rope to reward your labour.

70

If Pirithous had not gone down to hell,
His friendship with Theseus would be buried.
Nisus would not have died with such credit,
Had he not seen Euryalus when he fell:
The name of Pylades would not be heard
Without Orestes' fury, the loyalty of Pythias
Would not have been written about so much
If Damon had not behaved well, and returned:
And I should not have found you so fickle
If my fortune had not been so changeable.
What can I do to get my own back on you?
The worst I wish you is, there may be a day
When in like circumstances, but in a more generous way,
I make you see you were wrong, and what I said was true.

71

This hero who thinks that his coat of mail
Makes him a second Roland, this pretender,
So grand with his friends, with his enemies, a flatterer,
Makes out he is clever, but says nothing worth saying.
Don't believe him, Belleau, however he tries
To put a bold look on his lying face;
Discount all his big talk, for there never was
A man of any courage with a mouth of that size.
He talks of nothing but of who he is in with,
He sneers at his master and sucks up to a tribe
Who think nothing of him; he is greedy as hell,
Says he is a Christian, and you can't trust him an inch,
He pretends to be good with the girls, but I think
It is to hide another vice he'd rather not tell of.

72

However well one may be educated
In Greek and Latin subtleties, I think
The effect of this place is to teach something
One didn't know before one came this way.
Not that one finds here better libraries
Than any that the French have put together,
But that the atmosphere, and perhaps the weather,
Spirit away our less ethereal faculties.
Some demon or other, with his sacred fire,
Purifies even the worst of us, tempers and refines
Till our judgement is too wary to be misled.
But if one stays here too long, all one's strength of mind
Goes up in smoke, and leaves nothing behind,
Or so little that one loses the thread.

73

Gordes, I hate an old man who is vicious,
Who imitates the blind desires of youth
And, though the years have made his appetite cool,
Works himself up to sybaritic excess.
But I fear nothing so much as a young man with ambition
Who, getting himself up like a sham hermit,

And hypocritically concealing all his tricks,
Hatches his malice under a charming disposition.
There is, as the proverb says, nothing so dirty
As an old goat, and nothing so anxious to hurt
As a young wolf: or, to put it more politely,
When I consider the nature of the two beasts,
While a dirty swine cannot but displease,
It is of the elegant fox that one has to be wary.

74

You assert that Du Bellay worries about what people say
And that he is not concerned about his friends:
But I have no titles, or honours or anything,
And am the same today as yesterday.
So far, I don't know what ambition is,
And I am not ashamed not to be a great man,
Indeed my position is a constant one
Because it rests on a temperamental basis.
I have no idea how one should talk to one's boss,
How to be pleasant to him, and know still less
How to get on with the nobs, as people now live.
I am polite to everyone, and annoy nobody,
I bow four times if anyone bows to me,
And if people ignore me, I take no notice.

75

Much as I love you, Gordes, I must say
That nature, which has given us different faces
Has also made us different in behaviour,
And, what one of us likes, the other hates.
You say you cannot stand a bragging fool
Who gives himself airs with his inferiors,
Who likes to hear himself talk, shows off like a whore,
And sees himself as an exception to all the rules.
I'm quite different myself, and for this reason:
Those who are civil and always trying to please
Turn me into a courtier against my will:
But a man with a big mouth leaves me quite free,
There is no need to answer him politely,
I leave him alone and he goes on talking still.

76

Speaking ill is a hundred times more delightful
Than praising people, because it means telling the truth,
While praising means, often, that one cannot choose
And has to be servile to say anything at all.
Even when it is true, did it ever please you to read
The praise of some great man, or of some city,
As much as to hear somebody being witty
At someone's expense, and to laugh till you are in tears?
If therefore I may talk innocuously
About vices without mentioning anybody,
The reader can think me cracked or sound, as he likes:
But I think that nowadays it would be found
It is not the wisest who pass for being sound,
As would be seen if the mask came off and they were recognized.

77

I am not here revealing the sacred mysteries
Of the holy Roman priests, and I write nothing
That could cause any embarrassment to a virgin;
My concern is only with more public follies.
You may say it is wrong to call the book, *Regrets*,
Since half the time I'm trying to raise a laugh;
But I say that the sea is not always rough,
And that slings and arrows are not the only subjects.
If you find something here that looks like a joke,
Do not suppose that there is some mistake
And that my poems from Italy had all to be moans.
The moans I make, Dilliers, are authentic:
If I laugh, it is a sort of party trick,
And not a laugh I laugh when I'm alone.

78

I will not tell you about Bologna and Venice,
Padua and Ferrara, or about Milan,
Naples and Florence, and which of them are
Best equipped for conducting war, or commerce:
I'll tell you about the headquarters of the Church,
Which above all things values idleness,

And which, under the triple crown and its stuck-up-ness
Hatches ambition, hatred, pretence and worse.
I will say that here is good and ill fortune,
Vice and virtue, here is pleasure and pain,
Respectable learning and plain ignorance.
Indeed I will say that here is a great heap,
Pelletier, of all the world's bits and pieces
Of good and evil, as in Chaos once.

79

I do not write of love, I am not a lover,
I do not write of beauty, I have no mistress,
I do not write of kindness, here is uncouthness,
I do not write of pleasures, my pleasures are over:
I do not write of happiness, I am unhappy,
I do not write of favours, no one to give them,
I do not write of treasures, I am not rich,
I do not write of health, for I am poorly:
I do not write of the court, I am far from my Prince,
I do not write of France, I am in a strange province,
I do not write of honour, I see none here:
I do not write of friendship, all is here pretence,
I do not write of virtue, which also is absent,
I do not write of knowledge, where churchmen are.

80

If I go to the Vatican, I find only pride,
Dissimulated vice, and ceremony,
The sound of drums, a strange harmony,
And scarlet outfits flaunted on every side:
If I go to the Exchange, what I find there
Is the news of the day, and appalling usury,
A crowd of rich expatriate Florentines
And a few poor Sienese, who are close to tears:
If I go on, everywhere that I go
I find a plentiful supply of whores
Decked out to make the most of their attractions:
If I go further still, and from the new Rome
Enter the ancient Rome, I see the shame
Of monuments turned to a heap of stones.

81

It's good, Paschal, to see a packed conclave,
With one cardinal's room close to another,
Serving as antichamber, hall and kitchen,
For which the ten feet square is enough room:
It's good to see the Vatican walled in,
And all these holy men deep in intrigue,
One plain ambitious, another full of deceit,
And because they are jealous of one, another is adored:
It's good to see the town outside in arms,
Shouting a Pope is made, on a false alarm
Sacking a candidate's house, but better still,
To see who talks up one candidate or another,
And who supports whom when the talking's over:
Ten cardinals go for a pound in the final sale.

82

Would you like to know, Duthier, what Rome is like?
Rome is the public stage of all the world,
A theatre on which is seen and heard
All that can possibly happen to mankind.
Here is the wheel of Fortune, you may see
How one turn sends us up, another down:
Here each man's vice is plain to the whole town,
What ever pains he is at to conceal it.
Here false news travels fast, the true no less,
Here courtiers make love and their affairs progress,
Here cunning and ambition are plentiful:
Here anyone who wants may be audacious,
And idleness makes even good men vicious,
There is endless talk of affairs from the rogue and the fool.

83

Don't think, Robertet, that Rome as it is now
Is like the Rome which so pleased you once,
One gets no credit here, as in those times,
One does not make love as one used to do.
Peace and good times are here no more,
The music is silent and the dancing's stopped,

The air stinks, and violence is common,
Common too, hunger, suffering and care.
The tradesman shuts up, enticed away,
The lawyer has nothing to do all day,
The poor dealer has become a beggar:
There is nothing to be seen but soldiers in helmets,
Nothing to be heard but drums, and the noise of trumpets,
And another sack of Rome is expected.

84

We do not spend our time here writing poetry,
As you do, whose lives are undisturbed:
If you want to know what in fact it is we do do,
The next ten lines will make it plain as day:
Follow one's cardinal to the Pope, to the consistory,
To chapel, on visits, or to the congregation,
And honour some prince, or some nation,
By waiting on some ambassador in his glory:
Be in place in the train of one's master,
And do the usual honours to chance-comers,
Talking of the latest rumour, and seeming smart:
Go out in state, calling from door to door,
Borrowing money from Jews and talking to whores,
These my friends, are what the amusements of Rome are.

85

To flatter a creditor, for time to pay,
And to look promising to please a banker,
Not to speak freely as one does in France,
And, before answering, to worry about what one should say:
Not to suffer from too much drink and food,
Not to spend money rashly without reflection,
Not to say what one thinks to everyone,
And to manage foreigners without the right words:
To know dispositions and who wants what,
To be the more careful, the freer one is to talk,
In case one gets into trouble when it is known:
To keep in with everybody, to watch everybody:
That, dear Morel, I am ashamed to say
Is all I have learnt in three years in Rome.

86

To walk solemnly and with brows knit,
And welcome everyone with a solemn smile,
Weigh all one's words, answer and think as well
Whether 'Yes, sir' or 'No, sir' is what is wanted:
Often adding such expressions as 'And so'
And 'Your servant, sir', pretending to be civil,
And talking about Florence and Naples in a way that will
Sound as if the victories were one's own:
To treat everyone like a lord, and kiss his hand,
And, in the manner of an intriguing Roman,
To hide one's poverty under great elegance:
That is the highest virtue of this court,
From which, often ill-dressed and out of sorts,
Beardless and penniless, one goes back to France.

87

How does it happen, Mauny, that the more
One tries to escape, the more the spirit of the place
(It would take a god to effect such a change)
Holds us bound here with some attractive force?
Could it be love, luring us to stay,
Or some other poison, such that when we drink
We feel little by little, our minds shrink,
As under new skin the body may waste away?
A thousand times I have wanted to leave
But I feel my hair changing into leaves,
My arms into branches, my feet into a root.
Indeed, I am now nothing but a living trunk,
Objecting helplessly to the transformation
Like that Englishman who was turned into a myrtle.

88

Who will find me the root Ulysses had?
And who will stop me falling into the danger
That some Circe effects such a change
That I shall go permanently to the bad?
Who will put Medusa's ring on my finger,
To disenchant me as she did Ruggiero?

And will some Mercury not free me so
That I waste my time in love's service no longer?
Who will let me by without hearing the voices
And being subject to the Sirens' devices?
Who will drive these greedy harpies away?
Who will steal a thunderbolt from heaven
To give me back my sight and my good sense?
And who will ensure that I live peacefully?

89

Gordes, it seems to me I have woken up,
As someone frightened by a terrible dream
Wakes up with a start, and stretches anxiously,
Astonished that he has been asleep so long.
Ruggiero was struck with wonder in this way
And, just in the same way, I am ashamed,
As he was, to discover that the game
Was a lie, which he entered upon so blindly.
Like him now I want to change my style,
As he in the bosom of Logistilla,
Who gives susceptible hearts general support.
Come on then, Gordes, hoist the sail, seize the oar,
And let us hurry away from this shore
To where that Lady beckons us to her port.

90

Do not think, Bouju, that the Latin nymphs,
By giving their deceits a friendly look,
Or disguising their complexions with false beauty,
Are making me forget the girls of Anjou.
The Angevine sweetness, the divine speech,
The dress, so free of any exhibitionism,
The grace, the youth and the simplicity,
Make me disgusted with these tawdry bitches.
Looking at the outside, nothing could be finer,
But nothing so like the grave as the inside,
Without going into more sordid details.
What greed! and what squalid poverty!
And what a horror to find they are so filthy!
A young man has to see them to be saved.

91

O lovely silver hair, all twisted up!
O corrugated brow and golden face!
O beautiful glass eyes! O, the vast space
Of mouth, creased at both ends when it is shut!
O lovely ebony teeth! O precious treasures
Which raise a laugh from everyone taken in!
O throat inlaid with a hundred shapes,
And you great breasts, not least of all these pleasures!
O lovely gilded claws, on short fat hands!
Delicate thighs! Legs plumply elegant!
To say nothing of what I cannot name!
Lovely transparent body! Limbs of ice!
O divine beauties! Pardon, I dare not try
To enclose you in a mere mortal's embrace.

92

Doing her hair up in a thousand ringlets,
Plucking her eyebrows, and with special oils
Perfuming her mouldy body top and tail,
And covering her face with white and red:
Wearing a mask all night, talking through a mask,
Always pretending to be madly in love,
And whistling through screens all night to get enough,
Wanting some other than the one who asks:
Dancing, singing, chattering, rampaging in bed,
More often than not with two tongues in her head,
These are the ordinary occupations of whores.
But is there any need for me to tell you?
If you are curious, Gordes, you might as well
Ask La Chassaigne, who can tell you that, and more.

93

Goddess of Cyprus, sweet mother of Love,
Who compel all the powers to acknowledge your power,
And who, from the banks of Scamander, guided here,
With your son's help, the Trojan fugitives,
If I go back to France, lady of Ida,
As I came here, without falling into the danger

104

Of finding my skin unpleasantly changed,
And my French beard become the Italian kind,
Here and now I swear, I will hang upon your altar,
Not lilies, nor the amaranth which is immortal,
Nor the flower which is the colour of your blood:
No, but the tawny fleece which grows upon my chin,
And I shall boast to have done more than Jason,
Who brought another fleece when he came home.

94

Happy the man who can be long at the wars
Without death, wounds, or long years in prison!
Happy the man who can be away from home
Without going broke, or selling up land and all!
Happy the one who can acquire some favour
Without the risk of envy or treason!
Happy anyone who, without danger of poison,
Can swank with a cardinal's hat or the keys of Peter!
Happy whoever is safe far from dry land,
Or without lawsuits at the Vatican!
Happy the man who can die quietly at home!
Happy the man who can hold on to his fortune,
And his wife without suspicion, and still more
Happy he who can keep his hair for three years in Rome!

95

A thousand curses upon Hannibal
Who, having found a way to split the rocks,
Not only proved the Alps could not stop him,
But opened the road to Italy for all.
Without him, there would not have been that envy
Poisoning the hearts of Spaniards, and French soldiers,
And there would have been fewer people coming here
To lose their lives and their sense of honesty.
The Frenchman corrupted by foreign vice
Would not have changed his coat and changed his speech,
Nor changed the nature of his life and morals.
He would not have been diseased and lost his hair,
Or been the one they named the pox after,
Or found so often he had no money at all.

96

O Goddess Fortune, who can make a beggar,
Who has nothing but words, the equal of a prince,
You made a great king a schoolmaster once,
Pulling him down even to that level!
I do not ask you to include me
Among the gentlemen who do really well,
So that people talk of me, if at all,
As if I were one of the great names of history:
There are thousands of things I do not ask for,
All of them certainly well within your power,
I do not ask for any excessive fortune.
I only ask that my own doesn't disappear,
And that they don't call in the receiver,
So that I leave here absolutely broke.

97

Doulcin, when sometimes I see these poor girls
Who are possessed of the devil, or seem to be,
Making horrible movements of head and body,
Doing much the same as once those old Sibyls:
When I see the strongest of them suddenly weak,
Trying in vain to get back their insane energy:
When I see even the best doctors helplessly
In doubt as to what useful steps they can take:
When I hear the poor patients cry,
And roll their eyes till they show only the whites,
My hair stands on end, and I am silent.
But when I see a monk with his Latin,
Feeling all over their breasts and sexual organs,
My terror passes, I cannot restrain a smile.

98

Why is it that we so often see in Rome
Girls who have gone mad, most of them just children,
Or little more, Ronsard, and what is the reason
There is one convent especially that they come from?
Who talks through their voices? What devil is it forbids
That the girls should speak to people they don't know?

106

And why is it they are suddenly gone
And if a candle is blown out what accounts for it?
Why in these holy places do they get worse?
Why do so many spirits torment one girl?
If one is exorcised, what about the rest?
Tell me, Ronsard, you understand their natures,
What are they that so bedevil the poor creatures?
The highest sort of spirit, the middle, or the lowest?

99

When I go through the street, and see the crowds
Of priests, prelates and monks, tradesmen and bankers,
It strikes me as odd that there is a lack
Of what one sees in Paris, women wandering about.
It is as if, after the universal flood,
These parts were not properly populated;
To see the people here, you would have said
That God had only created half the world.
For the Roman lady, so decorous,
The wife of the lawyer or the man of business,
Does not walk about here, and all one sees
Is those who trade in sex, so there is a chance,
I am afraid, that when I get back to France,
I may take every woman for one of these.

100

Ursin, when I hear these old Roman names,
The great names which are known to the ends of the earth,
Applied to people who are of little worth,
The better sort and the rabble using the same:
I am furious to hear these rascals called
By the famous names which all the world holds in honour,
And, but for the name of Christian, which alone I adore,
I could wish that our saints had names as noble.
My own name annoys me, so does the name William,
And a thousand others which with us are common,
Seeing that here they call such unspeakable creatures
By the great names which belonged to old Rome and Greece,
But most of all, Ursin, it annoys me when I hear
A whore called by the chaste name of Lucretia.

101

Melin, what shall we say of this Roman court,
Where we see everyone adopting different methods,
And the least considerable reaching the highest honours,
Through vice, through virtue, by work, or without effort?
One spends a lot of money and gets nowhere,
Another spends, and becomes an important man,
One is severe, and so makes an impression,
Another finds that being kind pays better:
One makes progress by seeming to hang back,
Another pushes till he comes a cropper,
What does no good to one, propels another:
Some say that knowledge is the way to honour,
Others assert that ignorance does better,
Which of the two, Melin, is the more probable?

102

You can't make a silk purse out of a sow's ear,
So they say: but here we see any material
Will do to make a Pope or cardinal,
And three days are enough to change the features.
Princes and kings are accustomed to being grand,
And there is less danger it will turn their heads,
As it does those of these jumped up temporary gods,
Who have not got the habit of command.
Paschal, I have seen men who have been followed
By the whole of Rome, whenever they walked abroad,
Walking through the streets with no following at all:
And seen with great masses of attendants
Men whose fathers knew nothing of anything
Except following a plough and the ox's tail.

103

If the losses you have known, your mother's tears,
The family's regrets, any of these,
Has made you understand what mourning is,
Cupid, however cruel and heartless you are:
Now is the time to put aside your torch,
Now is the time to do without those arrows,

Now is the time to snap your bow in two,
As you did on the occasion of your original loss:
For it is not here that you should be mourning
The father of young Ascanius: now what needs doing
Is to mourn Ascanius himself, the little sod,
The Ascanius whom Carafa loved more than his eye-teeth,
Ascanius who in physical beauty exceeded
The Trojan cup-bearer who poured wine for the gods.

104

If fruit and grapes and corn and such-like things
Have shoots and stems, they certainly have seeds,
And if as gentle spring comes round, one sees
Violets and roses everywhere springing:
No fruit, nor grape, nor corn, nor any bloom
Will issue from the body that lies here:
Garlic, leeks, onions, and such stinking weeds
Will have their origins in this dark room.
Passer-by, therefore, if you cannot hope
To offer spices to this buried Pope,
Julius the Third, give him a whiff of this:
On earth he used to stuff his god-like body
With all the members of the onion family,
As Jupiter in heaven feeds on ambrosia.

105

To see the King's bum-boy a respected courier,
A young lad with orders and decorations,
A little nobody with a royal pension,
Is, Morel, after all, nothing particular.
But to see a little page, a child, an idiot,
Who talks about courage, made a cardinal,
And for having combed a pet monkey well,
A little bugger given a red hat:
To have been exhibited wearing a halter,
High on a scaffold, by a Spanish soldier,
And then to find oneself a Holy Pope:
A little squirt in three days like a king,
And in three days back where he was again:
These are the miracles you see only in Rome.

106

Who can deny, Gillebert, unless he flies
In the face of general opinion, that Peter's chair,
Which must surely be thought heaven on earth,
Has its great Jupiter, as have the skies?
The Greeks put the one upon Olympus,
From which his lightning falls upon men:
The other thunders from the Vatican,
Whenever some king has annoyed him enough:
The heavenly Jupiter had a Ganymede,
It takes fifty to meet the other's needs:
One gets drunk on nectar, the other on wine.
Both of them prefer eagles to doves,
But one hates tyrants while the other loves them:
In this the mortal differs from the divine.

107

Wherever I look, towards the Capitol,
The baths of Hadrian or of Diocletian,
Or at any more ancient monument
Which may survive within the city walls:
Secretly I detest the Reaper, the robber,
And heaven which has brought all to nothing:
But give the devil his due, I say, and think
What a fool I am to get so hot and bothered:
And indeed it is an impertinence
To accuse Time and say heaven has no sense,
All for a damaged medal or a broken column.
And who knows but all will come round again,
Since every day we see so many noblemen
Build on the Forum or the Coliseum.

108

Once I was Hercules, but am Pasquino,
As people call me now, yet I perform
The same labours as under my old name,
For with my verses I clobber dubious heroes.
My true vocation is to spare nobody,
But bawl out vices at the top of my voice:

Even though I cannot, however hard I try
Compete with the many-headed Roman fury.
I have borne on my shoulders the Palace of the Gods,
To help out Atlas, who was getting tired,
Holding up the complete outfit of heaven.
Now I have a more exhausting mission,
I hold up a gentle monk from the Inquisition
Who weighs as much as all the gods put together.

109

Unless a man who is cleaning out a cess-pit
Has something to give protection to his nose,
The stinking atmosphere may make him choke
And he may die there buried in the shit:
So good Marcellus, who pulled up the sluice
To let out all the vicious muck and slime
From which the last Holy Father, in his time,
Had for six years distilled his poisonous juice:
The poor fellow, knocked back by the stink,
Collapsed and died while working at this sink,
Before he'd even half cleaned the place out.
Anyone who can clean up all the rest
Will have done more than Hercules at his best,
For the Augean stables hardly count.

110

When Caracciolo chooses to describe
War, winds and winter: then at once we see
A violent storm, and a blazing fury
Agitate hearts, heads, everything besides.
When he will have no more of such disturbance,
No wars, no storms, no frost, an amorous heat,
A long, good-natured mildness is released,
Then hearts are put at ease and storms are curbed.
So he contrasts, in one age, peace and war,
Fine weather and tempest, spring and winter,
Comparing Paul the Fourth with Julius the Third.
Two centuries were never so different,
Nor could one better show what these two meant
Than is done here in Caracciolo's words.

111

I have never thought that there was constancy
Under the vault of heaven: now more than ever
It seems to me, Morel, that never, never,
Can anything here below be built firmly.
For he who dominated land and sea
With thunderbolts and terror, tired at last,
Wants to restrict his great actions to a cloister,
Give up the world and serve God quietly.
Then what shall we say of this other old man
Who, having spent his better days as one
In the service of God, now imitates the Emperor?
I don't know which of the two is more confused,
But think, Morel, it must be an illusion,
I distrust the one's wars and the other's prayers.*

112

When I see all these great men, who having given up
Sword and lance for this holy Roman pride,
And those others who find it exciting
To play at generals without ever having shown their courage:
When I see them, too grand to be spoken to,
And with a row of eight antechambers to prove it,
And with a footman in each, they all love it,
And the patience of Job will hardly see you through:
I often think of those enchanted palaces
In Amadis, Palmerin and such romances,
Where they put so high a price on getting in.
Then I say: the Papal Palace I am in
Seems to be different from the Palace of my King,
Where there is no door that is not wide open.

113

To have seen one monstrous triple crown go down,
A mild successor appear and disappear,
And the Caraffa that we now have here,
Set upon the tomb of the emperor Hadrian:
To see only soldiers go in, then out to battle,
To see great men imprisoned for doubtful crimes,

* Charles V retired to a monastery; Pope Paul IV became bellicose in his old age.

Exiles come back again, and all the time
The Pope from Naples laying the Spaniards flat:
Many new lords, and of them all the greatest
Closely related to His Holiness,
Many cardinals, whose names one hardly knows:
Many fine horses, and fine equipages,
And many favourites, who just now were pages,
This, my dear Dagaut, is the news from Rome.

114

Unhappy, oh, unhappy is the land
Whose prince sees only through other men's eyes,
Hears only what they hear, lets them reply,
Blind, deaf and dumb, and with no understanding!
So are those, my lord, who today are shut,
Idling, each in his room, as if in boxes
To keep them better, and so they won't feel the shocks
Which, overwhelmed by war, their people suffer.
Like children they love trumpets and love guns,
Bright flags and coloured banners, fifes and drums,
And their province at the mercy of the enemy.
They are like Nero, fiddling while Rome burned,
High in a tower, with the flames all around,
Singing about the fall of Troy, and happy.

115

Dagaud, you don't know how lucky you are
To have got out of the hands of this gang
Who, making out they have liked us all along,
Filch away all our money, lives and honour!
Where you are there is not this secret rancour,
The many-sided cares we have to cope with,
But here the endless hatred, envy, avarice
Of petty courtiers poisons every hour.
With you, idleness does not mean mischief,
And no one works without pay and reliefs,
Nor do they talk behind people's backs:
Justice is done, friendship is not fatal,
And no one knows what it is to calculate
Shares and percentages like a city hack.

116

Let us escape, Dilliers, from this cruel land,
This grasping city and inhuman people,
Before the angry gods make us all feel
The violence of the thunderbolts in their hands.
Mars is unleashed and the temple of war
Is opened as I write, the Roman high-priest
Strikes at the German heretics, and what he
Calls the kike Spaniards, enemies of Saint Peter.
Nothing to be seen but soldiers, flags and banners,
Nothing to be heard but trumpets, drums and cannon,
Horses and men everywhere down below:
The only talk now is of blood and fire;
Now if ever is the time to admire
The Roman ark, and see how the Pope can row.

117

He certainly knew something, the man who announced
That the divine seed of fire being the origin
Of all creatures that ever were living,
Our minds must be made of the same substance.
The body is the torch lit by that burning,
And, the finer the matter of it may be,
The more it blazes and the mind finds it the easier
To show the nature of its own concerns.
So this celestial fire, of humble birth,
Rises little by little to show its worth,
Until it has risen to its full size:
Then it grows smaller, its strength gone
For lack of matter only ashes remain,
And suddenly it feels its heat less.

118

When I see these characters, whose authority,
Each in his office, is so powerful here,
Advancing side by side to instil fear,
I think I am in the presence of some divinity.
But when I see them pale as His Holiness
Spits into a basin, and with white faces

Take a sly look to see if there are traces
Of blood, and smile that there is no danger yet:
I think, how pitiful the greatness I see here
Is beside that of a king and I despair
At those who buy honour at such a price.
The sword of Damocles, and a Rock also,
Hangs over the heads of these Vatican boys,
Since by this old thread hang their own lives.

119

Brusquet will tell you when he gets back, your Majesty,
How very grand these scarlet prelates look,
With their slippers, costumes, bows long and dramatic,
Difficult to describe, but he'll do them easily.
He will tell you, if he can do it properly,
The manners of this court, and the difference
Between these greatnesses and the greatness of France,
But it will make you laugh to hear what he's seen.
He will describe the looks and dress of the Holy Father,
Who, like Jupiter, can change the whole temper
Of the world with a wink; his flow of talk, his grace,
The nobility of his entourage, their generous manners,
The presents he gets, and with what loving hands
All your interests are taken into the Roman embrace.

120

The Carnival! Let everyone bring a girl,
Let's go to the masked ball, walk in the streets,
Hear the jesters jest and see clowns perform their feats,
And great men laughed at yet remaining amiable:
Let us see races run in the ancient style,
And the stupid buffaloes led by the nose,
Or, for those with a preference for war-like shows,
Let us see how skilful Italians are at a bull-fight.
Let us enjoy the shower of bad eggs,
And the air which is lit up with squibs and rockets.
Let us make the most of the dispensation:
Tomorrow we shall have to visit the holy places,
There we shall make love, but only by the looks on our faces,
To go further would be against regulations.

121

To be maddened all day by a maddening sport,
To see a courageous bull run round in circles,
Astonished to see so many men at the circus,
His courage challenged by fifty picadors:
To see him as he charges head down
Back away and then come on more boldly than ever,
And then to see him beaten in the end,
Covered in wounds, his blood all over the ground:
To see torches racing here and there,
And inept swordmanship in shining armour,
With a whole pile of Teutons looking on:
To make great preparations for a long wait
And, after all, a rotten entertainment:
That is what is called pleasure by the Romans.

122

While, in the Palace, you talk of law-suits,
Advocates, procurators, counsellors, presidents,
Instructions and decrees, and new appointments,
Corrupt judges, what other kind would they choose?
Here we talk about the odd victory,
Financial matters, and all the latest news,
More cardinals, attendants, lovely shoes,
And a whole lot of Roman haberdashery:
And then, Sibilet, as I am writing,
It is of bulls and buffaloes that we are talking,
Masks, banquets, entertainments and so on:
Tomorrow it will be of going to shrines,
Getting the right piece of paper at the right time,
Of the other sort of bulls, and dispensations.

123

We are not sorry to see the truce arranged,
Because although we are far away from France
We understand perfectly that this is a chance
For a country weary of war to have peace again:
Still, it disturbs us that the insolent Spaniard,
Who needs a respite even more than the French,

Can boast that he makes war or peace as it suits him best,
And that we are giving him the breathing space he planned.
We are sorry to hear our wretched allies
Complaining that we have lost our memories
And that we have forgotten the common interest:
But what we are most sorry for is that foreigners
Can once more say how light-headed we are
Not to understand when Fortune serves us best.

124

The King, or so say the Florentine exiles,
Will never now lay his hands on the sceptre of Italy,
And his hand will never now be so lucky
As to touch the Fortune of France and see her smile.
The Pope will not longer have confidence
In all those fine designs, so lightly made;
Remembering Siena, foreigners will be afraid
To put their trust in any French alliance.
The Emperor, weak now, will quickly recover
And the Empire will remain Spanish for ever,
And England be left more peaceful than before:
That's what people say, when they talk of the King:
What answer can we give them? Vineus, say something,
You who are such an expert on peace and war.

125

In that dark womb where was once enclosed
All that has since filled out the great void,
Air, earth and fire, and the elemental liquid,
The whole outfit that made Atlas's load,
The original atoms were still mixed up,
No separate hot and dry, or cold and wet;
The laws of science were not thought of yet,
And so the gate of Chaos remained shut:
It was as if war had filled the lock with dust,
Or age deformed the key with layers of rust,
The baby struggled but could not get free:
But when the truce announced we should have peace,
And found ways of effecting her release,
Then out she came, with love, so easily!

Welcome, welcome, and God bless the truce!
The truce is something for Christians to sing about,
For it alone can, as if by magic, wipe out
Memories of past labours and confusions.
It's supposed to last five years, I hope it wants to,
Because if through divine intervention it achieves
What is expected of it, then we may believe
That we can have a peace and a long one too.
But if the party with most reason to be content
Is given the opportunity to choose his moment
To renew his accusations and seize our territory:
If the peace everyone is asking for
Is to leave us worse off than we were before
Better fight on than make such a peace.

Bad faith here has not one disguise, but many,
Crime here is not thought something to avoid,
There are no penalties for homicide and poison,
And the way to get rich here is lend money:
It is the bastards here who found great houses,
And nobody believes in religion here
Where every time is the right time for pleasure,
Which is enjoyed more the less it is allowed.
You can imagine the rest. But perhaps after all
There are even here some legal scruples
And justice is not altogether banished:
Everything here is not done by bribery,
And perhaps great men are not always ready
To use force and fraud to enforce justice.

Carle, it is not my idea of sailing from Italy,
The way my ship flounders: but whatever I think
The wind drives it wherever it is blowing
Without a thought of the attractions you see.
I see nothing but rocks, and that is not the worst,
Consider what there is crashing on the rocks:

And the beacon to which I used to be able to look
Has disappeared completely, which is not re-assuring.
But if one day I do get away from the dangers
Of these foreign seas, and see for a change
An ocean composed of green fields for miles,
I will lay up my boat on the Gallic shore
And dedicate my efforts to the French Neptune or
Other appropriate mythological wiseacres.

129

Dilliers, I see the storm subside at last,
I see old Proteus shut up all his monsters
And green Triton desporting himself on the water
And Castor and Pollux blazing above the mast.
A favourable wind is springing up,
And I begin to row towards the harbour,
Now I see more friends than I can number,
Celebrating on the shore and holding their arms out.
There's the great Ronsard, I recognize him from here,
I see my friend Morel, and Dorat's another,
Now I see Delahaie, and Paschal too:
And further off, if I am not deceived,
The inspired Mauleon, whom I have never seen
But whom I admire for his grace and learning and virtue.

130

I too thought what Ulysses once thought,
That nothing could be pleasanter than to see
The smoke rising from my own chimney,
And to be again in the land where I was brought up.
I congratulated myself on having got away
From the Circes of Italy and the Sirens of sex,
And thought that once back in France I should find the respect
That is earned by faithful service, or so they say.
No good. After years of worry in Rome,
I come back here only to find trouble at home,
And to agonize because things will never mend.
So good bye, Dorat, I must still be a Roman
Unless you are willing to let me try my hand
With the bow the Muses gave you, to take my revenge.

TWENTY POEMS
OF PAUL VALÉRY

The Birth of Venus

De sa profonde mère, encor froide et fumante

From her profound mother, still cold and steaming,
Here on the storm-slapped threshhold, the flesh, see,
Bitterly cast up in the sun by the sea,
Shakes off the diamonds, done with their tormenting.

Her smile forms, following along white arms
The dawn of a bruised shoulder weeps upon;
The pure jewels of the moist Thetis gathers on
Tresses which ripple her flanks with alarm.

The cool gravel, drenched and escaping as she goes,
Crumbles, hollow and thirsty, and as it flows
Sand has drunk the kisses of her childish bounds;

But with a thousand looks, vague or deceitful,
Her mobile eye catches the dangerous ground,
Smiling water, waves dancing, deceiving all.

The Friendly Wood

Nous avons pensé des choses pures

Our thoughts were certainly quite pure
As, side by side, through the woodlands
We walked together, holding hands
Without a word... even the flowers obscure.

We went like a couple who are engaged,
Alone, through all the fields of green night;
We were sharing the fairy fruit of moon-light,
Friendly to those whose madness is unassuaged

And then, we died together on the moss,
Far away, alone while shadowy branches toss
Gently above us, intimate, murmuring,

And up there, in the brilliant immensity,
We found ourselves in our sudden weeping,
O my dear companion, sharing silence with me.

La Jeune Parque

To André Gide

For many years
I had abandoned the art of verse:
attempting to force myself to it again,
I have done this exercise
which I dedicate to you.
1917

Le Ciel a-t-il formé cet amas de merveilles
Pour la demeure d'un serpent?
Pierre Corneille.

Who is that weeping, at this hour, the wind?
Alone?... But who weeps, with extreme diamonds,
So close to myself at the moment of weeping?

This hand almost passes over my face, dreaming,
Inattentive, docile to some deep purpose,
Expecting a melting tear from my weakness,
And that of my fates, silently set apart,
The purest will reveal a broken heart.
The sea-swell, with a murmur of reproach,
Or drawing back into its rocky throat,
Like a disappointed thing, bitterly swallowed,
A rumour of complaint and heavy doubt...
What are you doing, tousled head, cold hand,
What traces of a dead leaf shudder and
Persist between the islands of my breast...
I scintillate, and heaven does the rest...
The immense bunch tempts my thirst for tragedy.

All-powerful strangers, stars which govern me,
You deign to shine upon the temporal
A light both pure and supernatural;
You who plunge into mortals, even to tears
Invincible arms, flashes of blinding fears.
These transports from your own eternity,
I am alone with you, I have tremblingly
Quitted my bed; on rocks bitten by wonder,
I ask my heart what pain it labours under,
What crime of mine, or consummated on me?...
...Or whether the trouble came from a dream
When (the golden lamp-light gone somehow)
I pressed my soft arms about my brow,
And waited for flashes from my tardy soul?
All of me? All my own, my flesh controlled,
Hardening its strange surface with a shudder,
And in sweet bonds, attentive to my blood,
I saw myself, sinuous, gilding the crests
From look to look, of my profound forests.
I was following a serpent who had bitten me.

A train of coiled desires!...What treasures he
Snatched in disorder from me, left me avid
And with how dark a thirst for something limpid!

O ruse!...Derelict in the light of pain,
I felt myself rather known than hurt again...
In my deceiving soul a poisoned thorn;
Poison, my poison, so is self-knowledge born:
It colours a virgin who is interlaced
With it, and jealous...Jealous, and by whom menaced?
What silence speaks to my only possessor?

Gods! In my heavy wound a secret sister
Burns, and prefers herself to all attentions.

'Go! I have no need of such a simpleton,
Dear Serpent...I embrace myself, my head spins,
Lend me no more the knots that you are in,
Nor your devotion, guessing and elusive...
My soul is quite enough, while I live!

She loses her torments on my shade and bites
The charming rocks my breast are, in the night;
And there she sucks the milk of reverie...
Therefore let fall this arm loaded with jewelry
Which threatens me with love said to be spiritual...
You can do nothing which would be less cruel,
Or less desirable... Bid these waves be still,
Retrieve this eddy, promising so much ill...
My surprise stops, and my eyes open wide,
I expected nothing less of all this pride
Than the birth of such a fury in my thoughts;
These passionate deserts glitter in their drought,
So far off, I advance and thirst to see
The pensive hells in which, hopelessly...
I know... Sometimes my weariness is pretence.
The mind is not so pure, so dull to sense,
It lonely passion with its bursts of heat
Should never see its prison-walls retreat.
Everything happens, if one waits for ever,
And agony makes even shadows waver,
The mean road half-opens, moved by desire,
Which twists and turns before a gate of fire...
And yet, prompt and capricious though you seem,
Reptile, your living coils caressed in dream,
Impatience may be close, and langour heavy,
But what are you, to my eternity?
You watched my lovely sleeping negligence,
But, threatened, I am not without intelligence,
More fickle, Thyrsis, and less sure than they.
Avoid me! Back along your viscous way!
Go, look for closed eyes for your massive dances,
Glide into other beds with your disguises,
Hatch out on other hearts their germs of ill,
And may the windings of your dream enthral,
All the night long, some anxious innocent!...
I keep awake. I go out, pale, intent,
Wet with many tears I have not shed,
Back to the shape of a girl cossetted
By herself alone... Breaking from a calm grave.
I relax uneasily, and yet I have
Sovereignty over visions of night and eye,
And my least movements answer to my pride.

But I trembled to lose a divine pain and
I kissed the fine tooth-marks on my hand;
I knew nothing of my athletic form
Except the fire that kept the surface warm.

Good-bye, I thought, SELF, mortal sister, lie...
Harmonious SELF, no dream, certainly,
A woman flexible, firm – a silent stare
Followed by pure action...Clear brown, and hair
Carried away so far by the waves
That it ends in a shaggy wind and behaves
As if in flight...I was the bride of the day,
Born aloft by my love in delicious play
To the all-powerful altitude, adored...

What flashes blind me with their golden hoard,
O eye-lids weighted by a treasured night,
I prayed in shadows which the gold made bright!
Porous to the eternal all around,
My velvet fruit devoured by it, I found
No hint at all that a desire to die
Could ripen in my pulp, in this blue sky:
As yet I had no taste of bitterness.
Only my bare shoulder was a sacrifice
To light; and upon my honeyed breast,
Which heaven had nurtured, the world's face sought rest
And came to fall into a half-slumber.
Then, in this sun, a wandering prisoner,
I shook myself and, on the sand, deep-pressed,
Bound and unbound the ghosts under my dress.
Happy! and, looking along the range of hills,
Saw all the joins and dips in them until
The valleys showed in their proud frailty;
And if, as if to check this liberty,
The linen catches where the bramble is,
My body quickly bends and so displays
Me naked underneath the swelling colours,
Where my youth wrestles with long lines of flowers.

I half regret this vain resilience...
One with desire, I was the obedience
Associated with these polished knees;

I felt my cause scarcely less prompt than they.
Towards my bright senses swam my blond clay,
And in the ardent peace of dreams so natural,
All these infinite steps appeared eternal.
If it is not, Splendour, that the enemy,
My shadow! the mobile and supple mummy
Skimming, where I was not, over the ground
Where the faint death I feared was to be found.
Between the rose and me, I see her sheltering;
On the dancing dust, she glides without touching
A single leaf, but passes, never insists...
Glide! Ship of death...

                          I, on my feet, exist,
Hard in the armour of my nothingness,
Yet one cheek inflamed by tenderness,
My nostril full of orange-blossom scent,
My look back at the light is half absent...
How in the curious night the secret part
Can grow, within my separated heart,
Its skill enhanced by its experiments...
Far from purity, I am in imprisonment
And by faint odours utterly undone,
I feel my statue shudder in the sun,
Its marble played on by capricious light.
But I know what is there for vanished sight;
My dark eye is before the house of the dead!
I think, letting the breeze give time its head,
My soul still on the bitter, shrubby bank,
At the gilded edge of the universe, I think
Of the taste for death felt by the Pythoness
In whom there howls the hope for nothingness.
I renew my enigmas and my gods,
And prayers interrupt my steps, my stops
Bearing upon my feet the weight of dreams
Following a mirrored bird in the wind's streams;
It changes, dips to nothing in the sun,
And burns, my gaping marble looking on.
O dangerously the prey of its own glance!

For the spirit's eye upon its silken sands
Had seen dawns and dusks so many days
Of which the colours were the same always.
The tedium of the shades that I could see
Gave me a taste of what my life would be:
The light revealed at once the hostile day.
I was half-dead; and yet was in a way
Half-immortal, dreaming the future no more
Than the last diamond on the crown that bore
So many chilling ills that were to be
Upon my brow, and fatally to burn me.

Will Time dare to resuscitate my past,
An evening full of doves, that with a last
Thread from a stray rag draws a touch of red
From my docile childhood, only to spread
Bland emerald over a long rose of shame?

Memory of martyrdom, surely the same,
When the wind from the stake made me crimson
As, stubborn, I refused my conversion...
Come, blood, redden the pale circumstance
Ennobled by the blue of holy distance,
Dull rainbow of the time that I adored!
Consume the tints this faded gift affords;
Come, let me recognise, and let me hate,
This sulky child abetting her own fate,
Transparent trouble bathing in the woods...
And from my frozen breast that voice obtrudes,
So strange, so harsh, so full of hidden love...
Charm sought the huntress flying down the grove.
Was my heart near a heart that would give way?

Was it I, with long lashes, who sought to play
In covert sweetness, laughing at your threats...
Tendrils clung to my cheek, or else you set...
A tissue of lashes and fluidity,
A tender evening light, where arms entwined me?

IN THE SKY, MAY MY EYES TRACE MY TEMPLE!
AND ON ME REST AN ALTAR UNEXAMPLED!

Cried from its stony pallor my whole body...
The earth is now a coloured scarf only,
Slipping, refusing my vertiginous brow...
The universe, on my stalk, rocks, trembles now,
The pensive crown escaping all my minds,
And Death would breathe this priceless rose in time,
Before the sweetness serves its shady end!

And if, O Death, my tender odour sends
Your empty head reeling, breathe this air,
Call me, unbind!... And drive me to despair,
Tired of myself, and a condemned idol!
Listen... And do not wait... The spring is full
Of new and secret movements in my blood:
The frost can no more hold me as it would...
Tomorrow, the good constellations sigh,
The spring unseals the fountains of the sky:
Surprising spring laughs, violates... Unheard,
Unseen. So sweet its stream of candid words,
Tenderness seizes the bowels of the earth...
The trees swell and forget their times of dearth,
So many branches, too many horizons,
They move their thundering fleeces in the sun,
Rise in the bitter air with all their wings,
Their leaves, in thousands, conscious of the spring...
Do you not hear the rustling, airy names,
Deaf as you are!... The loaded space becomes
Vibrating, living wood which no top bends,
For and against the gods the whole trees spends
Its strength; the forest floats on trunks and boughs
Which piously, on their fantastic brows,
Carry, as superb archipelagos pass,
A tender river, O Death, hidden under grass.

What mortal woman would resist this whirl?
What mortal woman?

I, an innocent girl,
Feel in my trembling knees how vulnerable...
The air is shattering. I hear a bird call
Like a lonely child...the shadow where my heart
Tightens, and roses! heave in a sigh, and part
The gentle arms which held the basket tight...
Oh, in my hair I am conscious of a light
Touch as of a bee, a sharpening kiss, to say
This is the dawn of your ambiguous day...
Light!...Or you, Death! The one that gets there first...
How my heart beats! I feel a burning thirst!
Let my breast swell, offer itself, this hard
Sweet captive that a net of blue veins guards...
Hard in me...but sweet to the infinite lips!...

Dear thirsty ghosts who have me in your grip,
Desires! Clear faces!...And you amorous grapes,
Did the gods give you this maternal shape,
These sinuous rims, these folds and chalices,
For life to touch the altar with a kiss,
Where the fresh soul joins the eternal round
And seed and milk and blood are always found?
No! Horror tells me, loathsome harmony!
Each kiss will bring another agony...
I see, the honours of the flesh are lost
For bitter millions of these powerless ghosts...
No to breath, looks, to tenderness...My guests,
A people thirsty for me, I protest,
You will get no life from me!...Spectres, now go,
You sighs nightly expended on a pillow,
Go, join the impalpable crowds of the dead!
Not on them shall a light of mind be shed!
I keep far from you and my mind is clear...
You will not find a flash of lightning here...
My heart denies its thunder, as it must,
I pity all of us, O clouds of dust!

Great gods! the benefits you give are slight!

I will ask nothing now but your faint lights,
Imminent tear, so long waiting to melt
Upon my cheek, you alone give me help,

Fear which makes tremble, to my human eyes,
Funereal ways of all varieties;
You proceed from the soul, the labyrinth's pride,
You carry from my heart this drop denied
At first, then drawn off from my precious juice,
To sacrifice my ghosts and to induce
A tender libation from the back of my mind!
From the cave of fear by which I am mined,
The mysterious salt sweats out its silent drops.
Where do you come from? What laborious lot,
Tear, draws you slowly from the bitter shade?
You climb the steps where my fortune is laid,
Forcing a passage through my burdened days,
All my life long, your dilatory ways
Have choked me... Yet you plod over the ground...
– And who asked you to dress a youthful wound?

But wounds, sighs, dark attempts, why these things, why?
For whom, hard jewels, do you mark this cold body,
Blind, with the spread fingers avoiding hope!
Where is it going, this body, as it gropes
In the dark night, astonished at its trust?
Troubled earth... And mixed with sea-weed which must
Carry me, do it gently!... Weakness of snow,
Until it finds its trap, can it still go?
Where is my swan, where does he seek to fly?
... Precious hardness... My footsteps could but try,
Such was their faith in you, sense of the ground!
But, under the living foot which thought it sound
And touches with horror the pact it made at birth,
My pedestal is reached by this firm earth.
Not far away there dreams my precipice...
The unfeeling rock, slippery with sea-weed, is
Escaping (in itself ineffably still),
Begins... And, through a shroud which the wind will
Weave, an unsteady web of sea-sounds,
Half ruined billows, half an oar swung round...
So many gasps, so long, such death-rattles
Broken, and then released... however they fall,
The varied fates will bring forgetfulness...

Alas, will anyone who finds the trace
Of my bare feet, long forget his own destiny?

Troubled earth, mixed with sea-weed, carry me!

And yet, mysterious SELF, you are still alive,
You will recognise yourself in the sun-rise,
Bitterly the same... A mirror of the sea
Rises... And upon the lip you see
Yesterday's smile, announced by fading signs,
Freezes in the east already the pale lines
Of light and of stone, and the full prison
Where there will float the ring of the horizon...
Look: a pure arm is seen, strips itself bare.
I see you again, my arm... You bring dawn... Air,
Waking a half-killed victim... O threshold,
So sweet... the running wave enfolds
Quietly the level shelf, washed by the swell...
The shade which leaves me, the imperishable
Host, shows me red with new desires,
On the fierce altar of remembered fires.

There, the foam makes an effort to be seen,
And, on the boat, at every half-careen,
An eternal fisherman reels at the impact.
Everything will complete its solemn act
Of seeming once more incomparable and chaste,
And showing the eager tomb once more placed
In the gracious state of universal laughter.

Hail! Divinities in rose and water,
And the first plaything of the young light,
Islands!... Soon bee-hives, when the flame, first bright,
Makes your rocks, islands I now foretell,
Feel as it reddens touched by the paradisal;
Tops fertilised by fire, with hardly a fear,
Woods which will buzz with insects and ideas,
The hymns of men whom the just ether fills,
Islands the murmur of the sea encircles,
Mothers ever virgin, even with these signs,

133

Kneeling, you are to me the Fates, divine:
Nothing in air equals the flowers you hold,
But, in the depths, your feet are icy cold.

My soul preparing, under a calm brow,
My death, a secret infant, half-formed now,
And you, divine disgusts which start my fears,
Chaste distancings from my predestined years,
O fervour, was not a noble term all?
Never did one whom the gods sought to call
Dare to paint on her brow their panting breath,
And, praying for the perfect dark of death,
Offer her lip to the supreme murmur...

   I bore the brilliance of death and was pure
As I had born the brilliance of the sun...
My naked torso offered its desperation
While the soul, drunk with self, silence and glory,
Ready to faint from its own memory,
Hears with hope, knocking on the pious wall,
This heart, – which is ruined as the blows fall,
Until it holds only by its own compliance,
As a last fluttering of a leaf, my presence...

Vain expectation, vain... She cannot die,
She who, before a mirror, tenderly cries.

Should I not have accomplished my strange end
Of making choice, for my own punishment,
Of this lucid contempt for so subtle a fate?
   Will you ever find death in a clearer state,
Or a purer slope for me to crawl to my doom
Than on this long look of a half-opened victim,
Pale, and resigned, bleeding without regret?
What does it matter, this blood no longer secret?
In how white a peace this crimson leaves her,
At the edge of being, lovely in disaster!
She calms the time which comes to see her gone,
The sovereign moment finds her no more wan,
Empty flesh so kisses a sombre spring...

She becomes ever more lonely, more distancing...
And I, in my heart approaching such an end,
I see the funereal cypress as a friend...
    The aromatic smoke that I shall be,
I am drawn towards, I offer, it consumes me,
All of me promised to the happy clouds!
Even, I seemed to be this tree, mist-shrouded,
Its majesty already slightly gone,
Its whole length given to amorous abandon.
The immense being has me, my heart warms,
The burning incense breathes an endless form...
The radiant elements tremble in my essence!...
No, no!...Do not provoke the reminiscence!
Dark lily! Shady allusion from afar,
Your vigour could not break a precious jar...
You were approaching the supreme moment...
– But who could win, without being spent,
Against the power avid to see through your eyes,
The day which selected you to light the skies?

Look, you say, see at least, by what paths led,
The night has brought you here, back from the dead?
Remember who you are, make instinct yield
This thread (your gilded hand disputes the field),
This thread, blindly followed – it needs no more –
Has brought your life back to this brilliant shore...
Be subtle...cruel...or more subtle!...And lie,
But know!...And tell me by what sorcery
A coward from whom smoke could not get away,
Nor regard for a breast of perfumed clay,
By what regression have you re-assumed,
Reptile, your cavern scents and all your gloom?

Yesterday deep flesh, commanding flesh
Betrayed me...Yet no dream, and no caress!...
No demon, no scent offered me the peril
Of imagined arms sinking upon a virile
Neck; nor, by the Swan-God's feathers caught,
His burning whiteness did not touch my thought...

And yet he would have found the softest nest!
For as, unanimously, my limbs thought best,
A virgin, in the shade, I was an offering...
But sleep was taken with so sweet a thing,
And tied to myself in the hollow of my hair,
I feebly lost control, and it was there,
In my own arms, I made myself another...
Who is not herself?...Who sprawls and turns over?
And in what hidden turn did my heart melt?
What shell has whispered of my new-found guilt?
An ebbing tide perhaps has carried me
Back from my pure and premature extremity,
And taken from me the sense of my vast sigh?
An alighting bird needs sleep, and so did I.

(*The low door is a ring...where the thin veil*
Passes...All dies, laughs as the throat tells tales...
The bird drinks at your lip...Of light, no crack...
Come lower, speak softly...Black is not so black...)

Delicious shrouds, my luke-warm confusion,
Lay where I spread myself, pose yielding questions,
Where I meant silence for my beating heart,
Almost a living tomb, dwelling apart,
Breathing in comfort for eternity,
Place, full of me, you have taken all of me,
O form of my form and the hollow heat
Consciousness sometimes finds in its retreat,
The pride which plunges into your recesses
Finally mingles with your dreamed excesses!
Under your covering, imitating death,
The helpless idol draws her sleeping breath,
Tired absolute woman, tears in her eyes,
When her charm's naked secrets and declivities
And this trace of love the body prizes
Corrupted her loss and mortal promises.

You secret ark, secret and yet so close,
This night my transports meant to break you open;
All I have done is rock with lamentations
You womb loaded with day and with creations!

What! my eyes coldly lost in so much blue
See perish there the star so rare and true,
And the young sun of my astonishments
Seems to light up a she-ancestor's torments,
It flame deprives remorse of its existence,
Composing out of dawn a much-loved substance
Which was already substance for the tomb...
On the sea, on my feet, beautiful doom,
You are coming!...I am still your chosen mate,
The mists that veil me now evaporate...

...Farewells vain if I live, were they then dreams,
No more?...If I come, naked as it seems,
To this edge, sniffing the foam, without distress,
My eyes drinking this laughing bitterness,
My being against the wind, where the air is keenest,
Receiving full in the face a call from the foam-crest;
If the intense soul blows, and furiously
Slaps wave upon broken wave, and the sea
Thunders upon the headland, sacrificing
A monster of candour, from the far depths flinging
On this rock, splashing even my own thoughts,
A shower of icy sparks the sun has caught,
And over my whole skin it bites and runs,
Then it must be, in spite of myself, O Sun,
That I adore my heart, where you find self-knowledge,
A pleasure of which being born is the image,

Fire, towards whom a virgin in revolt
Rises, her grateful breast a shower of gold.

Dawn

La confusion morose

The morose confusion
Which served me for sleep,
Dissipates as the sun
Makes its first rosy leap.
In my soul I advance,
Winged with new confidence:
It is my first prayer!
Scarcely out of the sand,
And reason is at hand
For me to follow, where?

Good morning! Still asleep
With your matching smiles,
The company words keep
Can be seen for miles!
To judge by the noise of bees,
I shall have all I please,
And on the trembling rung
Of my gilded ladder, the incense
Of my evaporated prudence
Is already hung.

What dawn upon these crests
Which begin to quiver!
Already some of them stretch
Who seemed asleep for ever:
One shines, another yawns,
Vague fingers in the dawn
Playing, they have no choice,
Over a comb, still close to a dream
Which this lazy-bones seems
To implicate in her voice.

What! it is you, cheerless mistresses
Of the soul, what did you do
All night, what so distresses
That boredom makes a whore of you?
– We always behaved, they say,

138

Never did we betray
Your dwelling! Though immortal,
We kept close, were unobtrusive,
Secret spiders who live
In you dark corners, that is all.

Will it not be a delight
To see thousands of silken suns
Woven from shady night
On your enigmatic precisions?
Take a look at our work:
Over your abysmal dark
We have stretched our primitive threads,
And in a web held in place
By trembling preliminaries,
We have captured nature naked...

Their web of intellect
I break and, seeking, go
Into my sensual forest
Where my poems grow.
Being! the universal
Ear! So the whole soul
Is trimmed to extreme desire...
She listens for her own fears,
And sometimes my lips appear
To follow her quivering fire.

Here are my shady vines,
The cradles of all my chances!
The images that I find
Numerous as my glances...
Not a leaf not offering
An accommodating spring
Where I drink this elusive murmur...
All is pulp, all is almond,
And every calyx demands
That I wait till her fruit matures.

I do not fear the thorns!
Waking is good, hard though it is!
Pillaging, this bright morning,

Does not call for certainties:
If a world is ravished
No wound but is relished
For it is fertile
To the ravisher,
And his own blood assures
The taker he has all.

I approach the transparency
Of this pool not seen but guessed
Where my Hope swims, and, see!
Water supports her breasts.
Her neck pops through the mist,
Stirring an amethyst
Wave, this neck as white a white . . .
She feels, beneath this flow,
The depths are infinite,
And shudders to her toes.

To the Plane-Tree

You bend, tall Plane-tree, offering yourself, stripped
As a young Scythian, white,
But your candour is caught and your foot gripped
By the strength of the site.

Resounding shadow in whom the same azure
Which moves you, is appeased,
The black mother ties down this foot, natal and pure,
On which the muck has seized.

The winds have no wish for your travelling brow;
The gloomy, tender earth is so wise,
O Plane-tree, she will never allow your shadow
Even a step of surprise!

This brow will have access only to the brilliant high
To which the sap raises it;

You may grow, candour, but not break the tie
Of what you fixedness thinks fit!

You should sense that there are other living creatures
Bound by the hydra, and never free;
From pines to poplars, your likes are not a few,
Holm-oak and maple, always stationary,

All as in the grip of death, their feet dishevelled
In the confused ashes,
Feel their flowers go from them, gently levelled
To the ground, sperm floating unused.

The pure trembling, the charm of this beech
Formed by four young women,
Never cease to beat the sky, out of reach
But the branches are useless.

They weep, confounded, they live apart
In a single absence;
To no purpose, their silver limbs part
At their sweet emergence.

When the soul, as they breathe out at evening,
Rises towards Aphrodite,
The virgin must find herself in the shadows, sitting
Hot with shame, silently.

She feels herself surprised, and pale, yet sure
Of this foreboding tenderness
Which a present flesh turns to the future
Through a young face . . .

But you, who with arms purer than animals', will
Plunge them into gold,
You who form in daylight the spectre of the ills
Which sleep and dreams hold,

High profusion of leaves, proud disorder
When the north wind keenly
Sounds, at the golden crest, the first blue of winter
On you harps, O Plane-tree,

Dare to groan... O supple flesh of wood,
You must twist and untwist,
Complaining without breaking, giving to the winds' mood
The voice on which their tumults insist.

Whip yourself!... Like the martyr who cannot wait,
Flay yourself and, lest the flame scorch,
Wrest it, before it is too late,
From the lips of the torch!

So that the hymn will rise to the birds of spring
And so that the pure soul aspire,
Making the leaves tremble, as still hoping,
Though the trunk may dream of fire,

I have chosen you, great figure in a park,
Drunk as you pitch and reach,
Since heaven works you, presses you, great arc,
To yield it speech!

May the Dryads' amorous rival,
The poet alone discourse
Flatteringly of your polished body, as he lets praise fall
On the thigh of the Horse!...

– No, says the tree. It says No *by the sparkling*
Of it superb head, blown aslant,
Which the storm treats universally as being
Just another plant.

Canticle of Columns

Sweet columns, so
Light-capped as to astound,
Decorated with a row
Of real birds walking round.

Sweet columns, O
An orchestrated flow!
Each shank passes on
Its silence to unison.

Why do you bear so high
Your dazzling equality?
Faultless desires will try
Our studied beauty!

We sing as one, rejoice
To bear up heaven's light!
O single and wise voice
Which sings only to sight!

Our limpid elements
Draw what sonority
From the light, to present
The candid hymn you see!

So cold and touched with gold,
A chisel, from our beds,
Drew us out, to unfold
These tall lilies instead!

From our beds of crystal
We were forced to appear,
And by claws of metal
We were bonded here.

That we might brave the moon,
Moon and sun, and prevail,
They polished us, each one,
To shine like a toe-nail!

143

Servants who have no knees,
Smiles with no face to lure,
The beauty of our lines please
Feels that her legs are pure.

Piously looking identical,
Our noses under head-bands
And our rich ears deaf to all
The white load which here stands,

A temple upon eyes
Black for eternity,
Without gods we shall rise
To touch divinity!

Our ancient youth with its
Mat flesh and fine shades
Is proud that number fits
Us for such subtle parades!

Daughters of the golden numbers,
Measured with heaven's rod,
Upon us falls, and slumbers
A honey-coloured god.

He sleeps happy, the Day
That each day's sacrifice
Upon love's table displays,
On our brows his device.

Incorruptible sisters,
Half-burning and half-cool,
We took dry leaves as partners,
And winds, in our dancing-school,

And centuries in tens,
And peoples dead and gone,
The past is deep and when
Past, not enough drifts on!

Under our equal love,
So heavy as it weighs,

As water flows above
Pebbles, we pass our days!

It is in time we walk:
Our dazzling bodies leave
Impressions not made in talk
Which only fables receive...

The Bee

How fine soever, how mortal
Your sting may be, fair bee,
I have thrown on my basket only
A dream of lace to cover all.

Pierce the lovely gourd in the middle,
So that love dies on it, or drowsily
Makes redden a bit of me
In the round, rebellious shell.

I have great need of a prompt torment:
A sharp pain well terminated
Is better than a torture never absent!

So may my sense be illuminated
By this minute golden alert
Without which Love sleeps or is inert!

Poetry

Surprised, and suddenly,
A thirsty mouth which grips
At the breast of Poetry
Takes away its soft lips.

– O my mother Intelligence
From whom I sweetly sup,
What is this negligence,
What lets the milk dry up?

Scarcely upon your breast
Overwhelmed by such whiteness,
The waves which gave me rest
From your heart conveyed your fulness;

Scarcely brought down to find
Your beauty, from your dark night,
I felt, as I drank, my mind
Filled with clear light!

God lost within his essence,
And deliciously
Docile to a wide sense
Of appeased supremacy,

Close to pure night, it seemed
I could no longer die:
Through me, unchecked, there streamed
A river like a cry . . .

Say, by what touch of spite
Or by what empty dread,
This marvellous vein, so bright
Once at my lips, was dead?

Rigour, you fall upon
My soul, marking its rue!
Silence flies like a swan
No more between us two.

Your eyes, immortal one,
Refuse, which gave so much;
The flesh now turned to stone
Once yielded to my touch.

Even from heaven you wean me,
Unjustly changing: why?

Without my lips what will you be,
Without love, what shall I?

The answer from the suspended Spring
Was not unkindly dropped:
– You bit me, when you were sucking,
So hard that my heart stopped.

The Steps

Your steps, the children of my silence,
Holy and slow, and one by one,
Move, to surprise my vigilance,
Icy and mute, in my direction.

Pure person, shadowy and divine,
Your circumspect advance, how sweet!
Gods!... all the gifts that I divine
Come to my bed on naked feet.

If you prepare, with lips advanced,
To appease the inhabitant
Of my reflections with the enhanced
True substance of the kiss it wants,

Take your time with this tender act,
Sweet when it is, and sweet when not,
For I have lived to seal this pact,
My heart and your steps had one thought.

The Sash

When the cheek the sky discloses
Allows the eyes to dwell on it
And, at the point when it will quit,
Gilded time plays in the roses,

Before one dumb with the delight
Such a scene cannot but bring,
Dances a Shade, and evening
Catches at her loose sash's flight.

In the breath of air
The final links between
My silence and this scene,
As the sash trails, shudder...

I am alone...Absent, present
And dark, bland cerement.

The Sylph

Unseen, unknown,
I am the scent,
Present and absent,
By the wind blown!

Unseen, unknown,
Is it chance or genius?
No sooner with us
Than its task is done!

Unread, not understood?
So the best minds could
Could look out for baffled wits!

Unseen, unknown,
As a bare breast is shown
When a shirt is pulled over it!

148

Insinuation

O curves, O meander,
The liar's trick, no less,
Is there art more tender
Than this of dilatoriness?

O know where I am going,
I mean to lead you there,
And my corrupt designing
Is to make all seem fair.

(For although she smiles
As proudly as may be,
With so much liberty
She ignores my wiles.)

O curves, O meander,
The liar's trick, no less,
I mean not yet to end her
Wait for my tenderness.

Sketch of a Serpent

Deep in a tree, the light wind rocks
The viper whose shape I assume;
A smile, pierced by a tooth which mocks
And talks of appetite, finds room
In this Garden for prowl and risks,
My triangle of emerald whisks
Its double tongue out; I am a beast,
Yes, but not a stupid one,
And one whose poison is at least
Better than hemlock, when I've done.

How bland this time of pleasure is!
Tremble, mortals! I am strong
Though not without deficiencies,
My yawn is more than three feet long!

The splendour of the sharpened blue,
The head, heraldic and not true,
A mask of animal simplicity;
Come to me, you headstrong race!
I stand up, alert, and see
Everything in its proper place.

Sun, O sun!... The great mistake!
You the mask that covers death,
Under the gold and azure lake
Where flowers none the less draw breath;
By impenetrable delights,
You, great accomplice of my sleights
And most exalted trap of all,
You deprive hearts of any sense
That the universe is only a flaw
In the purity of non-existence.

Great Sun, you who ring the alarm
For men, accompanying them with fires,
Who, in a dream that brings them harm,
Encloses them, and their desires
Are written in all that is there seen
Which subjects to the present scene
The obscure presence of the soul,
The absolute, that lie you tell,
Has always pleased me very well,
O king of shadows, flaming Whole!

Pour upon me all your crude heat,
There where my frozen idleness,
Thinking up some new deceit,
My twisted nature would impress...
The charming place where flesh may fall
And be joined up, is wonderful!
My fury, here, is ripening;
I give it tips and make it hot,
And hear, for I can hear a lot,
My meditative murmuring.

O Vanity! The Primal Cause!
Reigning in heaven, who with a voice

150

Which was the light and made the laws,
Which makes the universe rejoice.
As if tired of his spectacle,
God then removed the obstacle
Of his perfect eternity;
He made up his mind to dissipate
His principle and so create
Stars – and so, no more Unity.

Heavens, his mistake! Time is his ruin!
And the gaping animal abyss!...
What an inferior origin,
A spark in place of nothingness!...
But the first Word spoken by the Word,
I!... The proudest of stars yet heard
From the mad lips which spoke them all,
I am!... I shall be... I throw light
Upon the day now shrunk to night
Of all the fires which will make the Fall!

Radiant object of my hate,
You whom I love inordinately,
Who gave command beyond hell gate
To this spirit who loved you dearly,
Take a look now in my shadows!
In front of your funereal show
Which is the pride of my dark mirror,
So profound was your unease,
Your breath into the clay no more
Than giving your despair some ease.

In vain you moulded in the clay
Facile children who would sing
All your triumphs night and morning
Or indeed the livelong day!
No sooner moulded, given breath,
Master Serpent showed them Death,
Those fine children you created!
Hi! he said, you two are human,
Just a naked man and woman,
Smug white beasts who should be mated.

The execrated model you
Were copied from: how could you please?
I hate you as I hate him who
Made all imperfect prodigies!
I am He who modifies
And touches trusting hearts with lies,
My hand is not without its skill...
We will soon change these flabby things
And these evasive snakes, making
Reptiles with a furious will!

My infinite Intelligence
Touches, in the human mind,
An instrument of my vengeance
Which you prepared for your mankind!
And your concealed Paternity
Which, in its splendour, wants to see
Nothing but incense, none the less
May find that my excessive charms
Will yet sound some remote alarms
For his plan of Almightiness.

I go, I come, I glide, dive,
I disappear in a pure heart!
None was ever so hard in that part
That no dream could be made to thrive!
Be you who you may be, am I not
The complacency which is the law
Of every mind given to self-love?
I am the root of his favour,
This inimitable savour
You think you're the only to have!

Eve, formerly, I took by surprise
In the midst of her first thoughts,
Her lips half-open as her eyes
Saw what dreams the roses brought.
This perfect form appeared to me,
Her vast flanks shimmering goldenly,
Which neither sun nor man made fearful;
All is exhibited to air,
The soul, bewildered, stupid, null,
On the brink of flesh but not yet there.

O you mass of beatitude,
So beautiful, the fair prize
Of the entire solicitude
Of the intelligent and wise!
For them to hang upon your lips
It is enough for you to sigh!
The purest find no price too high,
The hardest feel the sharpest nips...
Even I am touched, and I
Love the blood the vampire sips.

Yes! from my observation-point
Among the leaves, reptile and bird,
My babbling, when it pleases most,
Is what is meant, not what is heard.
I drank you, do not take alarm,
Deaf, calm, clear, heavy with charm,
I dominated secretly
The eye in the burning gold of your wool,
Your enigmatic nape, so full
Of what you move to be.

I was present like a scent,
Like the aroma of a thought
Whose meaning cannot quite be caught
In all its depth and its intent.
I disquieted your candour,
A thing not difficult to do,
Without the need to frighten you
Into some tottering of you splendour!
Soon I shall have you, I am sure,
Your nuance shows you less secure.

(Such superb simplicity
Deserves the greatest of respect!
Transparent looks of course protect,
Helped by pride, silliness, felicity,
The approaches to the lovely city!
Let us know how to interject
A chance of two, which will subject
A pure heart to some difficulty;
It is my strong point, and my aim;
I have means to perform the same.)

So, out of a dazzling drivel,
Let us spin systems of deceit
In which Eve, idle and civil,
Finds vague dangers at her feet!
Under a load of silk the skin
Trembling, the prey so quiet in
The sunlight that she knew before . . .
But there is no more subtle gauze,
Nor any thread less seen, or more
Deadly than when I weave the flaws.

Gild, tongue, gild for her the sweet
Stories that you know how to tell,
Allusions, fables, tricks, as well
As chiselled silence; and repeat
Everything that does her harm:
Only what flatters and will charm
Her to be lost is my designs,
Docile to the inclinations
Which give back the deepest mines
Heaven's most exalted inundation!

O what incomparable prose,
And how much wit have I poured here
Into the downy maze
Of this so marvellous ear!
Nothing lost there, I thought;
A heart in suspense is soon caught!
A certain success! if what I say,
Importuning the precious soul,
Like a bee close to its prey,
Sticks close to this ear of gold.

'Nothing,' I whispered, 'is less sure
Than the divine word is, for, Eve.
A living science will undeceive
And knock down a fruit so insecure!
Don't listen to Him, the old and pure,
Who curses the short bite you will receive,
Unless your mouth dreams and you grieve
For this thirst for sap and for new leaves,
This pleasure which is half the future,
It is eternity melting, Eve!'

154

She drank up all I said
Which had the strange result her eye
Strayed from an angel overhead
To seek the foliage where was I.
The wiliest of the animals,
Who teases you for being hard,
O faithless creature, big with ills,
Is nothing more than a voice barred
By the foliage! – Yet how Eve
Listened below the moving leaves!

'Soul,' I said, 'sweet treasure-trove
Of all forbidden ecstasy,
Do you feel the sinuous lure
I have filched from the Almighty?
I have, with a delicate skill,
Treated this heavenly essence till
It tastes sweeter than any honey...
Take this fruit... This is the test!
It was to take what you think best
Your hand and arm were made so lovely.'

What silence, broken by an eye-lash!
But what a breath under the shadow
Of the dark breast the Tree bit now!
Like a pistil, the other showed a flash!
– *Whistle, whistle!* he said to me!
And I felt number shudder along
All the length of my whip, subtly,
Of these tiresome twists of the thong;
They rolled away from the beryl
Of my crest, as far as peril!

Genius! O the long impatience!
Time in the end for a new feat
And for a step towards new Science
Will spring as it were from these bare feet!
Marble aspires, gold is displayed,
These fair pillars of amber and shade
Tremble on the edge of movement...
It totters, this tall urn
From which must fall the full consent
Of her who appears taciturn.

Yield, dear body, to the baits
Of the pleasures you propose;
Let your thirst for novel states
Suggest to you pose after pose;
Around the Tree of Death you may
Come without coming! Make your way
Vaguely as if it were deep in flowers...
Dance, dear body... Do not reflect!
Here delights will fill your hours
Without the help of intellect.

Surely I was on the wrong track
To be content with the mere presence
Of the pure length of a long back
Shuddering with disobedience...
Already giving forth its essence
Of all wisdom and illusion,
The Tree of Knowledge   sense
Dishevelled with a crop of visions,
Stirred its huge body which seems
To dive in the sun and suck up dreams.

Tree, great Tree, the Heavens' Shadow,
Irresistible Tree of trees
Who, where the faults of marble show,
Pursue the juices which most please,
You who grow such a maze,
Embracing shadows which go their ways
To lose themselves among the sapphire
Of the eternal morning above,
Sweet loss, either scent of zephyr
Or perhaps a petulant dove.

O Singer, O secret drinker
Of jewels in the deepest mines,
Cradle of the reptile thinker
Who made the dream that all was fine,
Great Being troubled to know more
Who, to see further, dared to soar
As your topmost twig told how,
You who changed into fine gold
Your hard arms, your smoking boughs
And digging deep into earth's folds.

You can repulse the infinite
Which is made only of your growth,
And from the tomb up to the height
Feel all knowledge between both!
But this old dab hand at chess
In suns of golden idleness
Twists himself round your branchy head;
His eyes set all your dreams trembling.
He will rain down the fruits of the dead,
Despair, disorder and dissembling.

A fine serpent, rocked in the blue,
I hiss, but with delicacy,
Offering, for God's glory, the true
Triumphs of my melancholy . . .
Enough for me the breezes suit
Their immense hope of bitter fruit
And make your sons of clay insane . . .
– That thirst which makes you so impress
Exalts to Being the inane
Omnipotence of Nothingness.

The Marine Cemetery

This tranquil roof, on which doves stretch and walk,
Palpitates among pines, tombs white as chalk;
Just noon is there composing of its fire
The sea, the sea, in renewed sparkles caught!
What recompense, after so deep a thought,
Is a long look at absence of desire.

What fine work of sharp lightning here is doomed
And by how many diamonds is consumed,
What peace here appears to be conceived!
And when a sun rests over the abyss,
Created by whatever Cause there is,
Time scintillates, the Dream is not deceived.

157

Stable treasure, plain temple of Minerva,
A mass of calm and visible reserve,
Supercilious water, Eye which contains
So much sleep under a veil of fire,
O my silence! . . . Inner construction, higher
Than its thousand tiles and golden weather-vanes!

Temple of time, and summed up in a sigh,
I reach the top, with no surprised cry
Though all around the prospect is marine;
As if it were my holy offering,
The serene scintillation is scattering
On the height a contempt for what is seen.

As a fruit melts into its enjoyment,
Changing into delight when it is absent
Inside a mouth in which its form dies,
Here I inhale the smoke that I shall be,
My soul consumed as heaven sings to me
Of shores from which murmurs of change arise.

Beautiful sky, true heaven, see me change!
After so much pride, after so much strange
Idleness, but an idleness full of power,
I give myself over to this brilliant space,
Over the houses of the dead I trace
My shadow passing, tamed in this frail hour.

My soul exposed to the torches of the solstice,
I am with you, admirable justice
Of the light whose weapons are without pity!
I give you back pure to your original place:
Look at yourself! . . . But to reflect brightness
Supposes a half that is dull and shadowy.

O for myself only, to me and in me,
Near a heart, at the wells of poetry,
Between the void and the pure event,
I await the echo of my inner greatness,
Bitter, dark and sonorous emptiness,
Ringing in the soul a hollowness still absent!

Do you know, false captive of this leafy sill,
Gulf which eats greedily these meagre grills,
Upon my closed eyes, dazzling secrecy,
What body drags me to its lazy end,
What brow attracts it this bony ground?
A spark there thinks of those I do not see.

Closed, holy, full of fire without substance,
An earthly fragment offered to this brilliance,
This place is pleasing to me, torches everywhere,
Composed of gold, of stone and dark trees,
Where so much marble trembles under the sea
Faithful to so many shades, my tombs are there!

Splendid bitch, ward off the idolatrous!
When I, a smiling shepherd, companionless,
Patiently let my strange sheep feed as they will,
The white flock of my so tranquil tombs,
Here let no prudent doves be given room,
No empty dreams, nor any curious angel!

Once here, the future is all idleness.
The insect cleans and scratches at the dryness;
Everything burnt, undone, is taken here
Into the air, as some severe essence...
And life is vast, being drunk with its own absence,
Bitterness sweet, the intellect is clear.

The hidden dead are easy in this ground,
Warm and dry where no mystery is found.
Up there the Noon, the Noon forever Now,
Thinks to itself thoughts which could not be fitter...
O complete head and perfect manager,
I am the secret change you undergo.

You have none but me who can contain your fears!
Repentance, doubts, constraints, I have them here,
The only flaw in your great diamond...
But in their night, heavy now with marble,
Among the roots of trees a vague people
Has slowly come to be of your mind.

They have melted into darkness, out of mind,
Red clay has drunk the whiteness of their kind,
The gift of life has passed into the flowers!
Where are the familiar phrases of the dead,
The personal art expressing heart and head?
The larva spins where once there were tears.

The titillated girls with piercing cries,
Their teeth, their moistened eye-lids, and their eyes,
The breast, so charming when it plays with fire,
The blood which shines upon the yielding lip,
The fingers which resist the final slip,
Are underground, the players cannot tire!

And you, great soul, do you hope for a dream
Without the colours which to our eyes seem
To emanate from gold and brilliant waves?
Will you write poems when you are a mist?
Everything vanishes! You will not insist,
Even holy impatience finds its grave!

Frail immortality of black and gilt,
Consoler with the laurels meant to wilt,
Who speak of death as of a mother's breast,
What a fine lie, and what a pious ruse!
Who does not know, and who does not refuse
The skull where endless laughter is expressed?

Wise fathers, populated heads grown dull,
Who, weighed down by so many shovels-full
Are that earth upon which we lose our way,
The gnawing truth, worm irrefutable,
Is not for you who sleep under the table,
It is alive and does not go away!

Is it love, perhaps, or hatred of myself?
Does any name that you can call him help?
What secret tooth can be so close as this?
No matter! He can see, want, dream and touch,
My flesh delights him, where I lie, so much
That I live only that I may be his.

Zeno! Cruel Zeno! Zeno of Elea!
Have you transfixed me with that winged arrow
Which vibrates, flies, and yet does not fly?
The sound begets me and the arrow kills!
Ah, the sun... The stationary Achilles,
Bounding along, is a tortoise really!

No, no!... Get up! And into the next age!
Break, body, now this image of a sage!
Drink, lungs, the first traces of a wind rise!
A coolness which is exhaled by the sea
Brings my soul back to me... This god bites sharply!
Run to the waves and re-emerge alive!

Yes! Great sea rich in delirium,
A panther skin and mantle which the sun
Has holed with thousands of its images,
Absolute hyrdra, drunk with your blue flesh
Which your glittering tail bites, and then bites afresh
In a tumult which is more like silence than rage,

The wind is rising!... Try to live, for look!
The huge air flaps the pages of my book,
The powdered waves splash from the rocks above them!
Fly away, dazzled pages! They are gone.
Break, waves, break your reckless waters upon
This tranquil roof where sails feed like doves!

Palm

Scarcely hiding the brilliance
Of his fearsome grace,
An angel brings abundance,
Milk and bread, to my place;
His eyelid gives the sign
For a prayer which should be mine,
Speaking to my vision:
– Calm, calm, remain calm!
Feel the weight of a palm
Bearing its profusion.

161

As much as it bends
To accommodate its rich load,
It form achieves its ends,
It heavy fruit the goad.
Admire how it vibrates,
How a slow fibre dictates as it divides the moment
Decides without mystery
The force of gravity
And the weight of the firmament.

This fine moving arbiter
Between shade and sun
Has the look of being wiser
Than a sibyl, and sleeps like one.
Around the same spot
The ample palm does not
Tire of calls or farewells...
How noble it is, how tender,
Justly determined to surrender
Only a god compels.

The light gold which it murmurs
Sounds in the slightest breeze
A silken armour confers
On the living distances.
The eternal voice its leaves form
In reply to the sand-storm,
While the shower of grains falling
Serves as its own oracle
And is proud of the miracle
It troubles quietly sing.

While between sand and sky
It stands unconsciously
Each new day will supply
A little honey.
Its sweetness finds its measure
In the divine leisure
Which does not count the days
But which conceals them well
In a juice in which will tell
Rumours of amorous forays.

If one may sometimes despair
If the pleasing rigour,
Despite your tears, will yield your share
Only in the shade of languor,
Do not accuse avarice,
A Sage who is preparing this
God and this authority:
For this grave sap will bring
A hope that is everlasting
Which rises to its maturity.

The days which you think lost
To you and the universe
Have roots which will not be crossed
By any subterranean reverse.
The hairy substance identified
By the darkness, turns aside
For nothing, nothing can stop it,
Seeking out, however deep
Below the surface it may sleep,
The water sought by the summit.

Patience, O patience
In the blue sky! In the root
Every atom of silence
Is the chance of a ripe fruit!
Some happy surprise will come:
A dove, a breeze, or some
Other slight shock, maybe
A woman stretching her hand
For support, cause this shower and
Bid us kneel instantly.

Let a people now fall,
Palm!... an irresistible descent
Into the dust, and roll
On the fruits of the firmament!
These lost hours are a gain,
So light do you remain;
After this reckless drift
Like a man in thought
Whose long efforts have brought
Accretion to his gift.

Insinuation II

Demented and evil,
My lip is here,
Kissing as a bee will
The burning ear.

I love your frail
Astonishment,
Although only a pale
Ghost of love is meant.

What a surprise...
What hums is your blood.
It is my act supplies
The living breeze with food.

Among your hair
It is my tender mind
Which seeks more than its share
And is unkind.

To Dawn

At dawn, before the warmth of day,
When tender colour, after grey,
Scarce shaken over the world again
Astonishes and wounds our pain.

Night I have suffered all the night,
Suffer heaven's sudden gift, this smile,
And this immense flower offered to light
To rest upon day's brow awhile.

Great offering of so many roses,
Can evil bear you up, and see
The reddening surface earth discloses
Returning to us faithfully?

I have seen so many feigning dreams
Upon my shadows without sleep,
Even the strength of the sun sees
A product of the lying deep,

And I must doubt whether my mind
Should feel disgust or feel desire
At this young day the leaf will find
The virgin gold has touched with fire.

Equinox

Elegy

I am changing... Who escapes me?... The motionless leaves
    Now overwhelming the tree before my eyes...
Its great arms tire of rocking; my sibyls grieve:
    My silence has lost its voices.

My soul, if it once sang like a fountain
    Of which all the waters were heard,
Is nothing now but a pool, where the distant stone
    Marks the tomb of the birds.

On the simple bed of sand as fine as ashes
    My wasted footsteps sleep,
And living I go down among the shadows,
    Confused by traces so deep.

I am conscious of losing Psyche the sleep-walker
    Who disappears under her liquid veils;
The calm and time of the too pure water
    Disturbed by a bubble this tomb exhales.

Perhaps to herself She may speak a pardon,
    But giving way to her closed eyes
She flees from me, faithful, tender, to abandon
    All care of my lifeless destinies.

She leaves her loss without explanation,
	And my heart has no hope, although it beats,
Disputing with Persephone Eurydice, bitten,
	And her pure bosom the black serpent eats.

Gloomy and dying witness of our tender annals,
	O sun, as with our passion,
The invincible sweetness of the underworld calls
	You too to the unavoidable destination.

Autumn, transparency! O solitude
	Big with sadness and liberty!
Everything, as soon as gone, is understood;
	It is by non-existence that we see.

While I value my stony gaze
	In the fixed hardness of its 'Why?'
A dark trembling the eyelid betrays
	Quivers between me and eye.

An eternity of spontaneous absence here
	Has just been shortened by the fall
Of a leaf which, dividing the year,
	Is yet hardly an event at all.

You leaves, so weak and dry, yet hot and fierce,
	Bowl your frail murmur towards me,
And you, Sun, with your last arrows, pierce
	This time, which dies so gently.

Yes, I am awake at last, feeling an autumn stirring
	Which raises a red, sad drift,
A whirling panic of gold and crimson, so astonishing
	That it angers me, and I exist.

The Caress

My warm hands, bathe them
In your own...Nothing calms
So much as the ripples when
Palm is engaged with palm.

Familiar as they are,
Your rings with their long stones
Melt at once in the shudder
Which makes the eye-lids close.

The trouble spreads, much as
A tile is polished,
Extended by a caress
Until melancholy is touched.

Chanson à Part

You do what? Nothing.
And are worth? I don't know,
Attempts, forebodings,
Strength, disgust, so...
You are worth? Don't know
And you want? Nothing now.

What d'you know? I'm bored.
What d'you do? Dream.
Dreams, in a word,
To make day what night seems.
What d'you know? Dreams,
A change from being bored.

What d'you want? That's all.
What should you do? Know,
Let the world come when I call
Nothing but a fiasco.
What do you fear? The will.
What are you? Where I go.

Where is that? I go to death.
To do what there? To finish,
To draw no more the breath
That fate will not replenish.
You are going where? To finish.
What's to be done? Death.

CATULLUS

Preface

Catullus walked in the Campus Martius.
He had seen all he needed to see,
Lain on his bed at noon, and got up to his whore.
His heart had been driven out of his side
By a young bitch – well, she was beautiful,
Even, while the illusion was with him, tender.
She had resolved herself into splayed legs
And lubricity in the most popular places.
He had seen Caesar who – had he not been, once,
The drunken pathic of the King of Bithynia? –
Returning in triumph from the western isles:
Nothing was too good for this unique emperor.
Against these fortunes he had nothing to offer
– Possibly the remains of his indignation,
A few verses that would outlive the century.
His mind was a clear lake in which he had swum:
There was nothing but to await a new cloud.
We have seen it. But Catullus did not;
He had already hovered his thirty years
On the edge of the Mediterranean basin.
The other, rising like a whirlwind in a remote province,
Was of a character he would have ignored.
And yet the body burnt out by lechery,
Turning to its tomb, was awaiting this,
Fore-running as surely as John the Baptist
An impossible love pincered from a human form.

I

To whom shall I offer this charming new volume,
Just smartened up with dry pumice?
Cornelius, to you: for you have been accustomed
To think that there is something in my trifles
Since the time when you, alone of the Italians,
Were bold to explain all ages in three volumes;
They were learned books, produced with much industry.
So take and keep for yourself this little book,
Whatever it amounts to. And Patroness, Virgin,
May it still be read after more than one century.

II

Sparrow my Lesbia likes to play with,
The one she likes to hold in her lap
To whom she gives her finger tip
To make him bite, as she likes, more sharply,
When, shining because of my desire
She finds it a precious thing to play with
(I think, when her grave fire acquiesces
She finds it a solace for her pain).
If I could play with you just as she does
I'd have a way of lightening my cares.

IIA

This is as sweet as the golden apple
Was, so they say, to Atalanta:
It loosed her girdle too long tied up.

III

Time for mourning, Loves and Cupids
And any man of wit and love.
The sparrow's dead, my girl's own sparrow
That she loved more than her eyes:
For it was sweeter and knew her better
Than any girl might know her mother;
The bird would not move from her lap!

172

But hopping here and hopping there
Chirped for its mistress, no one else.
Now it goes to the darkened pathway
Out of which, they say, none comes back.
But curses on you, cursed darkness,
Orcus, you eat everything up.
You have taken my little sparrow away.
Oh, badly done! Oh, poor little bird!
It's all your doing, my poor girl's eyes
Are heavy and red with weeping now.

IV

That yacht, as I was telling my guests,
Regards herself as the fastest of ships.
There is nothing afloat that she could not pass
Whether she was driven with oars or sail.
She says that the windy Adriatic will agree,
The Cyclades, Rhodes and the bleak Thracian strait,
Or the dark bay of Pontus
Where, before she was a boat, she was long-haired woodland:
For on Cytorus, on the hill-back,
She gave out a rustling with her speaking leaves.
Pontic Amastris and Cytorus
Green with box, all these, she says, were well known to her.
From her beginning she stood on that summit;
It was here she first dipped oars;
And from there she brought me over so many uncontrolled seas
To port or starboard as the wind called
Or with Jove blowing astern on both sheets;
And she had never cried mercy from any god ashore
When she came from the last salt to this limpid lake.
But these events are past: now, hidden away,
She grows old quietly, offering herself up
To the twin Castor and to Castor's brother.

V

Living, dear Lesbia, is useless without loving:
The observations of the censorious old
Are worth a penny every piece of advice.

173

One day follows another, the sun comes back
But when once we have gone away we do not;
Once night comes for us, it is night for ever.
Give me a thousand kisses, and then a hundred,
Then give me a second thousand, a second hundred
And then another thousand, and then a hundred
And when we have made up many, many thousands
Let us forget to count. Better not to know –
It will bring someone's jealous eye upon us
If people know we give so many kisses.

VI

Flavius, I know that you would tell me your pleasures
If they were not – shall we say? – a bit on the rough side;
If they were not, you would not know how to keep quiet.
It is obvious to me that you have chosen some female
Not quite in condition, and that no doubt makes you silent.
But you don't lie alone; that is plain as such a thing need be.
Your bed cannot speak, but it shouts: it has garlands,
Is scented with Syrian olives, the bolsters and pillows
Pressed down, thrown this way and that; it is shaken,
It is tremulous, goes up and down. So nothing, but nothing
Can possibly hide what you're up to. When you flop down
      exhausted
It is plain that you do so because of your amorous diversions.
So tell us whatever you've done. And was it successful?
I should very much like to make Flavius and Flavius's pleasures
The subject of some of my more agreeable verses.

VII

You ask me, Lesbia, how many kisses
Make enough kisses for me to take from you.
As many as there are sands in the desert
In Libya, the drugged sands of Cyrenaica
Between the oracle of that burning Jove
And the monument of the mythical Battus;
As many as there are stars, in the quiet night
Looking on furtive copulations.
That would be kisses enough for Catullus

To kiss you with, that would be more than enough:
A number which could neither be counted by the inquisitive
Nor put under any spell by malevolent tongues.

VIII

You had better stop playing the fool, Catullus,
And accept that what you see is lost, is lost.
Once your days were shining
When you used to go wherever the girl led you,
She loved as none will ever be loved.
Then those many pleasant things were done
Which you wanted and the girl was willing to do;
Certainly then your days were shining.
She wants those things no more: you had better not want them,
Nor ask for what will not be given, nor live in pain.
Be patient, harden your mind.
Good-bye, girl. Already Catullus is hardened.
He does not seek you, and will not, since you are unwilling.
But you will suffer when you are asked for nothing at night.
It is the end. What life remains for you?
Who now will come to you? Who will think you pretty?
Whom will you now love? Whose will you say you are?
Whom will you kiss? And whose lips will you bite?
But you, Catullus, accept fate and be firm.

IX

Veranius, of all my friends
The best of all of them
And are you here again?
Back to your aged mother and
Your unanimous brothers?
Those messengers were welcome!
And shall I see you safe,
Talking over Iberia
Its places, facts and peoples
As your way is; draw your neck to me
And kiss your smiling mouth and eyes?
No one is luckier than I
At this moment, or happier.

175

X

Varus had taken me from the Forum
Where I was idling, to see his mistress,
Not at all a bad little whore, as it seemed to me
– Quite good looking.
When we got there we started talking
About various things; among them what sort of place
Bythinia was now, how things were going there,
In particular, whether I had made any money.
I said how it was, that there was nothing in it
Either for ourselves, the praetor or his cohort,
To enable anyone to come back with his hair well oiled –
Especially since the praetor was a bastard,
Not caring a damn for his cohort.
Still, they said, you must have got a few men to carry your litter
That's the country they come from.
I, to make myself out to be one of the lucky ones,
Answered that I hadn't managed things so badly
Poor as the province was
That I couldn't find eight men who could stand upright.
In fact I had no-one, in Rome or in Bythinia,
Who could lift the broken leg of a camp-bed on his back.
The girl said – what can you expect of a whore? –
Would you be kind enough to lend me those men
To take me just as far as the temple of Serapis?
Half a minute, I said to the girl,
When I said that just now I was forgetting
They actually belong to Gaius Cinna.
Of course, whether they are his or mine, it's all the same,
I use them as if they were my own.
But you are a nasty tactless creature, you are;
One can't make the slightest mistake without getting into trouble.

XI

Furius and Aurelius, friends of Catullus,
Whether he has a mind to go to India
Where the eastern ocean beats upon the shore
Echoing far off

176

Or to the Hyrcanians and the soft Arabians,
To the Scythians or the arrow-bearing Parthians,
Or to those plains which the seven-fold Nile
Dyes with its mud.

Whether he will climb across the High Alps
To view the memorials of great Caesar,
The Gallic Rhine, or the ultimate recesses
Of the barbarous Britons.

Ready although you are to do all these things
And indeed anything else that the fates direct,
The service I ask is only that you take a message,
Not a very nice one.

Tell my girl to enjoy herself with her lechers,
I hope she may manage three hundred at one time,
Not loving any properly, but leaving all of them
With ruptured arteries.

Tell her not to expect my love any more
And that it is through her fault that it has fallen
Like a flower at the edge of a meadow
When the plough passes.

XII

Marrucinus Asinius, your left hand
Could be better employed at table
Than in stealing people's napkins.
Do you think that a joke? It is an extremely poor one,
About as silly and witless as such a thing can be.
If you don't believe me, perhaps you will believe Pollio,
Your brother, who would give a talent to buy you off from your
      thieving,
For he has a better idea of what is amusing.
So now you will get three hundred hendecasyllables
Unless you send me back my napkin;
It is not for the value of the thing in money
But because it reminds me of my friends.
Fabullus and Veranius sent me some Saetaban napkins

As a present from Iberia
And I am as fond of them, necessarily
As I am of Veranius and Fabullus.

XIII

Certainly you shall come to dinner, Fabullus,
And in a few days, if you are lucky,
Provided that you bring your supper with you,
A decent one, and don't forget a girl,
A bottle, your conversation and some laughter.
If you bring all these, I say, dear friend, you will dine well –
For your Catullus
Has nothing in his purse at the moment but cobwebs.
In return I will give you the essence of love
Or something more balmy and elegant than that;
I will give you an unguent
Which my girl had from the Loves and Cupids.
When you smell that you will ask the gods
To make you, Fabullus, nothing but nose.

XIV

If I did not love you more than my eyes,
My witty Calvus, for this present
You would deserve a Vatinian hatred.
What have I done, what have I said
To bring all these poets on myself?
To hell with that client of yours
Who sent you so many rascals.
But if, as I suspect, this splendid and novel gift
Comes to you from Sulla the lecturer,
I am not at all upset, but content;
It means your efforts have not been lost.

But, gods! what a ghastly anthology!
Yet you send it to your friend Catullus
So that he dies of it on the Saturnalia
Which should be the best of days.
You shall not get out of it so easily.
In the morning I will go to the booksellers' boxes,

Collect Caesius, Aquinus, Suffenus and all such poisonous stuff.
It will be your turn to receive a present.
Meanwhile you, the poets of the anthology,
Take your horrible feet back where they came from.
I count you among the diseases of the age.

XIVA (Fragment)

If any of you will be readers of my performances
And yet not fear to move your hands towards me

XV

I commend to you myself and my love,
Aurelius, and make a modest request:
If you have known what it is to desire
One whom you wanted left untouched
Then keep this boy untouched for me.
It is not the great world that I fear;
Those you go up and down the street
Are lost in their own pre-occupations.
What I fear is you and your penis
Which is after boys, good-looking or not.
Exercise it as much as you like
Out of the house, however you like:
But spare this one, it is little to ask.
If your ill mind and rapacious fury
Carry you on to such a point
That you do not stop at this injury
Then you shall suffer, with feet tied up
And mullet and radishes stuck up your arse.

XVI

All right I'll bugger you and suck your pricks
Aurelius and Furius, you pair of sodomites
Who imagine, on the strength of my verses
That I am lacking in reserve as they are.
But although the sacred poet ought to be chaste
It does not follow that his verses should be.

XVII

So the Colony would like a long bridge,
One they can dance on, but fear the rickety
Joints of the one they have got, patched with second-hand timber,
Which might collapse and sink in the depths of the marsh.
You can have as good a bridge as you wish,
One fit even for the rites of Salisubsilus,
If you will give me the chance of a good laugh.
There is one of my fellow-citizens I should like to see
Go head-over-heels from your bridge into the mud,
In the deepest, most stinking place of the whole marsh.
He is a man with no more sense than a small boy,
A two-year-old rocked to sleep by his father.
He has married a girl in the very flower of her youth;
The girl is more delicate than a tender kid,
She deserves to be kept like a bunch of the blackest grapes
And he lets her play as she will, and is quite indifferent.
He does not stir himself, but lies like a log
In the ditch where it has been felled by a Ligurian axe.
With as much sensation as if nothing existed, anywhere,
The clot sees nothing, he hears nothing;
What he is, whether he is or not, he does not know.
Now he is the man I should like to throw from your bridge
To see whether he can be roused from his lethargy.
And leave his supine mind in the dirty sludge,
Much as a mule might leave her shoe in the mire.

XXI

Aurelius, father of hungers,
Not of these only, but of all that were
Or are, or will be in other years,
You want to turn pederast with my boy.
Not surreptitiously; you are with him, you joke together,
You stick beside him and leave nothing untried.
It is no good you plotting against me,
I'll see you buggered first.
If you were satisfied I would say nothing;
As it is, you teach my boy to have an appetite.
Leave off while you may do so with decorum
Or you'll end up buggered.

XXII

Suffenus, Varus, whom you know so well,
Is not only witty, polite, acceptable,
He even writes more verses than other people.
I believe he has at least ten thousand, perhaps more,
All copied out, not just on bits of paper
– Royal parchment, beautiful bindings,
Lines ruled with lead, and all smoothed out with pumice.
But when you read him, the elegant Suffenus
Turns out to be a goatherd or a ditcher,
He is so unlike himself, so changed.
What can one make of it? This charming wit,
This expert in civilised conversation
Is about as dull as a row of turnips
Once he touches poetry. However
He is never so happy as when he is writing it;
Then he can love himself and admire his talents.
Still, we all imagine that we have gifts,
And everyone is a bit like Suffenus;
Everyone has his special delusion –
Our view of ourselves is a bit different from other people's.

XXIII

Furius, you have no slave, no money,
Not a bug, not a spider, and no fire;
You have, however, a father and a step-mother
Whose teeth could eat up flint-stones.
It is delightful, the life you lead with those two,
The old man and his mahogany wife.
No wonder; you all enjoy good health;
Your digestions are good; you fear nothing,
Not fire, or houses falling on your head.
Or thieving, or plots to poison you
Or other occasions of danger.
But your bodies, drier than bones
Or anything drier you can think of,
Are made so by sun, cold and hunger.
Why should you not be well and contented?
You have no sweat, no saliva;
Your noses are absolutely free from snot.

To this purity one may add a more impressive one:
Your anus is cleaner than a salt-cellar.
You don't shit ten times in a whole year
And then it is harder than beans or pebbles.
If you press it or rub it with your hands
You can't even dirty your fingers.
You should not scorn advantages like that, Furius,
Or reckon them to be small ones.
You should stop asking for a hundred sestertia,
Really you are well off enough already.

XXIV

O flower of the Juventii, not only
Of those now living, but your ancestors
And those who will be in the years to come,
I would ratherr you gave the riches of Midas
To that man without slave or money
Then that you should allow him to love you.
'Well, is he not polite?' you ask. He is:
But this polite man has neither slave nor money.
You can say it does not matter if you will;
The fact remains, he has neither slave nor money.

XXV

Thallus you pansy, softer than rabbit's wool,
The down of a goose or the lobe of an ear,
Softer than an old man's penis and the cob-webs hanging from it.
Thallus none the less rapacious as the wind,
Give me back my cloak, you stole it,
And my Saetaban napkins and Bythynian tablets.
You clot, you show them off as if they were heirlooms.
Unstick your claws from them and send them back
Or you may find your dear little body and hands
Inscribed in shameful fashion by a horsewhip
And yourself tossing around in an unusual way
Like a small ship caught in an enormous storm.

XXVI

My little villa is exposed to the blast
Not of the south wind or the west wind
Or even of the north wind or the east wind
But of fifteen thousand two hundred sestertia,
A horrible and penitential wind.

XXVII

You are looking after the Falernian
So pour me out stronger cups;
I am sure Postumia would tell you to do so;
She is fuller of wine than a grape herself.
The water can go as far away as it likes;
It ruins wine, it had better trickle off to the sober.
This is pure Thyonian.

XXVIII

You who have been with Piso, which is not the way to grow rich,
Have no difficulty with your baggage, it is easily lifted;
Veranius and Fabullus, I am glad to see you, how are you?
Were you cold and hungry enough with that sour bastard?
Were all your winnings in the wrong direction
As mine were, when I was with my praetor?
My only credits were debits.
Memmius, you had me down and properly buggered,
Slowly, with your whole great beam.
You two seem to have been in like case,
Filled up with a prick of the same size.
Friends in high places!
May the gods and goddesses give you every kind of bad luck.
Blots on the names of Romulus and Remus.

XXIX

Who can see this, who can suffer this,
Except the shameless, the rapacious, the gambler –
Mamurra in possession of what before
The hairy Gaul had and the far-off Briton?

Depraved Romulus, can you see this and bear it?
Now he walks proud in his superfluity
Through everyone's beds like a leching pigeon
Or a handsome Adonis.
Depraved Romulus, can you see it and bear it?
It is because you are shameless, voracious, a gambler.
Was it for this, unique emperor
That you went to the last island of the west?
Was it so that this worn-out cod-piece Mamurra
Could squander twenty or thirty million?
What is that but the liberality of a pervert?
Has he spent little on lust and gluttony?
First he ran through his paternal estate,
The spoils of Pontus next, then, those of Spain.
You should hear what is said in the Tagus gold-fields.
Is this the man feared throughout Gaul and Britain?
Why do you keep such a man?
He is a general devourer of patrimonies.
Is it for this you and Pompey have thrown away everything?

XXX

You forget your friends, Alfenus, you let them down,
You have no pity for me, though we have been close.
Betrayal, deception, seem to you quite normal?
You think this sort of thing pleases the gods?
It seems so, and you desert me in my need.
What can men do, in whom are they to trust?
You told me I could rely on you, it is unfair
Leading me on to love, as if all were safe.
Now you draw back and all your words and deeds
Are carried into nothing like the clouds and winds.
You may forget, the gods will not forget;
Faith will remember and you will suffer for it.

XXXI

Of all peninsulas and islands
The inner and the outer Neptune
Bear upon lakes or the great sea
Sirmio is delectable. With what pleasure

I see it again, hardly believing that I have left
The plains of Thynia and Bythinia.
What is more pleasant than to dispense with trouble?
The mind puts down her load and, tired with travel,
We come to our Lares and rest in our own beds.
This is really all we undertake these toils for.
Elegant Sirmio, I salute you.
Be glad your master has come.
Be glad, waters of the Lydian lake.
Laugh, whatever laughter there is in the house.

XXXII

Please darling, dear Ipsithilla,
All my pleasure, my only attraction,
Order me to you this afternoon
And if you do order me, please arrange also
That no-one shall get in my way as I enter
And don't you go off either at the last moment.
But stay at home and organise for us
Nine copulations in rapid series.
If there's anything doing, send round immediately
For here I am, lying on my bed;
I have had my lunch, the thing sticks out of my tunic.

XXXIII

The most accomplished thieves at the baths
Are old Vibennius and his pansy son;
The father has the dirtier hands,
The son the more voracious anus.
Why not go into exile now?
Since everyone knows about father's thieving
And, honestly, son, you'll never sell
Your hairy buttocks for more than tuppence.

XXXIV

We are Diana's children,
Girls not yet adolescent,
Boys not yet adolescent;
We sing Diana, Diana.

O Latonian, O noble
Daughter of Jove, your mother
Dropped you beneath the Delian
Olive, beneath the olive

So that you might be mistress
Of mountains and bursting woodland,
The mistress of hidden valleys
And echoing, echoing rivers.

You are called Juno Lucina
By women moaning in childbed;
You are called Trivia, and powerful
And Moon with the counterfeit light.

Goddess, you measure the annual
Course of the year with your cycles;
You fill up the farm and the cottage
With your beneficent produce.

With whatever name you may favour
Be hallowed, and may you continue,
As you did in the past, so in future,
Your comfort and help to the Romans.

XXXV

I ask this paper to tell Caecilius,
The tender poet, and my friend,
To come to Verona and leave New Como
And leave the shores of Larius.
For there are certain cogitations
I want to put to him from a friend.
If he is wise he will certainly come
However often his candid girl
Calls him back and, throwing her two arms
Round his neck implores him to stay.
She now, if all that I hear is true,
Loves him with lunatic desperation
For since the time she read the beginning
Of his poem on Cybele, the fire has been eating

186

Away at the poor girl's inmost marrow.
But I forgive you, you wiser Sappho,
It's perfectly true they're extremely good,
The opening lines of the 'Magna Mater'.

XXXVI

Annals of Voluisius, fresh from the lavatory,
Discharge the promise my girl made.
She made a vow to Venus and Cupid
That if I were given back to her
And ceased to brandish my sharp iambics
She, for her part, would give to Vulcan
The choicest works of the worst of poets
To be burnt with wood from an unlucky tree.
Now, goddess born of the blue, blue ocean,
You who inhabit sacred Idalium,
The bubs of Uria, Ancona,
Reedy Cnidos, Amathus, Golgos,
Dyrrhachium, the Adriatic drink-shop,
Chalk this vow up as one completed
Unless it seem to you in poor taste;
But meanwhile, you lot, into the fire
– Full of crudity, full of witlessness –
Annals of Volusius, from the lavatory.

XXXVII

Less pub than brothel, and you, the regulars
The ninth pillar from Castor and Pollux
Do you think you are the only ones equipped with a penis,
That you are the only ones licensed for fucking
And that the rest who do it are merely goats?
Do you think, as you sit waiting in rows
A hundred or two hundred together, that I shall not dare
To do the whole lot of you, two hundred together?
Think again: I will draw scorpions
All over the walls of the place.
For my girl, who has escaped from my arms,
Who was loved as much, and more than any is loved,
From whom I have expended all my forces,

She is there. You, the great and the good, all love her,
You the valueless, corrupt, adulterous all love her;
You above all Egnatius
Long-haired son of a rabbit-toothed Celtiberian,
Only made good by your beard
Your teeth whitened by Spanish piss.

XXXVIII

Things go badly with me, Cornificius;
They go badly all right, they are more excruciating
Every day and every hour.
Easy for you to console me if you will, but you will not.
A few words, that is all that is needed.
I am angry with you. Is that how you treat my love?
Why will you not utter a few words of comfort,
A small poem, with a few tears, like Simonides?

XXXIX

Egnatius, because he has white teeth,
Smiles all the time. In court,
When the lawyers are reducing everyone to tears,
He smiles. At a funeral,
When a mother is mourning the death of an only son,
He smiles. Whatever is happening, anywhere,
Whatever he is doing, he smiles. He has this disease,
Not an elegant one, I think, nor very polite.
Let me give you warning, Egnatius.
If you were a city man or a Sabine or Tiburtine,
A pig of an Umbrian or a fat Etruscan,
Or a dark Lanuvian with a fine set of teeth,
Or a Transpadane (not to forget my own people)
Or anyone else with reasonable oral hygiene.
Still I shouldn't really want you to smile all the time
For nothing is stupider than a stupid smirk.
But you are a Celtiberian. Now the Celtiberians
Are accustomed to rub their teeth and gums every morning
With their matutinal micturations
So that, the more highly polished your teeth are,
We must assume, the more piss you drink.

XL

What folly, you wretched Ravidus,
Throws you into the path of my iambics?
What god have you stupidly invoked
To work up to an idiotic quarrel?
Do you want to be talked about? What do you want?
A little notoriety, no matter how it is come by?
You shall have it. You have set your desire where mine is;
The penalty shall be enduring.

XLI

Ameana, the worn-out bitch,
Is asking for a whole ten thousand,
That girl with the flattened nose
That used to go with the Formian bankrupt.
Her family, or whoever looks after the girl
Had better call in her friends and doctors:
The girl is mad, she has never enquired
What a mirror would have to say about her.

XLII

I can do with hendecasyllables,
All the lot of them, as many as they like.
The filthy whore has thought of a joke:
She will not give my tablets back,
Which is more than a little hard to bear.
Better follow her, better beg them back.
Who is she? Over there, there she is,
Strutting like an actress and grinning like a cur.
Now surround her, and now call for them:
'Give them back, dirty bitch,
Give back the tablets, dirty bitch.'
You don't care? You shit, you whore-house,
Or any improvement on those terms.
But it's no good thinking that is enough.
Oh well, if we get nothing else
Let's force a blush from the bitch's muzzle.
Shout together, but louder this time:

'Give them back, dirty bitch,
Give back the tablets, dirty bitch.'
But nothing happens, there's not a movement,
The method of asking had better be changed.
If you want to make progress you'd better try:
'Chaste and honest, give them back!'

XLIII

Girl with the not inconsiderable nose,
Sizeable feet and eyes not exactly jet-black,
With fingers scarcely long and mouth which can hardly be called
    dry,
And a tongue you are in the habit of sticking out,
You who go to bed with the Formian bankrupt:
You are reported in the Province to be beautiful?
My Lesbia is compared with you?
What an uncultivated age we live in!

XLIV

My farm, either Sabine or Tiburtine
(Those who do not want to annoy me call it Tiburtine,
Those who do, bet anything it is Sabine)
– But whether it is Sabine or Tiburtine
I was glad enough to be there, more or less in the country,
And to get rid of my horrible cold on the chest.
My belly had given it to me, not undeservedly,
While I was trying to get to a rather splendid dinner.
For, wanting to be invited to Sestius,
I read his speech *In Antium petitorem*
– It is full of poison and undoubtedly infectious.
Anyway I had a shocking head and coughed all the time
And this went on till I got back to my farm
And a course of idleness and stinging nettles.
Now I am better, I am thankful the farm apparently forgave me.
If ever I look at those beastly compositions of Sestius again
I hope the cold will produce a frightful head and a cough
Not in me, in Sestius himself
Who only asks me when I have read one of his stupid books.

190

XLV

Septimius, Septimius holding Acme
In his arms, says to her: Acme, Acme,
If I don't love you, hopeless and headlong
And go on loving you for ever and ever
As much as ever, in desperation,
I hope I may end in Libya or India,
Eaten alive by a green-eyed lion.
At this Love gave, to left and right hand,
Two small sneezes of approbation.
Acme, however, turning her head round
And kissing the sweet boy's fluttering eye-lids
With her red, red lips, said: Septi darling
I swear, I swear, as we serve one Cupid
My fire is worse, for my bones are tingling.
At this Love gave, this time left-handed,
A further small sneeze of approbation.
Starting from these most favourable omens
They live together and love one another,
Poor young Septimius fonder of Acme
Than of all the wealth of Britain or Syria;
Acme finding in poor Septimius
All she could want of amorous pleasure.
Who ever saw such a pair for loving
Or imagined that Venus could be so docile?

XLVI

Already it is spring, the days are warmer;
The fury of the equinoctial sky
Gives way to gentle breezes, Zephyrus.
Catullus, now they leave the Phrygian plains,
Nicaea, with its rich and burning fields:
Now I can see the famous towns of Asia.
My mind is trembling at the thought of travel;
I am so eager that my feet feel strong.
I say good-bye to all the friendly cohort
Who came together from their far-off home
And wander back through individual ways.

XLVII

Porcius and Socration, two left hands of Piso,
Who operate like scurvy and famine
Has ballocky Priapus preferred you
To my Veranius and Fabullus?
Are you eating and drinking with the rich
In the middle of the afternoon while my friends
Wander the streets and wait to be sent for?

XLVIII

If I should be allowed to go as far as kissing
Your sweet eyes, Juventius,
I would go on kissing them three hundred thousand times
Nor would it ever seem I had had enough,
Not if I harvested
Kisses as numerous as the ears of standing corn.

XLIX

You are the best orator, Marcus Tullius
There is or ever was among the Romans,
The best orator they ever will have.
Catullus tenders you his warmest thanks,
Catullus, who is the worst of all the poets
– As much the worst of all poets
As you are the best of all orators.

L

Yesterday, Licinius, was an idle day:
We amused ourselves with my tablets,
Giving ourselves up to being agreeable.
In turn we wrote verses in different metres,
Simply as something to go with the laughter and wine.
But I came away so alight with your wit,
Lucinius, and the pleasure of these diversions,
That I was not interested in food
And sleep could not cover my eyes with quiet
But, uncontrollably, from one side of the bed to the other,

192

I tossed and turned, longing to see the light
So that I could be with you and talk.
But when I was worn out with this activity
And lay on the bed hardly conscious,
I made this poem for you, agreeable friend.
You can see from that the nature of my pain.
Take care: if I beg and pray do not spit,
There is always Nemesis, my darling,
Who may well get her own back on you.
She is a difficult goddess; beware of annoying her.

LI

He seems like a god, that man,
He seems to subdue the gods, if I may put it that way;
He is sitting opposite you and yet repeatedly
Looks at you and hears
Your delightful laughter. I should be completely senseless.
When I look at you, Lesbia, there is nothing left of my voice.
My tongue is frozen, a thin flame descends through my limbs,
There is ringing in my ears, my two eyes
Are covered with night.

LIA

Leisure is no good to you, Catullus;
You are elevated and perform extravagantly.
Leisure has destroyed kings before now
And cities that have been so fortunate.

LII

What reason is there for not dying, Catullus?
Nonius nurses his wen in the curule chair;
Vatinius perjures his way into the consulship.
What reason is there for not dying, Catullus?

LIII

I laughed at that chap in the crowd:
When Calvus was holding forth in his best manner
About the series of charges against Vatinius,
He listened admiringly and lifting up his hands
Said, 'Gods, what a clever little cock he is!'

LIV

Otho's head is a very little one,
It is as if Erius had waded in from a pig-sty,
While Libo has a trick of lifting his leg.
It is impossible that you should like everything about them,
You and Fuficius, that old man warmed up.

LIVA

Again you will be angry at my iambics,
Harmless although they are, my one and only general.

LV

Perhaps, if it is not a nuisance to you,
You would be good enough to tell me where you are hiding.
I have looked for you in the lesser Campus,
In the circus, and among the lost property;
I have looked for you in the temple of Jove
And in Pompey's walk
I stopped all the women and asked them
But they looked at me with the utmost innocence.
These are the women I begged:
'Give me Camerius, you indelicate girls.'
One of them said, pulling open her dress:
'He is here, somewhere between my nipples.'
Really it is a labour of Hercules to put up with you.
If I were as mobile as the giant of Crete
Or could fly through the air after the manner of Pegasus,
If I were Ladas, or Perseus with wings on his feet
Or the white horses of Rhesus;
You may name all the feather-footed and volatile

194

And at the same time invoke the course of the winds.
But, Camerius, though you produce the whole lot
My bones would ache, I should suffer repeated fainting fits
Before I succeeded in laying hands on you.
Why do you keep yourself from me? It is insolent.
Tell me where you expect to be. Give over,
Be brave, make up your mind, tell the news.
Have those sleek girls got you?
If you keep your face shut and say nothing
You are losing all the pleasure you had from them.
Venus likes to be talked about.
Still keep quiet if you must, but on one condition
That you give me a share of whatever it is you have found.

LVI

Cato, I will tell you a funny thing
Worthy of your ears and loud cackle;
Laugh, as much as you love Catullus, Cato:
The thing is ridiculous, really too funny.
I caught a small boy jogging a girl
So, love forgive me,
I set about him with my rigid rod.

LVII

They suit one another well enough
The pathic Mamurra and the pathic Caesar.
The stains in them are about equal,
One from the city and one from Formiae,
And in neither will they ever be washed out:
Both alike sick, both lying on one bed,
A pair of twins, both of them even writers
You could not say one was more adulterous than the other.
They fight over little girls and then share them.
They certainly suit one another well enough.

LVIII

Caelius, our Lesbia, Lesbia, that Lesbia
More loved by Catullus than any besides.

– More than he loves himself and his pleasures –
Is now, in the alley-ways and even at cross-roads
Fucked by the noble sons of the Romans.

LIX

Rufa of Bononia sucks Rufulus?
The wife of Menenius, whom you have seen in the graveyards
Snatching her supper from the funeral pyre?
– She would run after a loaf as it rolled down out of the flames
And be thumped for it by the half-shaven undertaker's assistant.

LX

Did a lioness from the Libyan mountains
Or Scylla barking out of the mouth of her womb
Give birth to you? You are so hard and inhuman.
Your suppliant's voice crying in its last need
You treat with contempt, so very cruel is your heart.

LXI

Sprung from Urania
You inhabit Helicon;
Young girls you carry off
To men, O Hymenaeus,
O Hymen Hymenaeus.

Put flowers in your hair,
Sweet smelling marjoram,
Put on a veil and come,
Happy, with yellow shoes
On your white feet.

Excited on this day,
Sing all the wedding songs
At the top of your voice;
Dance, and jump about,
A pine torch in your hand.

Vinia is marrying Manlius;
Like Venus from Idalium
She comes to have her beauty judged.
She is a good girl and
The omens are good.

Like the Asian myrtle,
All her branches shining
As if the Hamadryads
Had poured their dew upon her
To amuse themselves.

So make your approach,
Leaving without delay
The caves in the Thespian rock
Which Aganippe waters
Coldly from above.

And call the lady home.
She, wanting her new husband,
Tangles her mind with love
As the persistent ivy here and there
Clings vaguely to a tree.

You with me too, you girls
Whose turn is coming;
Take up the chant together with
O Hymenaeus Hymen.
O Hymen Hymenaeus.

Hearing himself so called
No doubt he'll come more gladly
To do his part which is
In turn to bring in Venus:
He connects up the love.

What god could be more sought
By those who love and are loved?
What god is there more worshipped?
O Hymenaeus Hymen,
O Hymen Hymenaeus.

The tremulous old man
Calls on you for his children:
The girls take off their clothes:
The bridegroom in a dither
Listens for your approach.

To the wild youth you hand over
The girl who is just florescent
Straight from the arms of mother
O Hymenaeus Hymen,
O Hymen Hymenaeus.

Venus can do nothing without you,
That is, nothing respectable;
She can get nothing out of it; but with you
She can. No one should dare
To compare himself with you.

Without you no house can have children
No father can see the succession
Continued: but with you
He can. So no-one should dare
To compare himself to you.

A country without your rites
Will find no protectors
To stand at the frontiers: but with you
It will. So no-one should dare
To compare himself to you.

Open the door, she is coming
And in she comes, the torches
Shake their hair
· ·
But shyness holds her back.
· ·
Preferring to listen to this
She cries because she must go.

Do not cry. There is no danger
For you, Aurunculeia,
That any beautiful woman

Will see the clear day rising
Out of the sea.

In the varied garden
Of the expensive householder
The hyacinth stands so.
You waste time, day is going:
Bride, come out.

Bride come out! If you can bear to,
At long last, if you can hear us;
We are speaking. Come out and see
The torches shake their hair:
Bride, come out.

Your man will not be flippant
And, giving himself over
To mean adulteries,
Want to lie elsewhere than
Between your gentle breasts.

But as the vine embraces
A tree that's planted near it
So he will be entangled
In your embrace. The day goes:
Bride come out.

O bed, which everyone
. . . .
White foot in bed
How glad your man will be
In the passing night, how glad
He will be, in the afternoon!
And yet, this day runs out:
Bride, come out.

Boys, lift the torches up:
I see the bridal veil.
Go, chant together now:
Io Hymen, Hymen Io
Io Hymen Hymenaeus.

Do not prohibit now
The Fescinnine impertinences;
And let the boys have nuts.
The boy that went to bed
With Manlius, gives them out.

You pansy boy, give nuts;
You've played nuts long enough
And now your time has come
To serve Talassius:
You pansy boy, give nuts.

And only yesterday
The country girls seemed nothing!
But now you get a shave;
Hard luck, you pansy boy,
Hard luck, but give the nuts.

Seeing the bridegroom oiled
And combed, one wonders, can
He leave the slippery boys?
But leave them. Io Hymen,
Io Hymen Hymenaeus.

We know what you allowed
Yourself, was once allowed,
But husbands are not free.
Io Hymen, Hymenaeus Io,
Io Hymen Hymenaeus.

And bride, be sure you give
Your husband all he asks
Or he will go elsewhere.
Io Hymen Hymenaeus Io.
Io Hymen Hymenaeus.

This is the house, a large
And pleasant one; it's his
And it will serve for you
(Io Hymen Hymenaeus Io.
Io Hymen Hymenaeus).

Until extreme old age
Forces your head to nod
Assent to everything.
Io Hymen Hymenaeus Io.
Io Hymen Hymenaeus.

And with good omen now
Carry your golden feet
Across the threshold, through
The polished doorway, Io,
Io Hymen Hymenaeus.

Inside, your husband rests
Upon a Tyrian couch,
His mind intent on you.
Io Hymen Hymenaeus Io,
Io Hymen Hymenaeus.

The fire burns in his heart
As much as in your own
But deeper, certainly.
Io Hymen Hymenaeus Io,
Io Hymen Hymenaeus.

The child who leads the girl
Lets go her slender arm;
Go to your husband's bed.
Io Hymen Hymenaeus Io.
Io Hymen Hymenaeus.

You married women now
Whose husbands have grown old
Put the girl in her place.
Io Hymen Hymenaeus Io,
Io Hymen Hymenaeus.

Now, bridegroom, you may come;
Your wife is in the bed,
Her face shines like a flower,
Like a white daisy or
A golden poppy.

Husband (so help me gods)
You are as beautiful.
Venus did not forget
You either. The day goes;
Go on, and lose no time.

You lose none; here you come.
Kind Venus help you since
You now so openly
Take what you want
And do not hide your love.

You could more quickly count
The sands of Africa
Or the glittering stars
Than find the total of
Your many thousand games.

Play as you will and soon
Produce a child. A name
As old as yours must not
Be left without an heir;
The tree must fruit.

A baby Torquatus
I want, at his mother's breast,
Stretching his tender hands
Towards his father, and smiling
With half-parted lips.

May he be so like
His father Manlius
That the instant he appears
Nobody will doubt where
His mother got him from.

May his name be as good
As now his mother's is
So from Penelope
Telemachus derived
And left, a noble fame.

Girls, close the door. For we
Have played enough. But you,
The married pair, good luck;
Play out assiduously
Your vigorous youth.

LXII

Young men:

Evening is here, young men. Stand up and look. From Olympus
Vesper at last has raised the light you awaited so long.
It is time to get up from the couch and the luxurious tables.
The bride is now coming in, the prayers of Hymen are said.
Hymen O Hymenaeus, approach Hymenaeus.

Girls:

Girls, do you see the young men? Let us stand up and face them;
Surely the Star of Night shows its Oetaean fires.
That for sure; do you see how dangerously they have jumped up?
It was not for fun; they will sing; there'll be something to watch.
Hymen O Hymenaeus, approach Hymenaeus.

Young men:

It is not easy for us, the young men, to win the prize:
Look, the girls are going over the part that they have learnt.
They are not doing that for nothing; what they've learnt is a thing
    to remember;
No wonder they turn it over so deep in their minds.
What we learnt went in at one ear and out at the other:
Serve us right, we shall be beaten; to win you've got to attend.
At least let us try to see if our brains are as good as theirs:
Already they've started to speak; it will be for us to reply.
Hymen O Hymenaeus, approach Hymenaeus.

Girls:

Hesperus, what crueller star than you is there up in the sky?
You don't mind taking girls away from their mothers?
Taking a girl away when she's holding tight to her mother?
And giving a girl that is chaste to an ardent young man?

Do the enemy soldiers do worse when they capture a town?
Hymen O Hymenaeus, approach Hymenaeus.

Young men:

Hesperus, what pleasanter star than you is there in the sky?
You are the one who sees that the promise comes true,
The contracts the bridegroom has made, and the families before
    that,
Cannot be carried out until your fire is up.
Is there any time the gods give which is an improvement on this?
Hymen O Hymenaeus, approach Hymenaeus.

Girls:

Hesperus has taken one of us girls away
*   *   *   *   *   *   *   *   *   *   *   *   *

Young men:

When you come up the watch-dogs are always let off the chain
For thieves can hide in the night, and you often find them out
When you go back in the morning, having changed your name to
    Eous.
Hymen O Hymenaeus, approach Hymenaeus.
*   *   *   *   *   *   *   *   *   *   *   *   *
The girls complain about you but we don't believe a word;
We know that, if they complain, they want you all the same.

Girls:

As a flower springs up unknown behind a garden wall
Where the beast can't eat it and can't be convulsed by a plough.
The breezes stroke it, the sun makes it stronger, the rain brings it on
*   *   *   *   *   *   *   *   *   *   *   *   *
Many boys would like to have it, and many girls would too.
Once torn up by sharp nails, it loses its flower,
Then no boys want it, and no girls want it either:
While a girl remains chaste, her family are fond of her
But if she loses her flower, her body is not so nice;
She finds she's no catch for the boys, and even her girl friends go.
Hymen O Hymenaeus, approach Hymenaeus.

Young men:

As a vine which grows on its own in the open field
Never climbs at all, or produces a decent grape
But its tender body bends with its own dead weight
So that the top of it practically touches the root
No farmer comes near it, no oxen plough up the ground.
But if it happens to find a tree to support it
Many farmers will care for it, many oxen will plough.
So a girl, as long as she's virgin, grows old in neglect
But when she is suited in time with the right sort of marriage
She is dear to a man, and not such a trial to her family.
Hymen O Hymenaeus, approach Hymenaeus.
So, girl, it is really not wise to resist such a husband.
You should not resist, since your father has given you away;
Your mother and father decided, you should do as they tell you.
Virginity isn't just yours, it is partly your parents' as well.
A third is your father's, a third is your mother's, a third is your own.
That is all you have. Better not resist the two others.
They have given their rights with the dowry, and you go with that.
Hymen O Hymenaeus, approach Hymenaeus.

LXIII

Carried in a fast ship over profound seas
Attis, eager and hurried, reached the Phrygian grove,
The goddess's dark places, crowned with woodland.
And there, exalted by amorous rage, his mind gone,
He cut off his testicles with a sharp flint.
She then, aware of the limbs without the man,
While the ground was still spotted with fresh blood
Quickly took in her snowy hands a tambourine
Such as serves your initiates, Cybele, instead of a trumpet
And, shaking the hollow calf-hide with delicate fingers.
Quivering, she began to sing to the troop this:
'Go together, votaresses, to the high groves of Cybele.
Go together, wandering herd of the lady of Dindymus.
Quick into exile, you looked for foreign places
And, following me and the rule I had adopted,
You bore with the salt tide and the violence of the high sea
And emasculated your bodies from too much hatred of Venus:
Delight the lady's mind with your errant haste.

Overcome your reluctance: together
Go to the Phrygian shrine of Cybele, to her groves
Where the voice of cymbals sounds, the tambourines rattle,
Where the Phrygian piper sings with the deep curved pipe,
Where Maenads wearing ivy throw back their heads,
Where they practise the sacred rites with sharp yells.
Where they flutter around the goddess's cohort:
It is there we must go with our rapid dances.'
As Attis, the counterfeit woman, sang this to her companions,
The choir howled suddenly with tumultuous tongues.
The tambourine bellows, the cymbals clash again;
The swift troop moves off to Ida with hurrying feet.
Crazy, panting, drifting, at her last gasp,
Attis with her tambourine leads them through the opaque groves
Like an unbroken heifer refusing the yoke:
The swift votaresses follow their swift-footed leader.
When they reach Cybele's shrine they are feeble and worn.
Sleep covers their eyes with a heavy blanket;
Their rabid madness subsides to a girlish quiet.
But when the golden sun with his streaming eyes
Purified the white sky, hard land, wild sea,
And drove away the shadows of night with his thundering horses,
Attis was aroused and Sleep went quickly from her
Back to the trembling arms of the goddes Pasithea.
Then from her girlish quiet, with no hurrying madness,
Attis remembered what she had done
And saw in her lucid mind what was missing and where she was.
Tempestuously she turned back to the shore.
There, looking at the open sea with tearful eyes,
With grief in her voice she addressed her native land:
'Land which begot me, land which brought me forth,
I am abject to abandon you like a runaway slave.
My feet have carried me to the groves of Ida
To be among snow in the cold lairs of wild beasts;
I shall visit their violent haunts.
Where, O my land, can I imagine you are?
My eye desires you and narrows as it turns towards you
In this short interval when my mind is unfrenzied.
Shall I be carried to the forests, from my far-off home?
Away from country, goods, friends, family?
From the Forum, palaestra, race-course and gymnasium?
There is nothing for me but misery.

What shape is there that I have not had?
A woman now, I have been man, youth and boy;
I was the athlete, the wrestler.
There were crowds round my door, my fans slept on the doorstep;
There were flowers all over the house
When I left my bed at sunrise.
Shall I be a waiting-maid to the gods, the slave of Cybele?
I a Maenad, I a part of myself, I impotent?
Shall I live above the snow-line on green Ida?
Shall I pass my life under the rocky peaks of Phrygia
Where the doe runs in the woods, where the bear mooches in the
    glades?
I regret now, now, what I have done, I repent of it, now!'
As these words hurried away from her pink lips,
Bringing a new message to the ears of the gods,
Cybele, letting her lions off the leash
And urging forward the beast on the left hand,
Said: 'Get on, be fierce, see that he's driven mad;
Make him insane enough to return to the forest;
He has had the impertinence to want to be out of my power.
Come on, lash around with your tail till you hurt yourself:
Make the whole neighbourhood ring with your bellowing roar.
Be fierce, shake the red mane on your muscular neck.'
Thus the threatening Cybele, and she wound the leash round her
    hand
The beast stirs up his courage and rouses himself to fury.
He is off, he roars, he breaks up the undergrowth.
When he came to the wet sand on the whitening shore
He charged: Attis, mad, flew into the wild woods:
There, for the rest of her life, she lived as a slave.
Great Goddess, Goddess Cybele, Goddess lady of Dindymus,
May all your fury be far from my house.
Incite the others, go. Drive other men mad.

LXIV

Pines from the summit of Pelion,
It is said, floated in the running seas
As far as Phasis and the shores of Aeetes
When elect youths, the pick of Argive manhood,
Seeking to relieve the Colchians of the golden fleece,

Had the courage to run over salt waves with a rapid craft,
Sweeping the blue deep with pine-wood oar-blades;
The goddess who keeps the city fortress-tops
Herself devised this chariot which would fly with the wind,
Joining the pine-wood structure to a bending keel.
It was the first ship that attempted a voyage.
As soon as the prow cut through the windy sea
And the waves whitened as the rowing churned them up
The Nereids came out of the whiteness,
Amazed at this new form of marine animal.
On that day at least mortals did really see
Naked sea-nymphs sticking out of the water showing their tits.
It is supposed to have been then that Peleus became mad about
    Thetis,
That Thetis decided she wouldn't despise human marriage
And that the Father admitted to himself that Peleus would have
    to have her.
O heroes, born in that most happy age,
I salute you, race of the gods, I salute you
O excellent offspring of excellent mothers.
I shall often address you in the course of my song:
And you, notably multiplied by fortunate marriage torches,
The pillar of Thessaly, Peleus, on whom Jupiter himself,
Who begot the gods, bestowed his love:
Did Thetis embrace you? She was the most beautiful of the Nereids.
Did Tethys allow you to marry her grand-daughter,
And Oceanus, who wraps up the whole world in the sea?
    At last the waiting was at an end and the day came.
All Thessaly poured into the house;
They come in, presents first, and wear looks of rejoicing.
Cieros is deserted; they leave Phthiotic Tempe,
The houses round Crannon and the walls of Larissa,
And crowd indoors at Pharsalus.
Nobody works on the land, the oxen go soft round the neck,
The vine is left struggling and the hoeing isn't done.
The pruning-hook has a holiday and the trees grow thick;
The ox stops dragging the plough-share through lumps of earth
And rust begins to develop on the deserted equipment.
    But Peleus's house, as far as you can see inside that millionaire
        palace,
Shines brilliantly with every kind of gold and silver.
The seats are of ivory, and the cups on the table gleam.

The whole house is gay with splendid paraphernalia.
In a central position is the golden bed,
Polished elephant tusk, with the hangings dyed purple with
    shell-dye.
The bed-spread, worked with figures from former times,
Illustrating the deeds of the heroes, is a remarkable production:
Ariadne, looking out from the wave-beaten shore,
Sees Theseus disappearing with his rapid boats.
She has fury in her heart and cannot believe her eyes,
For awakened at last from deceptive sleep
She sees herself miserably alone on the lonely sand.
But the youth is in flight and the oars fall in time on the water;
He leaves his empty promises to the winds and squalls.
From among the sea-weed the daughter of Minos
With tears in her eyes looks out like a stone bacchanal.
She looks out, alas, washed by great waves of care,
Not keeping her fine scarf in place on her yellow head
Nor her breasts covered with the light material;
The band had given way and there they are, full of milk.
All her clothes slipped down and the salt waves
Moved them gently as they floated about her:
But she was not bothered about her scarf of drifting clothes.
Her whole heart was on you, Theseus,
Her whole mind, her whole consciousness, were fixed
    immoveably.
Poor girl, whom Erycina made wild with continuous sorrow,
Sowing prickly cares in her heart
From the moment when Theseus
Setting forth from the curved shores of Piraeus
Reached the Gortynian temple of the unjust king.
    The story is that once, forced by a cruel plague
To compensate for the death of Androgeos,
Cecropia used to give as food to the Minotaur
Selected youths and the best of the unmarried girls.
When his narrow walls were troubled with these evils,
Theseus decided to offer his own body for Athens
Rather than that such living funerals should be carried to Crete.
So, pressing on with light ship and suitable breeze,
He came to the hero Minos and his superb residence.
When the princess saw him, which she did with eagerness,
A scented single bed kept her safe as in her mother's arms,
As the rivers of Eurotas mother the myrtles

Or the spring breeze brings out the different colours:
She did not lower her burning eyes
Till she had caught fire all over her body, and deep inside
Her secret marrow grew hot.
You, miserable boy, who stir up frenzy in your hard-hearted
    fashion
And mix the joys of men with trouble;
And you, queen of Golgi and green Idalium,
On what waves you threw the burning mind of that girl
As she sighed repeatedly for the yellow-haired visitor.
What fears she had in her fainting heart!
How often her face was a cold glitter
When Theseus, anxious to measure himself against the violent
    monster,
Sought either death or the reward of his heroic operation.
Useless though they were the sacrifices she offered were not
    unpleasing
As she prayed in silence to the gods.
As a hurricane on top of Taurus
Twists to the centre an oak or a sweating pine-tree
And fells it (and it falls, torn up by the roots,
Far off, breaking everything in its way)
So Theseus threw down the monster, its body inert,
Its horns thrown back useless in the empty wind.
He came back safe from that, having performed his feat,
Relying on the fine thread to guide his footsteps
So that as he came out of the twisting labyrinth
The unobservable confusion of the building did not frustrate him.
    But why should I digress from my original song
To mention these particulars: how the daughter fled
From father, sister and finally from her mother
Who cried her eyes out for the wretched girl;
How she preferred the love of Theseus to all her relations;
How the ship sailed for the breakers on the shores of Dia;
Or how her husband left her when she was asleep
Going away without a though?
It is said that frequently, in her fury, her heart blazing,
She expressed her inmost feelings with resounding screams.
First she would sadly climb up the steep hills
From which she could extend her gaze over the wide sea;
Then she would rush out into the trembling waves,
Lifting her skirt up to her knees

And so, in her final misery, she would say,
Her face wet, her sobs growing cold:
　'So, Theseus, you cheat, having taken me from my father's
　　house.
You leave me alone on this remote bit of coast?
So you go away as if there were no gods
And take home nothing but your perjury?
Could nothing have any influence on your cruel mind?
Had you no pity, could you feel nothing at all for me?
You talked blandly enough when you gave me your promises;
You didn't tell me that I was going to be miserable,
You talked about a happy engagement and a desirable marriage:
But all that has been scattered now by the wind.
In future no woman should believe any man's assurances
Or hope that anything a man says will come true.
When they want something and are keen to get it
Men will swear anything, and promise anything you like.
But as soon as desire is satisfied
It doesn't matter what they've said, they don't mind perjury.
Yet I saved you when you were caught in the whirlwind of death
And made up my mind to let my brother go
Rather than fail you, but you let me down.
For this I am left to wild beasts and birds of prey
Without decent burial.
Were you born of a lioness under a desert rock?
What sea brought you forth out of the foaming waves,
What Syrtis, rapacious Sylla, monstrous Charybdis,
That you should make such return for saving your life?
If you could not find it in your heart to marry me
Because you were afraid of your peevish father
You could still have taken me home with you
So that I could be your slave, I shouldn't mind the work,
Pouring water gently over your white feet
Or setting the purple cover on your bed.
　'But why should I complain to the ignorant winds?
It is useless; I am mad; and the air has no sense –
It can neither hear what I say nor return an answer.
He is already away on the high seas
And there is no soul among all this sea-weed.
Even fortune in this extreme hour
Refuses to listen to what I have to say.
　'Almighty Jupiter, I wish the Cecropian ship

Had never got so far as the Gnosian coast
Bringing the wild bull its terrible tribute
Or that the cheat had never tied up his boat in Crete
Nor, hiding his cruel designs in a fair appearance
Had ever been a visitor in our house.
Where shall I go from here? What hope shall I entertain?
Shall I take refuge in the hills of Sidon?
The sea is broad and fierce that divides me from them.
Shall I look for my father's help? I abandoned him
To follow the young man who killed my brother.
Shall I console myself with the faithful love of my husband?
He is leaving me, bending to dip his oars in the sea.
Here I am on the shores of a desert island;
I am surrounded by sea and there is no way out.
There is no possibility of escape; no hope; all is silence;
All is deserted and everything looks like death.
But I will not allow my eyes to sink into darkness
Nor my tired body to become insensible
Before I have demanded vengeance from the gods
And prayed for the faith of heaven in my last hour.
   'Eumenides, avengers of what men do,
Your foreheads decorated with snaky hair
Makes public the anger steaming from your hearts:
Come this way now, listen to my complaints
Which I, poor girl, extract from my inmost marrow.
I am driven, I cannot help it, blazing and blind
With mindless fury. Since these griefs come from my heart
Do not let them vanish;
But as Theseus had a mind to leave me
May that mind, goddesses, destroy him and all who are with him.'
   When she had poured out these words from her mourning heart,
Demanding that the man who had hurt her should be made to
      suffer,
The ruler of heaven nodded his powerful assent.
At that the sea and land trembled together;
Earth shook the glittering stars.
Theseus himself, lost in a blank perplexity,
His mind forgetful, failed to keep any hold
Of the instructions he had carried carefully for so long.
He gave no signal to his mourning father
To show that he was safe in sight of the Erechthean harbour.
It is said that when Aegeus entrusted his son to the winds

And the young man left the goddess's town
He embraced him and gave him these instructions:
   'My only son, dearer to me than long life,
Given back to me at the end of old age,
Son, whom I was forced to send on a difficult mission,
Since my fortune and your courage
Took you away from me in spite of my unwillingness
And although my eyes could not see enough of you before they
     failed:
I will not let you go cheerfully
Nor allow you to bear the marks of a favourable fortune
But first I will express from my mind many complaints,
My grey hair covered with earth and ash to dirty it;
Then I will hang dyed sails on your swaying mast
So that the canvas may show, by its steely blue
My grief and the fire in my heart.
But if she who inhabits the sacred Itonus,
Willing to defend our race and the land of Erechtheus,
Allows you to spray your right hand with the blood of the bull
Be sure that these instructions sprout in your heart
And that no passage of time kills them:
As soon as you set eyes on our hills
Haul down the funereal canvas from your mast
And let the twisted cords run up white sails
So that at the first glance I can see the news is good
When in a happy time you are carried home.'
   At first Theseus kept these instructions steadily in mind:
Then, like clouds moved by the breath of winds
From a snowy peak, they left him.
But the father, as he looked out from his rock on the Acropolis
Consuming his eyes with tears, for he wept continually,
As soon as he saw the canvas of the inflated sail
Threw himself headlong from the top of the rock
Believing Theseus lost by ungentle fate.
So ferocious Theseus, entering his father's house,
Found it in mourning, and himself received
Such grief as by forgetting he had given Minos's daughter.
She meanwhile, mournfully watching the ship recede
Stricken, felt her many cares turn in her head.
   In another part the flowering Iacchus was wandering
With a dance of Satyrs and Sileni from Nysa
Looking for you, Arjadne, and burning with love.

. . . .
Who then, now here, now there, out of their minds, frenzied,
Shouted Euhoe we are drunk, Euhoe, and their heads swayed.
  Some of the women shook long rods with covered points,
Some of them threw in the air the parts of a bull,
Some pulled round themselves a belt of twisted snakes,
Some thronged around the box which held the orgies,
The orgies which only initiates may be told of;
Others struck timbrels with their palms uplifted
Or made slight tinklings with the polished brass:
Many blew horns and made a raucous noise
And barbarian pipes screamed out their horrible tunes.
  A covering decorated with figures like these
Hung round the bed and wrapped it up in its folds;
The youth of Thessaly had to have a good luck:
When they had done, they began to make way for the gods.
Then as, scaring the sea with his morning breath,
Zephyrus wrinkles the surface of the water
When Dawn rises on the threshold of the journeying sun;
The waves come softly at first, driven by a light wind;
They sound lightly and their complaint is like laughter
But, the wind rising, they grow bigger and bigger
And shine brilliantly as they swim far from the crimson light:
So here, leaving the gates of the royal palace,
The guests depart, each his own way, and scatter.
  When they had gone away, from the top of Pelion
Came Chiron with silvan gifts:
Flowers of the field, flowers from the towering mountains
Of Thessaly, flowers which, by flowering rivers,
The warm, productive breath of Favonius opens:
All these he brings woven together in garlands;
Their pleasant, soothing odour makes the house smile.
Suddenly Peneus is there: he has left Tempe,
Green Tempe, surrounded by hanging forests,
And thronged with Doric dancers:
Not empty-handed, for he was carrying immense beeches
Torn up by the roots, and bay-trees with upright stems,
Luxuriant plane-trees and tall cypresses
And swaying poplars, sisters of the sun.
With all these he decorated the house
So that the doorway was covered with gentle foliage.
After him came Prometheus, who had thought deeply

214

And was still marked by the penalty he had paid
When chained to the rocks he was left hanging from a peak.
Then came the father of the gods, the goddess his wife, and his
     sons,
Leaving you alone in the sky, Phoebus,
With your sister who also lives on the mountains of Idrus,
Like you, your sister regarded Peleus with contempt
And declined to celebrate the marriage of Thetis.
     When they had relaxed on the white couches
At tables piled with a varied wedding breakfast,
Then, shaking their bodies weakly,
The Parcae began to emit their reliable chants.
The white gown enfolding their trembling bodies
Came down to the ankles with a purple border;
Their white hair had roses in it;
Their hands, duly engaged in their eternal labour,
The left hand held the distaff covered in wool;
The right hand pulled down the threads while the fingers moulded
     them.
Then the thumb twirled the spindle with a smooth twirl
And all the while they bit off the straggling ends
And the ends they bit off stuck to their dried-up lips
As before they had stuck out from the smooth yarn.
At their feet fleeces of shining wool
Were stored in wicker baskets.
The Parcae struck them and poured out with unmistakeable voice
These prophecies in their divine song.
A song the truth of which no time will question:

     'To your distinguished name you add great deeds,
Guardian of Thessaly, friend to the child of Ops:
Accept what this happy day the sisters open to you,
The true oracle. And the fates that follow:
     Spindles run on, and draw the future out.

     'Soon he will come who brings the married what they want,
Hesperus; your wife will come with that happy star.
Like dew upon your mind she will bend it down
And then she will join you in the softest sleep
With her smooth arms under your robust neck.
     Spindles run on, and draw the future out.

'No house has ever covered loves like these:
No love has ever joined two with such trust
As is between Peleus and Thetis now.
　　Spindles run on, and draw the future out.

'Achilles shall be born, and know no fear;
His enemies will never see his back.
How often will he run long distances,
His feet like flames, and faster than a stag.
　　Spindles run on, and draw the future out.

'No hero shall withstand this man in war
When all the streams of Phrygia flow with blood
And the third heir of perjured Pelops comes
After long war to break the walls of Troy.
　　Spindles run on, and draw the future out.

'His virtues and remarkable performances
Mothers will know of when their sons are buried;
They will let down their hair from their white heads
And bruise their withered breasts with their weak hands.
　　Spindles run on, and draw the future out.

'For as the farmer chops the ears of corn,
Harvesting yellow fields in the hot sun,
His hostile sword will cut the Trojans down.
　　Spindles run on, and draw the future out.

'Scamander's waters shall be witnesses
Where they pour out upon the Hellespont,
For he is going to block their way with corpses
And warm the deepest of them with his slaughter.
　　Spindles run on, and draw the future out.

'The last witness shall be his prey in death
When the round barrow in its heaped up mound
Receives the white limbs of a girl struck down.
　　Spindles run on, and draw the future out.

'For when fortune gives the weary Argives strength
To break the chains about the Dardanian town
They will wet the great tomb with Polyxena's blood.

She, like a victim falling to a sword
Will let her body go and bend her knee.
  Spindles run on, and draw the future out.

'Come therefore, join the loves you so desire.
Husband, now take the goddess in all trust:
Bride, give yourself now to your impatient husband.
  Spindles run on, and draw the future out.

'When the nurse comes to see her in the morning
She will find that yesterday's thread won't go round her neck
Nor will her worrying mother have to fear,
Because the girl has slept alone, she will have no grandchildren.
  Spindles run on, and draw the future out.'

  Such happiness was pronounced for Peleus
And so the Parcae sang from divine hearts.
For in those days the Fates appeared in person,
Visited chaste homes and showed themselves to mortals
But that was before religion was despised.
The father of the gods, visiting his bright temple
When the annual rites came round on his festal days,
Would watch a hundred bulls felled to the ground.
Often Liber, wandering on the top of Parnassus,
Drove before him the Thyades with streaming hair,
When all the Delphians racing out of their city
Received him gladly and with smoking altars.
Often in the middle of a murderous battle Mavors,
The mistress of swift Triton or the Rhamnusian Virgin
Appeared in the armed bands to encourage them.
But when the whole world was imbued with crime
And so put justice out of its greedy mind
Brothers dipped their hands in brothers' blood,
The son no longer mourned his father's death,
The father wished for the death of his vigorous son
So that he could enjoy the flower of the bride,
The mother, getting secretly underneath her son,
Did not scruple to sin against the ancestral gods.
Then right and wrong were confused in an evil frenzy
And that turned from us the just minds of the gods.
So they no longer deign to come among us
Nor can they bear to be touched by the clear light.

LXV

Although I am exhausted by continual grief
And sorrow calls me away from the Muses, Hortalus;
Nor can what is in my mind be expressed in verse
So great is the trouble that shakes me:
For my brother has descended to Lethe,
The water is lapping his pale foot;
Under the coast of Rhoeteum the earth of Troy
Lies heavily on him, and he has gone from our sight.
. . . .
I shall never again speak to you or hear you speaking
Nor shall I ever, brother dearer than life,
See you again. But certainly I shall love you,
I shall always have you in mind in my poems
As among the branches and in heavy shadows
Daulias cries over the fate of Itylus.
Yet in the middle of this mourning, Hortalus, I send you
These translations from Battiades,
So that you will not think I have forgotten what you said
Nor that it was as if you had spoken to the wind.
It is as if an apple sent to a girl by her lover
Fell out of her decorously covered bosom
When she, having put it in a fold of her gown and then forgotten it,
Is startled by the approach of her mother:
Then see how quickly it rolls down and away
And a self-conscious redness creeps over her regretful face.

LXVI

He identified all the stars in the sky,
Finding out when they rose and when they set,
How the brilliant flame of the sun is eclipsed,
How the stars withdraw at determined times,
How Trivia is to be found in a cave on Latmus
When sweet love calls her down from her aery circuit.
This was Conon: then he saw me in the stars,
I who am the hair from Berenice's head,
Shining brightly. She vowed me to many goddesses
Stretching her gentle arms up as she did so
At the time when the king, in the honour of his new marriage
Had gone to devastate the Assyrian frontiers,

Still dishevelled from the nocturnal struggles
He had lately waged to strip and despoil a virgin.
Do brides indeed hate Venus, and when their parents
Show joy, do you suppose it is genuine blubbering
They make as they enter the door of the marriage chamber?
No, help me gods, their moaning is all dissembled.
My queen at least taught me that with her lamentation
When her newly married husband went off to the war.
But you of course weren't bewailing an empty bed;
The loss of a brother gave you something to cry about!
And how profoundly that sorrow ate at your heart!
You were so anxious the whole of you seemed involved;
Your senses left you, your mind gave way. Yet I for certain
Knew you had courage enough as a little girl.
Have you forgotten the magnificent crime you committed
Which no one else would have dared, for a royal marriage?
But in sending out your husband what words were spoken!
Jupiter, how your sad hand rubbed at your eyes!
Some great god must have changed you! Or may be lovers
Don't like their favourite body too long away?
So I with the blood of bulls had to be sacrificed
For your dear husband, to all the gods if he came back.
That was the vow. It didn't take him very long
To capture Asia and add it to Egypt's territories.
And so it was done: and I was given up to the divinities
And paid for yesterday's vow with an offering today.
I was not very anxious, queen, to come off the top of you,
Not anxious: I will swear that by you and your head
And if anyone forswears that, let him have his deserts.
But who is there, after all, who can stand up to steel?
Even that mountain was turned upside down, the biggest there
    was
In all the shores the son of Thia drives over,
When the Medes produced a new sea, and the youthful barbarians
Took their fleet right through the middle of Athos.
What can you expect of hair, when steel makes things like that
    shudder?
O Jupiter, let the whole race of the Chalybes perish
With the man who began it by looking for veins underground
And first invented the way of making pig iron!
The sister hairs were just bewailing the fate
Of me that was taken from them, when Ethiop Memnon's

Brother appeared, and flapping about with his wings,
Carried me off – he is Arsinoe's flying horse.
He bears me aloft through the ethereal shadows
And dumps me down in the chaste bosom of Venus.
Zephyritis herself had despatched her man on the mission,
The Grecian lady who lives on the shores of Canopus.
So Venus, who thought that the light of heaven should have
    something
Beside the golden coronet of Ariadne
And that it would be a good thing if we also shone there,
We the sacrificed spoil of your yellow head,
Put me all wet with weeping in the temples of the gods
As a new constellation among the old ones: she was a goddess.
You will find me among the stars next to Virgo and Leo,
Quite near to Callisto who was the daughter of Lycaon.
I turn to the west, and get there before Bootes
Who even at a late hour will hardly dip in the sea.
However, at night, the steps of the gods press upon me,
I am back with the white-headed Tethys when the day comes.
(I hope you'll allow me to say this, Virgin of Rhamnus,
You will not find me afraid of telling the truth.
And though the stars will tear me apart with their gossip
I feel I must plainly say what is in my heart.)
I am not so happy, with all this, that I don't suffer
Terribly at being away from the head of my mistress
With whom (although, when a virgin, she didn't use it)
I have, I assure you, drunk many thousands of perfumes.
Now you, when the wedding torch has been lit for you,
Before you give your bodies to your enthusiastic husbands
Or even pull back your dress to show your nipples,
Make me a pleasant gift from your onyx jar
You who are devoting yourselves to the rights of a chaste bed.
But of course if anyone gives herself up to adultery
I hope that the dust will swallow her worthless gifts
For I certainly don't want offerings from people who aren't
    respectable,
Rather, express a hope that they will live in harmony
And that they will be blessed with an assiduous love.
You, queen, when you look at the stars at evening
And are going to propitiate Venus with festal lamps,
Do not leave your old servant empty-handed
But rather seek my favour with out-sized gifts.

Why do the stars keep me here? If I were the queen's once again
Orion could blaze as he liked and be next to Aquarius.

LXVII

CATULLUS

Pleasing enough to the husband, and pleasing to the father,
Hullo, front door, and Jupiter's blessings on you!
They say that you served Balbus kindly enough
When the old man was alive and had this house.
Now they report you're serving the son unkindly
Since the old man is stiff and the bride has come here.
Tell me, how is it you are said to have changed
And abandoned your dutiful conduct towards your master?

DOOR

No offence to Caecilius, whose property I now am,
But it's not my fault, although they say it is;
No-one ever caught me doing anything wrong.
Of course people will say the door does it all;
When anything goes wrong they all shout out,
There you are, front door, at it again!

CATULLUS

It isn't enough just to put it like that:
You have to try and make yourself understood.

DOOR

What can I do? Nobody seems to want to know.

CATULLUS

I want to know, so don't mind telling me.

DOOR

In the first place it's not true that she was a virgin when she came
	here:
Her husband wasn't the first to touch her.
His dagger hung limper than a stalk of beet

And never had the strength to make his tunic stick out.
But the father is supposed to have been busy in his son's bed
And to have done worse than bring the house into disrepute;
Either because his beastly mind was in a flaming passion
Or because the son, coming from bad stock, was impotent
And it needed someone with a bit more courage
To loosen a virgin's belt and get her clothes off.

CATULLUS

That's a fine story of parental devotion,
The old man pissing in his son's lap.

DOOR

But that is not the only thing Brixia knows
– The town that lies under the old look-out
And through which Meo flows with its yellow water,
Brixia the mother of my beloved Verona;
It also has stories about Postumius and Cornelius
With whom that woman also had her adventures.

CATULLUS

Someone will say: Hey, door, how can you know all this?
After all you never get away from the house;
You can't hear the talk of the town, fixed to that door-jamb
With nothing to do but to open and shut.

DOOR

I have often heard that woman whispering to her maids
And telling them all about her goings-on,
Naming the people I have spoken of, hoping no doubt
That I shouldn't be able to hear or repeat what she said.
She also mentioned another name which I won't tell you
In case the man should raise his ginger eye-brows.
He is a tall man, and was once involved in a big law-suit,
Something to do with misrepresenting a birth and a wrong
     mother.

LXVIII

That, oppressed by fortune and a bitter event,
You should send me this note written in tears,
That, ship-wrecked and ejected by the foaming waves
You look to me to carry you on shore
When divine Venus refuses her sensual sleep
– For you lie alone in an empty bed
And have not the consolation of reading over the old poets
When your anxious mind keeps you awake –
I am glad of it, since you treat me as a friend
And ask me for provisions from Venus and the Muses:
In case you do not know my own troubles, Manlius,
And think I make a poor return for your hospitality,
I had better tell you I myself am under the waves of fortune
So that you do not look for happiness in this direction.
At the time when I first put on an adult toga
And my flowering years were at their agreeable spring
I played well enough: that goddess is not unknown to me
Who mixes a delightful bitterness with our cares:
But with my brother's death all pre-occupations of that kind
Have left me. In sorrow, my brother, I accept your loss;
Dying, you have deprived me of my advantages.
With you all our house is buried;
With you all those joys have died
Which your love kept going while you were alive.
Since your death I have put out of my mind
All such concerns and every kind of pleasure.
You write that I ought to be ashamed of myself staying at Verona
When all the young men about town
Are keeping themselves warm in the bed that used to be mine.
That, Manlius, is not a disgrace but a misfortune.
You will pardon me, therefore, if I do not, because I cannot
Give you those gifts which grief has taken away.
For I haven't got many authors with me here.
That is because I live in Rome. That is where my house is,
My home, that is where I pass my life:
All I bring with me here is one box of books.
In these circumstances I hope you will not consider me ill-natured
Or think I am acting ungenerously
If I have not provided you with either of the things you ask for.
I would provide them unasked, if I had any.

I cannot remain silent about how Allius helped me,
Goddesses, what it was and how much he helped.
I do not want time, flying in forgetful centuries,
To bury his efforts in darkness.
So I will tell you, and you hereafter can tell it
To many thousands, when my book grows old.
. . . .
Let him become more and more widely known after his death;
And let no spider weaving its delicate web
Cover the name of Allius with forgetfulness
For you know with what cares the ambiguous Amathusian
Visited me and how she oppressed me.
I was burning like the Trinacrian rock
And the Malian waters at Oetean Thermopylae,
My eyes were wasted with continual tears
And my cheeks always wet as if I'd been out in the rain.
As from the top of a high mountain
A stream springs brightly out of the mossy rock
And rolls headlong into the valley,
Then crosses a road thronged with people
And freshens the traveller in his weary sweat
When summer cracks the burning fields:
Or as to sailors caught in a dark storm
Comes a gentler wind blowing from the right quarter
– For which they have prayed to Pollux and then to Castor –
That is what Allius's help was to me.
He threw open the gate into a closed field;
He gave me a house and a mistress
With whom we could practise our pleasures in common.
It was to this house that my candid goddess
Came with soft step and placed her shining foot
On the common threshold, pressing it with her thin shoe,
As once, flaming with love for her husband,
Laodamia came to the house of Protesilaus
Which was never complete, because the blood of a victim
Had not yet pacified the masters of heaven.
May nothing please me overmuch, Rhamnusian virgin,
Which is undertaken without the will of those masters.
How the starved altar desires the blood of sacrifice
Laodamia learned when her man was lost,

Force to let fall her arms from the neck of her bridegroom
Before the coming of one winter and then another
With their long nights should give her enough of love
So that she would live on with her husband gone.
The Parcae knew he would shortly be lost
If he went as a soldier to the Ilian walls.
For it was then that, because of the rape of Helen,
Troy began to excite against herself all the Argive nobles,
Troy the foul common grave of Asia and Europe,
Troy the bitter ash of men and all their actions
Which also brought pitiful death to my brother.
Brother, you were taken from me, I am unhappy;
The kind light was taken from you, you are unhappy.
With you all our house is buried;
With you all those joys have died
Which your love kept going while you were with us.
Now so far, and not among known tombs,
Having found no place near the ashes of the family,
Obscene Troy, cursed Troy keeps you buried
In the extreme soil of an alien land.
To this town at that time all the youth of Greece
Were hurrying, deserting the family shrines
So that Paris should not enjoy his whore in a quiet bed.
By that event, beautiful Laodamia,
Your husband dearer than life or mind was taken from you.
The tide of love sucked you down abruptly,
Carrying you away into its caves and channels
As, the Greeks say, near Cyllenian Pheneus
The soil is drained from the rich marsh-land
Where the so-called son of Amphitryon
Is supposed to have dug away the bones of the mountain
At the time when he struck the Stymphalian monsters
With a sure arrow on the orders of a worse master
That the gateway of heaven might be thronged by more gods
And Hebe might not long remain a virgin.
But your deep love was deeper than that gulf
And taught you although untamed to bear the yoke:
For not so dear to the man who has completed his age
Is the head of the grandchild whom his daughter nurses,
Who has come at last to inherit the ancestral wealth,
Provide a name that can go in the will
And put an end to the expectations of relatives,

So driving the vulture from the old man's head:
Nor did ever dove so delight its white mate,
Though they are said always to be snatching kisses
With their mordant beaks, and more shamelessly,
Though women are notably inconstant.
But you alone outdid the madness of all these
When you were brought together with your golden husband.
Little or not at all less deserving was my light
When she gave herself into my lap.
Running around hither and thither Cupid
Shone brilliantly in his saffron cloak.
Yet although she is not satisfied with Catullus alone
I will bear with the rare deceits of this modest lady
Lest I become tiresome like stupid men.
Often indeed Juno, the greatest of the goddesses,
Chokes back her flaming anger at her husband's faults,
Knowing the numerous deceits of all-desiring Jove.
And I must not compare men to gods

. . . .

Bear the unpleasing weight of a tremulous father.
Still I did not take her from her father's hand
Into a house fragrant with Assyrian odours
But she gave me her furtive gifts in the marvellous night,
Stolen from her husband's bed.
Therefore it is enough if she gives me alone
The day she marks with a white pebble.
This gift, the best I could, set out in verse
Is given you, Allius, for your many kindnesses
So that your name shall not be touched by rust
On this day or the next nor yet the next.
To this the gods will add the many gifts
Themis in former times gave to the pious.
I hope that you and your life may be happy,
The house we played in and its mistress too,
And he who first offered me the earth,
From whom came all the good things I have known.
And far before all, she I love more than myself,
My light, for I am happy as long as she is alive.

LXIX

It should not surprise you, Rufus, that no woman
Wants to put her gentle thigh under yours,
That you cannot bribe them with presents of clothes
And that even the most dazzling jewellery is no temptation.
Your trouble is an unfortunate rumour, which reports
That there is a powerful goat under your armpits.
They're all afraid of him. No wonder, he is nasty, without a doubt,
That beast, and not one a beautiful girl would go to bed with.
So, either you should slaughter this cruel offence to their noses
Or cease to express surprise when they run away.

LXX

My woman says there is no-one she would rather marry
Than me, not even if Jupiter were to propose to her.
She says: but what a woman says to an eager lover
Ought to be recorded in wind and water.

LXXI

If ever a damned goat got in a man's way
Or anyone was ever tortured and impeded by gout
It is the rival who practises love in your bed.
It is marvellous how this chap has got both of them.
When ever he has a fuck, they are both in agony.
She is knocked back by the smell and he nearly dies of the gout.

LXXII

You used to say that you knew only Catullus,
Lesbia, and that you thought nothing of Jove as compared to me.
I regarded you then not simply as an ordinary girl-friend
But as a father regards his sons and sons-in-law.
Now I have got to know you: and although I burn more than ever
I regard you as a much less valuable person.
How can that be? you ask. Such injuries to a lover
Force him to love more, but to be less benevolent.

227

LXXIII

Give up wishing to do anyone a kindness
Or thinking that anyone could ever return thanks.
All is without return: to have acted kindly is nothing.
So with me, whom no one oppresses harder or more bitterly
Than the man who until just now called me his one and only friend.

LXXIV

Gellius had heard his uncle was very censorious
If anyone mentioned pleasure or indulged in it.
To keep out of trouble he fucked auntie,
Which worked wonders in keeping uncle quiet.
He did what he liked: for even if he had a go as uncle himself
He could count on uncle never saying a word.

LXXV

So low is my mind brought by your fault
Lesbia, and has so destroyed itself in serving you
That it can neither regard you benevolently if you behave well
Nor stop loving you whatever you do.

LXXVI

If recalling his good deeds is a pleasure
To the man who thinks he has been pious,
Has not broken his word, nor in any arrangement
Abused the majesty of the gods to deceive men,
You should have a lot to delight you in your old age, Catullus,
From this thankless love of yours.
For whatever good things men can say or do to anyone
You have said and done those things.
But they have all gone for nothing in an ungrateful mind.
Why then do you torture yourself any more?
Why do you not make up your mind to retreat
And, since the gods do not wish it, cease to be miserable?
It is hard to give up a long-established love.
It is hard, but certainly you must do it somehow:
You must do it whether it can be done or not.

O Gods, if you ever have pity, if you ever gave anyone
Assistance at the last in the very moment of death,
Look at me in my trouble, and if I have lived purely
Take away this plague and injury from me.
Alas, how numbness creeping inside my limbs
Expels all happiness from my heart.
I do not ask now that she should love me in return
Or, what is not possible, that she should want to be chaste:
I wish only to be well and to be rid of this unspeakable disease
O gods, grant me this in return for my piety.

LXXVII

Rufus whom I trusted as a friend
Pointlessly, or at a great and sinister cost,
Have you not crept up upon me and, burning my intestines
Taken away, alas, everything that kept me alive?
You have taken everything, cruel poison of my life,
Ah, ah, plague of my friendship.

LXXVIII

Gallus has brothers; one has a charming wife,
The other a charming son.
Gallus is a man of refinement: he arranges a love affair
And the handsome girl is in bed with the handsome boy.
Gallus is a fool not to remember he is married
When he shows his nephew how to seduce an aunt.
But what hurts me is that you have slobbered filthily
Over the delicate lips of a delicate girl.
You shall not get off scot-free. For all centuries
Shall know you and fame in her old age shall announce what you
    are.

LXXIX

Lesbius is handsome: why not? and Lesbia loves him
Better than you and all your family, Catullus.
But this handsome chap can sell Catullus and his family
If he can find three backers to vouch for him.

LXXX

How can I explain why your ordinarily red lips
Gellius, become whiter than winter snow
When you leave home in the morning or wake from your siesta
In the long hours of the idle day?
There is something wrong somewhere: is it true what they say
        about you
That you like to devour an extended male member?
It must be that: as is declared by the unfortunate Victor's ruptured
        groin
And your lips smeared with the sperm you have milked from him.

LXXXI

Is there nowhere in all this crowd of people, Juventius,
Some handsome man you could decide to love
Other than this man you have let in from moribund Pisaurum?
He is paler that a gilded statue
And yet you love him and dare to prefer him to me:
Do you not realise what an appalling crime that is?

LXXXII

Quintius, if you want Catullus to owe his eyes to you,
Or something dearer than his eyes,
Do not take from him what is dearer than his eyes
– If there is something dearer to him than his eyes.

LXXXIII

In the presence of her husband Lesbia talks to me abusively:
And the fool thinks it is something to laugh about.
Mule, you have no sense. If she were to ignore me
She would be all right: the fact that she whines and scolds
Means that she not only remembers but – what is worse than that –
She is angry. That is, she burns as she talks.

LXXXIV

He used to say *h*onours when he meant honours
*H*ambush when he meant ambush.
That was Arrius. He thought it was marvellous
If he said *h*ambush at the top of his voice.
I imagine his mother and his uncle Liber,
His grandmother and his maternal grandfather spoke that way.
It gave everyone's ears a rest when he went to Syria;
Words were pronounced softly and lightly
And it seemed we were free of that sort of thing for the future.
Then suddenly the horrible news arrived:
The Ionian sea, as soon as Arrius got there,
Stopped being Ionian and became *H*ionian.

LXXXV

I hate and I love. You may well ask, why I do so.
I do not know, but I feel it and suffer.

LXXXVI

Quintia is said to be beautiful. I would say tall, good complexion,
Well-built. I admit these attributes singly
But deny that they add up to beauty. She is not attractive:
In the whole of her large body there is not a grain of salt.
Lesbia is beautiful, totally and extremely so;
She has stolen all the attractions of all other women.

LXXXVII

No woman can say she was so much loved as you were,
Lesbia my darling, no one has loved as I have;
No trust was ever kept with such faith before
As, on my side, my love for you was kept.

LXXXVIII

What's Gellius up to? When he's with his mother and sister
He itches, and spends the evening with his clothes off.
What is he up to, not letting his uncle be married?

231

Do you know the extent of his turpitude?
There is so much of it, Gellius, that not even the ultimate Tethys
Can wash it away, or Oceanus who produced the nymphs:
There is no turpitude beyond it.
Not even if he were to put down his head and suck himself.

LXXXIX

Gellius is thin: why not? with such a kind mother
So fit and well, and such an attractive sister,
Such a very kind uncle and all those girls in the family,
How could he be otherwise than emaciated?
If he touched nothing but what it is not legitimate to touch
There would still be plenty of reasons why he should be lean.

XC

A magus should be born of this unspeakable union
Of Gellius and his mother, and he should learn Persian fortune-
    telling:
For a magus has to be born of a mother and her son
If the blasphemous religion of the Persians is true
Or the child's hymns are not acceptable to the gods
As the guts melt greasily in the flame.

XCI

It was not, Gellius, that I hoped you would behave like a gentleman
In the matter of my miserable and uncontrolled love,
Nor because I knew you and imagined you were a solid character
Who could restrain your mind from any baseness,
But because it was neither your mother nor your sister
I was eating out my heart for:
And although we had been close friends
I did not think that would be reason enough for you.
But I was wrong: so much you delight in any weakness
In which there is a trace of vice.

XCII

Lesbia is always talking scandal about me
And never stops: which proves that Lesbia loves me.
How does it prove it? I am in the same case: I abuse her
All the time: and one could not say I do not love her.

XCIII

It is indifferent to me whether I please you,
Caesar, or what is the colour of your hair.

XCIV

John Thomas fucks. What could he do but fuck?
Do they not say, the pot finds its own stew?

XCV

Cinna's Smyrna, finished at last after nine summers
And given to the world after nine winters.
While meanwhile Hortensius has produced half a million lines
. . . .
Smyrna will be diffused to the deep waters of Satrachus;
Grey-headed centuries will read Smyrna.
But the Annals of Volusius will end at Padua
Providing loose wrappings for mackerel.
My friend's small production will remain in my mind;
Let the public amuse themselves with the swollen Antimachus.

XCVI

Calvus, if there is any pleasure for the dead
In our grief, or in the desire we have
To renew old loves,
Or in our mourning for our lost friendships
At least Quintilia must feel less grief at her early death
Than joy that you love her so much.

XCVII

So help me gods, I didn't think it mattered
Whether I smelt Aemilius's mouth or his arse:
One is no cleaner or dirtier than the other.
As a matter of fact the arse-hole is cleaner and pleasanter
Because it has no teeth. The mouth has teeth eighteen inches long,
Gums like an old waggon-box,
And gapes like the cunt of a pissing mule in summer.
This man fucks a lot of women and thinks himself charming:
He would be better employed driving a donkey round a mill-stone.
Any woman who touches him would be capable
Of licking the arse of a sick executioner.

XCVIII

It can be said of you if of any man, stinking Victius,
What they say about windbags and half-wits:
With a tongue like that, you could, if you get the chance,
Lick arses and farmers' boots.
If you want to kill the lot of us, Victius,
Whisper: you will achieve your objective perfectly.

XCIX

I kissed you while you were playing, sweet Juventius;
It was sweeter than the sweetest ambrosia.
I did not do it with impunity: for more than an hour,
I remember, it was as if I was hung up on a cross
And I could not talk myself out of it with tears
Or get the slightest reduction of your anger.
As soon as it was done you rinsed your lips with a lot of water
And wiped them with every joint of your fingers
So that nothing contracted from my mouth would remain
As if it were the filthy spit of a dirty whore.
. . . .
Besides you forthwith handed me over to hostile love
And tortured me in every way
So that from being ambrosia that kiss was changed
Into the sharpest of sharp hellebore.
Since that is the penalty you exact for my unfortunate love
I will never steal kisses from you again.

234

C

Caelius is desperately in love with Aufilenus,
Quintius with Aufilena – the flower of Veronese youth,
The brother and the sister. This is indeed
The proverbial sweet companionship of brothers.
Which of them shall I favour? Caelius, you, because
You showed yourself pre-eminently friendly
When the insane fire was burning my marrow.
Be happy, Caelius, and potent in your love.

CI

Having come through many countries, over many seas,
I am here at last for these sad rites, my brother,
So that I may give you gifts of death
And uselessly address your silent ashes:
Since fortune has carried you off
Alas, my brother, wrongfully taken from me,
Now take these offerings which, by ancestral custom,
Are given as a sad gift to the shades;
They are wet with your brother's tears:
And then forever, brother, hail and farewell.

CII

If any secret was ever told to a friend
And kept with profound loyalty,
You will find that I am of that persuasion,
Cornelius; you can think of me as a complete Harpocrates.

CIII

Please either give me back my ten sestertia, Silo,
And then be as fierce and proud as you like
Or, if you're fond of money, give up, I beg of you,
Being a pimp and at the same time fierce and proud.

CIV

Do you believe I could have spoken ill of my life
Who is dearer to me than my two eyes?
I couldn't; and wouldn't love her so desperately if I could:
But you and Tappo make everything sound preposterous.

CV

Old cock tries to climb the Piplean hill;
The Muses however chuck him out with forks.

CVI

If you see a pretty boy with an auctioneer
Isn't it reasonable to think that he's for sale?

CVII

When something happens you wanted and never hoped for
That is, in the exact sense, a pleasure to the mind.
And so to me it is a pleasure more precious than gold
That you, Lesbia, return to me who desire you,
Desire but have given up hoping; give yourself back
To me: it is a day for a whiter mark.
What man alive is happier than I, or could say
There is anything more to be desired in this life?

CVIII

If, Cominius, by the will of the people your grey age
And filthy practices were brought to an end,
I have no doubt that first, your slanderous tongue
Would be cut out and given to a hungry vulture,
Your eyes gouged out and devoured by a black-throated crow,
Your entrails given to the dogs, the rest to the wolves.

CIX

My life, you promise that this love of ours
Shall be agreeable and last forever:
Great gods, arrange for her to speak the truth
And make this promise without reservation
So that we may protract though all our life
This treaty of inviolable friendship.

CX

Aufilena, kind girls are always well spoken of;
They get the money and they do what they say they will.
You are more a girl-enemy than a girl-friend:
You promise, lie, give nothing and take all.
You are entitled either to do it or to be chaste and not promise,
But, Aufilena, to snatch all you can get
And then cheat, is to be worse than a greedy whore
Who prostitutes herself with her whole body.

CXI

Aufilena, it is creditable in the highest degree
For a bride to be content with one husband:
But it is better to lie down with all comers
Than to produce brothers who are also cousins.

CXII

You are a stuck-up, Naso, and the man who is not stuck up
Goes down with you: you are stuck up and a pathic.

CXIII

In Pompey's first consulship, Cinna, two men
Frequented Maecilia: now that he is consul again
The two are still there, but beside each of them has sprung up
A thousand. Adultery is very fruitful.

CXIV

Cock is said to be rich with his estate at Firmum.
It is true, there are all kinds of marvellous things on it,
Game of all kinds, fish, plough-land and pasture.
It is no good: the expenses outrun the produce.
So I admit he is rich, but somehow everything is lacking.
We can admire the wealth of the estate as long as he remains poor.

CXV

Cock has something like thirty acres of pasture,
Forty arable, and the rest is salt water.
How could he fail to surpass Croesus in wealth
Who possesses so many things on one estate,
Pasture, arable, immense woods and then marshes
Stretching to the Hyperboreans and the Great Sea?
They are very big, but he is the biggest of all,
Not a man at all but a huge menacing cock.

CXVI

I have often considered in my studious way
How I could possibly send you some poems of Callimacius
Which would soothe you, so that you did not attempt
To threaten me all the time with your hostile weapons.
Now I see that I have done all this work for nothing,
Gellius, and that my prayers have got nowhere.
I will draw my cloak about me to avoid your weapons
But fixed by mine you shall be put to the torture.

Valediction

Catullus my friend across twenty centuries,
Anxious to complete your lechery before Christ came.

MARTIAL

Epigrammaton liber

I, ii

Here is the author that you read and ask for,
Known throughout all the world, Valerius Martial,
For witty epigrams in little books:
To whom, judicious reader, you have given
In his life-time, while he could be aware of it,
The fame that comes rarely to poets when they are dead.

I, iii

You who want to have my books with you everywhere
And take them to keep you company on a long journey,
Buy them with the parchment divided into small pages.
Keep book-boxes for the big ones; I can be held in one hand.
So that you are not uninformed about where I am to be bought
And wander all over the town, let me tell you where to go:
Look for Secundus, the freedman of the learned Lucensis,
Beyond the temple steps of Peace and the Forum of Pallas.

I, iv

Do you prefer to hang around in the bookshops
Although there is room for a small book like you in my cases?
Obviously you don't know how scornful Rome can be.
Believe me, the local populace knows too much.
Nowhere are there louder snorts: young men and old
– Even the boys – have the noses of rhinoceroses.
While you are acknowledging their applause
You will find yourself tossed into the air in somebody's cloak.
But you, lest you should suffer improvement at your master's
    hand
Or his grave pen should correct your indiscretions
You want to fly away irresponsibly over the roof-tops.
Go, wander away. But you might have been safer at home.

I, viii

The pigeon which is the delight of my Stella
– I will say it although Verona is listening –
Outdoes, Maximus, Catullus's sparrow.
Stella is as much bigger than your Catullus
As, compared with a sparrow, a pigeon would be.

I, xxxiii

I do not like you, Sabidius, I can't say why
But certainly I can say that I do not like you.

I, xxxiv

When she is alone Gellia does not weep for her father.
If anyone is about, the tears leap out like water-spouts.
It is not mourning if you are looking for praise, Gellia:
A mourner is one who mourns when there are no witnesses.

I, xxxv

With all the doors open, Lesbia, always,
You perform your misdeeds, there is no concealment.
The spectator gives you more pleasure than the adulterer;
There is no delight unless it is taken in public.
A prostitute takes the trouble to draw the curtain,
Only late at night you will find an occasional bolt drawn:
Learn a little restraint from Chione or Ias;
Old whores take refuge even in the cemetery.
Does my reproof strike you as a little hard?
I only forbid you to be caught, Lesbia, not to be fucked.

II, iii

You owe nothing, Sextus, you owe nothing at all;
One does not owe anything unless one can pay.

II, vi

Well, it was you told me to publish these books.
And having read hardly two pages, Severus,
You turn over and look at the design at the end
And emit a series of yawns.
These are the things I have read over to you
And you used to snatch from me to copy – in elegant format.
These are the things you used to carry round one by one
To parties or the theatre;
These are the same things, or better ones you haven't seen.
What good does it do me to have a slim volume
No thicker than a roller-stick
If you take three days to read it?
Enthusiasm could hardly show less energy.
Do you give up so rapidly when you are travelling
And, when you have to drive to Bovillae,
Do you ask to change horses at the Camenae?
It was you who told me to publish these books.

II, xiii

The judge wants money, your lawyer also wants money.
I advise you, Sextus, simply to pay your debts.

II, xxi

To some you give kisses, Postumus, to others your hand.
'Choose which you like,' you say. I prefer your hand.

II, xxiii

I will not say, however often you ask me,
Who is Postumus in my little book.
I will not say: for why should I make trouble
For those kisses which can so well take their revenge?

III, li

When I praise your face, when I admire your legs and hands,
You say, Galla: 'I shall please you more when I am naked.'

And yet you always avoid taking a bath with me.
Surely, Galla, you are not afraid I shan't please you?

III, lii

You bought your house, Tongilianus, for two hundred;
It was destroyed by an accident too common in the city.
Compensation tenfold. I ask you, might it not seem,
Tongilianus, that you had set fire to it yourself?

III, liii

And I could dispense with your face
And your neck and your hands and your legs
As well as with your breasts, your buttocks, your hips
And – not to particularise too much –
I could dispense with the whole of you, Chloe.

III, liv

As I cannot give the price you set on yourself
It would be much simpler, Galla, if you said 'No.'

IV, xxi

There are no gods and heaven is empty,
Segius says: and proves it, because
As he denies them he grows rich.

VII, ix

Now that he is sixty Cascellius is a clever man:
I wonder at what age he will be convincing?

XIV, cxcv

Great Verona owes as much to her Catullus
As little Mantua does to Virgil.

VIRGIL

A Reading of Virgil's Eclogues

Eclogue I

Meliboeus:

You, Tityrus, lean back below
The shadow of a spreading beech.
There are the trees your tuned notes reach.
But we must take our sacks and go
And leave these gentle fields and go.
We leave our homes but when you lean back
Content to sing of what you lack.
Dear Amaryllis. The woods know.

Tityrus:

How, Meliboeus, did this peace
Come to me? It was from a god
For he will always be a god.
I will hang up the softest fleece
For him. The gentlest blood will flow
Exact about his altar. So.
He lets me pipe my own release.
It is by his permission too
The heavy cattle wait on me.

Meliboeus:

I am amazed at what I see.
Elsewhere the people come and go
On all the wide fields restlessly.
Sick, I can hardly lead along
My herd of goats. Among
The hazels this one drops her twins.
They fell on flints, and that is that.
Oh, I was warned, dull wit. Heaven spoke
When I say lightning rip the oak.
But, say, who is this god of yours?

Tityrus:

I thought the city they call Rome
Was like another – our home

247

Town to which we drove our flock
On market days. I knew a puppy
Was like a dog, a kid was like
Her mother and I rather thought
A big town would be like a small.
And yet it is not so at all.
For Rome is not a city caught
By such comparisons. I see
A cedar in a shrubbery.

Meliboeus:

What took you there to Rome?

Tityrus:

I went when I was called by liberty.
It did not happen till the day
The barber found my hair was grey
But it did happen. Not before
Amaryllis took me on
And showed the other one the door.
The other, Galatea, had
From me whatever I could earn.
With Galatea, every turn
Screwed me down tighter. Though I bred
Cattle enough, and rich cheeses
Were pressed in my dairy,
There was never any money.

Meliboeus:

I wondered, Amaryllis, why
You sadly let the apples hang
Untouched against the autumn sky.
Tityrus was away. So rang
Your name, Tityrus, and so sang
The fountains, and the orchards sighed.

Tityrus:

What could I do? I could not leave
My slavery or find reprieve
From any other powerful god.

Our altars smoke twelve times a year
For that young man. I saw him here.
He spoke. And so the oxen trod
Once more across my fields. No fear.

Meliboeus:

You are an old man with good luck.
You stir around in your own muck
And cut yourself on your own flints.
Your lambs without disturbance suck
At the right teat. Your cattle munch
A cleanly hay.
Yes, some old men have all the luck.
Familiar rivers find their way
Past you. You watch the shadows play
And cool yourself. You hear the bees
Engaged upon your neighbour's trees
So willow blossom brings you sleep.
Your man sings at his pruning, you
May sit and hear the pigeons coo.
If there is any moan, or love
Expressing pain, it is a dove.

Tityrus:

Have I not reason to be glad?
The deer may graze on cloud, the sea
Recede and let the fish go bad,
Frontiers may switch, the Parthians all
Drink at the Tigris if they will.
I'll not forget that young man's look.

Meliboeus:

We are not wethers for his crook
We must leave what we love and go
To warm ourselves in Scythian snow
Or quench our thirst in Africa,
Cut off from all the world, exile
Ourselves beyond the Britons' island.
For that young man will have it so.
And shall we ever see again
Our frontiers and our flat-roofed huts?

And see the few poor ears of grain
The alien soldier roughly cuts
From our dear fields? This is the gain
Of all these years of civil war.
This is what we have laboured for:
Now, Meliboeus, plant your vines
And sow your beans in ordered lines.
Come on, my flock, once fortunate,
You have not been so soothed of late
I shall not see you hang upon
My rocks. But you can still eat stone.
I shall sing no more songs, my goats
Hold no more clover in their throats.

Tityrus:

You could have passed the night here, spent
A few green hours before you went
And shared my apples, chestnuts, cheese.
The cottage chimneys smoke, and please
The parting shepherd most of all.
See, from the mountains shadows fall.

Eclogue II

I do not think that anyone
Ever loved as Corydon
Alexis. Yet he understood
Enough to find his way to the woods,
Deep in which, out of the sun,
He regularly would make
To beeches and mountains
This complaint:
'Alexis, do you not care? Complain
I say but you drive me to death.
While I lack breath
The lizards look for shade.
The cattle cool themselves, made
Restless. Thestylis
Pounds for the reapers dishes
With thyme and garlic. While the sun burns

I seek for you by twists and turns.
There are, however loud I cry,
Only the grass-hoppers and I.
I should have had more sense and borne
With Amaryllis and her scorn
Or had Menalcas, though I knew
He was less beautiful than you.
But do not trust your beauty. White
Shoots end as withered twigs, the night
Falls on the hyacinth and rose.
Think, would you not do well to ask
How many fattened cattle bask
Under my trees, what honey flows
Out of my hives? Who, when it snows
Has butter still? Does not my voice
Conjure up luxuries at choice?
Nor am I so bad-looking when
Reflected in a pool or glass.
If Daphnis is the rival then
You might well think that I should pass.
Will you not lie upon my grass?
We have poor huts; you may come in.
I will cut you a switch.
You may drive your kids
Musically to their green meal
Or send arrows after the deer.
There are woods where we may sing
Like Pan, until he fears
A rival. Pan first found
Sweetness in pipes, he glued several
Together, he who cares for all.
Nor should you mind scorching
Your lip, as Amyntas did, with piping.
I have a pipe with seven stems
Damoetas gave me when he died.
Foolish Amyntas envied them.
I have two roebucks besides,
Found in a dangerous valley, they
Suck the ewe's udders twice a day.
Thestylis begs them. She shall
Have them if you turn away.
Come here you lovely boy, and all

The nymphs shall bring you basketsful
Of the chestnuts Amaryllis loved.
Add too the plum; honour that fruit.
And let the laurel have repute
Close to the myrtle. They have proved
Sweeter together. Corydon,
You know Alexis is not won
With presents, nor would presents make
Iollas give him up. No doubt
I was a lunatic to wish.
The storm has put my flower-beds out
And the pigs root among my fish.
Why run away? Alexis should
Know even gods may haunt the wood.
Pallas had founded cities, she
May well be true to them, but we
Have our obedience in the wood.
The lioness will track the wolf,
The wolf will track the goat, myself
Will have Alexis. Pleasure could
Have it no other way. Now look!
Over the plough circles the rook
And sees the sun go down in doubt
Which, ending, pulls the shadows out.
My love still burns. Ah Corydon,
What folly are you bent upon?
You leave the vine half-pruned, the dust
Gathers upon your withered lust.
There are toads under every stone.

Eclogue III

Menalcas:

Whose flock is that, Damoetas?
Meliboeus's?

Damoetas:

                No. Aegon's, or
It was, at any rate, before
He thought that I might manage as well.

Menalcas:

Then hard luck on the sheep.
While Aegon feeds on air, and tries
To touch Neaera with his lies
You milk the sheep till they are sore.

Damoetas:

Be careful what you say. The goats
Looked at you with the eyes of stoats
While you did certain things. And yet
The nymphs laughed. Or do you forget?

Menalcas:

You mean perhaps when Micon found
His vines all cut back to the ground?

Damoetas:

Or when you broke up Daphnis' bow
And pipe, because he liked them so
And they were not your gifts? Your spite
Exacerbated by delight?

Menalcas:

I can recall another time
When I saw you in a sublime
Attempt at thievery. There was a bark
And someone running in the dark.
I called to Tityrus and knew
The rascal he would catch was you.

Damoetas:

I was just getting back my prize,
I won that goat. Damon admits
It yet he tries
To blame me for it, thinking this
Another competition he
Might win a bit more easily.

253

Menalcas:

You sang against him? When did you
Play something we could recognise?
The only art you ever knew
Was whistling for a drink.

Damoetas:

You're too
Sure of yourself. Do you want to try
A competition presently?
If you win you shall have this cow.
She's a good milker. All right. Now,
What will you give me if I win?

Menalcas:

From the flock, nothing. My father and
My stepmother are close at hand.
They count the flock three times a day.
Still, I will give you something. Say
This pair of patterned goblets, done
In silver by Alcimedon.
Do you see this engraving? Vine
And ivy closely intertwine.
Conon stands in the middle, or
Maybe some other astronomer.
He marked the stars out, showing how
To tell the time to reap and plough.
The cups, you see, are quite brand-new.

Damoetas:

I have two cups as well as you,
Made by Alcimedon likewise.
Acanthus creeps round the handles.
To one side
Is Orpheus with his following woods.
Why should I want your cups? I would
Rather have my cow.

Menalcas:

You won't get off like that. Now
Here is someone who can judge,
Palaemon. He can take the pledges.
I'll show you what it's like to sing!

Damoetas:

So sing. If you have any choice
Favourites your voice
May sound them now. As referee
Whom you like. Palaemon, listen intently.

Palaemon:

Now let us sit. The grass is soft
And every tree a miracle.
The time of year when all is well!
Begin, Damoetas, and as often
As he pauses, Menalcas,
You follow in, for that is as
The Muses like it: each in turn.

Damoetas:

And what does Galatea fear?
She drops her apples, then she goes.

Menalcas:

But my Amyntas comes to prove
The value of the gift he throws.

Damoetas:

I have found presents for my love
A nest, and in the nest, a dove.

Menalcas:

What could I do? My gift is this –
Ten golden apples, then ten more.

Damoetas:

I had her promises before
And may the gods remember me.

255

Menalcas:

But what use will Amyntas be?
He leaves me to pursue the boar.

Damoetas:

Send Phyllis to me, Iollas,
Yet come yourself when you would see
A heifer slain.

Menalcas:

                    She cried 'Alas'
When I left her. 'O Iollas,
Good-bye, good-bye, you handsome boy.'

Damoetas:

No wind or hailstorm can annoy
Like Amaryllis in a rage.

Menalcas:

Amyntas in his golden age
Is like a pleasant spring-time shower.

Damoetas:

Pollio has given my muse a shake:
Then feed a heifer for his sake.

Menalcas:

Pollop himself has singing hours:
Then lead a bull to feed on flowers.

Damoetas:

He who loves Pollio will see
The honey dripping from the tree.

Menalcas:

Bavius and Maevius sing like cats:
So plough with foxes and milk rats.

Damoetas:

You who pick flowers and strawberries,
Avoid the cold snake in the grass.

Menalcas:

And sheep, be careful how you pass
The crumbling bank where the stream is.

Damoetas:

And turn the goats back, Tityrus,
The water here is dangerous.

Menalcas:

Round up the sheep, before the heat
Dries all the milk up at the teat.

Damoetas:

My bull is weak and thin; the same
Love gnaws the master and the herd.

Menalcas:

My weakness is not love. A game
Of magic strikes my young lambs dead.

Damoetas:

A riddle: in what land can eye
See no more than three feet of sky?

Menalcas:

In what land flowers are crowned, and you
Show Phyllis something you can do.

Palaemon:

I cannot judge who has sung best.
Not only both deserve to win
But anyone who has been in
The light or shade of love and pressed
Out verse should have a heifer. But
It is time the gates were shut.

Now higher matters entertain
This muse than shepherds and the plain:
Forests the consul would approve.
     The last age comes of all. Again
As Sybil prophesied, there move
The great chains of the centuries.
The Virgin is. And Saturn sees
His kingdom come like standing corn.
A new race now descends. And, please,
Lucina, when the boy is born,
Favour him. Let our iron give way
To all Apollo's gold that day.
     And you be consul, Pollio. Let
The months begin their process till
We lose the footsteps of ill will.
These are the fears we should forget.
He will have life from heaven, yet
Will mix with us and rule an earth
Made peaceful by his father's worth.
     But first for you, the child, foxgloves
And ivy demonstrate their loves.
Bean-blossom and acanthus laugh.
The goats come home uncalled, their milk
Serves itself for you. Lions eat chaff
And leave the herds untouched. The silk
Of your young cradle turns to flowers.
The serpent ends its poisonous hours.
The night-shade withers; in its place
Grow nutmegs, cinnamon and mace:
When you can read, the glory of
Your father, and the sombre race
Of patriarchs will guide your love
And all will ripen gradually –
The yellow corn, the blackberry.
Even the stubborn oak will prove
Its gentleness, by yielding honey.
Expect a few deceptions still.
There will be Argonauts to fleece
And how could there be perfect peace
With a new Troy, a new Achilles?

But, when you are firmly grown
You shall see trade and travel cease
And every country bear its own
Fruit and yet tillage be unknown,
The ox be loosened from the plough,
The sheep wear colours as they feed.
Run on the centuries which need
No spinning fates to tell them how.
　　Now it is time for the new seed
To sprout and turn into a Jove.
The whole bent world bows down, and love
Enters the age that is to come.
Let it not find that I am dumb.
Whatever Orpheus sang in Thrace
Or Linus by Apollo's grace
Let me out-sing, to show that man
May now out-do Arcadian Pan.
　　Time for you. Your smile
Eludes your patient mother who
For ten long months has carried you.
Time for you, for while
You dawdle, how can you be Lord
Of our expectant bed and board?

Eclogue V

Menalcas:

Why not, Mopsus, since both of us
Have our abilities, sit down
Under the elms, and sound
You your pipe and I verses?

Mopsus:

You are older than I, there is
No better rule of obedience.
Whether we sit in this pretence
Of shade, moved by the wind, or this
Cave across whose mouth the vine
Straggles, is for you to say.

259

Menalcas:

Does anyone sing more finely
Than you? Amyntas perhaps may.

Mopsus:

There is Apollo, the divine.

Menalcas:

Begin, Mopsus, whatever way
You like. With love for Phyllis or
Praises for Alcon, or a whine
Against Codrus if that is more
To your taste. Tityrus minds the goats.

Mopsus:

Something I wrote upon the bark
Of the green beeches, which I mark
With music. As Amyntas notes.

Menalcas:

As willows to the pale olive,
Reeds to roses, I give
You preference before Amyntas.
We are in the cave. Let that pass.

Mopsus:

The nymphs were weeping for your death,
Daphnis, hazels and rivers saw
Your mother hugging your last breath
And wriggling under the fates' paw.
No shepherd drove his flock that day
To the cool water, cattle lay
Parched at the edge and would not drink.
They bit no grass. The mountains think
Even the lions moaned that day.
Daphnis put the Armenian
Tigers to chariots and brought in
Bacchic dances, with leaves and ears
Of corn twisted round the harsh spears.

The vine lights up the tree, the grape
Lights up the vine, the dark shape
Of the bull dominates the herd;
Corn crowns the field, so your word
Impresses as the word of all.
The fates who took you were the fall
Of everything. As darnel grows
Instead of barley in the furrows,
For gentle violets and narcissus
There is the sharp thorn and the thistle.
Spread leaves upon the ground, bring shade,
Shepherds, where Daphnis is laid.
Heap up the mound and add a song:
'I, Daphnis, in the woods and long
Towards the stars was known. A fair herd,
Yes, but a fairer shepherd.'

Menalcas:

Your song is such to me, divine
Poet, as sleep upon the grass
Or the shooting spring we pass
A summer day. You not alone
In music but in words surpass
All but your master. Though I own
You next to him, fortunate
Boy, I will imitate
You and raise Daphnis to the stars.
He loved me also. He was fate.

Mopsus:

Now I lack nothing. He was far
The best shepherd and you are
A singer praised by Stimichon.

Menalcas:

Now he has heaven at his feet
He wonders as he gazes on
The constellations in retreat.
And Daphnis now makes the woods glad,
The other countryside, Dryads,
Pan and the shepherds. So the deer

261

And flocks may wander without fear.
Daphnis loves easiness. The hills,
Where every tree still stands, may shout,
The groves, the very rocks, call out
'A god, a god, Menalcas.' Be
Kind to your servitors and we
Will raise four altars, of which two
For Phoebus, two, Daphnis, for you.
Two cups of frothing milk each year,
Two goblets of rich oil, and here
Upon the hearth, in winter-time,
Bacchus, and at the harvest-time,
Bacchus. It shall pour out. Then sing
Lyctian Aegon. Play for us
The satyr, Alphesinoeus.
These are the rites. Each year praying
The nymphs that they will bless our plough.
While boars run in the woods and fish
Swim in the rivers, then as now,
Bees sink their long tongues in the fresh
Thyme, and cicadas feed on dew
We will perform this rite for you.
Your name shall stand, the farmers say
Grace to you. Bind them as they pray.

Mopsus:

That was a song which gave me more,
Menalcas, than I can repay.
Like quiet waves reaching the shore,
Like water among rocks, a breeze
Sibilant and quiet among trees.

Menalcas:

I give you this frail pipe, which played
'Much loved Alexis' and 'Whose flock'.

Mopsus:

Menalcas, take this crook I made
With my own hands for my own flock.
Antigenes shall not have it
Though once I would have thought him fit.

Eclogue VI

She sang Sicilian songs at first
And did not redden at the name.
Why should she? Muses are of the same
Mind as Apollo, that the worst
Poems are those with too much fat.
Spin thinly. Knowing what he was at
He took me by the ear and said
'Not kings and battles: sheep instead'
Now I (and, Varus, you will find
Plenty of poets to your mind
To sing of your heroic deeds)
Stick to this verse on country reeds.
But I will sing of you, and bind
Bearers to honour you, the grove
Shall sing of you and bring you love.
The name of Varus guarantees
That everything I write will please.

     You may sing, Muses. Chromis and
Mnasyllos saw Silenus lie
With swollen veins and outstretched hands,
His garland fallen on the floor
And his mouth open in a snore
The empty pot will tell you why.
The boys approach and quickly tie
Him in his ivy. Drivelling head
That should have sung to them instead.
And Aegle paints it. May not she
The loveliest naiad, well feel free
With this old lump of lechery?
She plasters him with mulberry stains.
Silenus as he wakes complains
But says the boys shall have a song
And the girl something before long.
Then he begins. And see the fauns
Dance on the daisy-covered lawns.
The beasts in measure run, the oaks
Themselves bob to the tune. Phoebus
Is not more musical, or Orpheus,
Than the unbraced bellowing Silenus.

     For he sang how, through emptiness

The first beginnings of things pressed
The seeds of everything, and how
From this first fistful grew the world.
It was not then as it is now.
But the ground hardened, and the curled
Water receded to the sea
And soon all shapes wrenched themselves free.
The new sun is astonishing,
New clouds drop rain. The first time spring
Comes to the forests. Animals
Prowl on the new-cut mountain slopes
And are not recognised at all.

      Then he reports on Pyrrha's stones
And how the thief Prometheus
Was eaten in the Caucasus.
He adds how Hylas dies, and all
The fountain echoed with the call;
Pasiphae was fortunate
Until she met her milk-white bull
And took him for a natural mate.
Proetus' daughters lowed like cows
But never tried to copulate
With beasts, although they feared the plough
And thought horns grew upon their brows.
Unhappy girl, upon the hills
You wander, while your lover fills
His belly up with hyacinths
And casts a licorous eye upon
Some heifer that he hopes to win.
'Then close the glades up, nymphs, he's gone
But you may tempt the animal
With grass or cattle to a stall.'

      He sings how Atalanta swerved
For apples from her virgin mark
And how those three young girls were served
Who found their limbs grow bitter bark.
And then he sings how Gallus wanders
Musing along poetic rivers
And all the choir rise to their feet;
To make the honour more complete,
Linus, a shepherd whose divine
Songs, locks and laurels intertwine,

Cries with an adulatory nod
'Here are the pipes of Hesiod.
He brought the ash-trees down the hills
With music and what you sing fills
Apollo's groves. It pleases him
Considerably to hear your hymn.'
Shall I say also how he sang
Of Scylla, by whom the waters rang
With yelps about the Ithacan
Ships to the wreck of craft and man?
Or what he told of Tereus
Whose body changed its carriage as
He flew from Philomela's feast;
She circled upwards and, released
From human form, paused at her roof.
So every song that Phoebus brooded
Over once and musically
Or that Eurotas told her reeds
Silenus sings, until the far
Echoes go up and wake the stars.
Vesper comes out, Olympus sees
The darkness come reluctantly.

Eclogue VII

Meliboeus:

Under an ilex Daphnis sat.
The wind spoke in it. Corydon
And Thyrsis drew their flocks to one
Place and accord. Corydon had
His goats distent with milk. Thyrsis
His sheep, and each their several ages
Green. Arcadians ready to sing
Both, and ready for answering.
To this place the great goat that led
My flock had wandered, and that is
How Daphnis saw me. 'Quickly' he said,
'Come over Meliboeus. Your kids
And goats are safe. If you can stay
Rest under this shade now. This way

265

Your steers will come to drink. The river here
Winds the reeds and your ear
Is entertained, listen, with bees.'
What could I do? I had no Phyllis
At home to look after my new lambs,
But the contest between Thyrsis
and Corydon, could hardly please
Less than my proper work. So these
Two started, with alternate tune.
One began, the other answered.

Corydon:

You nymphs, my loves of Libethrus,
Either let me sing like Codrus
(Who, after all, is next to Phoebus)
Or if this cannot be, I hang
My pipe up here, where he sang.

Thyrsis:

Shepherd, with ivy decorate
Your post. Codrus will envy
Him or it may be
Praise more than reason. From this state
Protect him. If there are evil tongues,
Add foxgloves to the crown.

Corydon:

To you, Delian, a boar's
Head, and the many-branched
Antlers of an old stag.
And if the fortune holds,
Diana, you shall stand
In marble, head to ankles.

Thyrsis:

Priapus, a pail of milk
And these cakes are all
We can offer yearly.
This garden is poor.
Be marble also. If fortune holds
You shall yet be golden.

Corydon:

Nerine Galatea, come,
Sweeter than thyme, whiter than some
White swan, more delicate
Than ivy. When the bulls come late
From pasture, do you also come.
Certainly my bed waits.

Thyrsis:

May you indeed be free to hate
Me more than thistles, gorse or sea-weed
If this day does not bleed
More slowly away than the year.
Go home quietly, my steers.

Corydon:

Moss at the springs, softer than sleep,
Grass, the arbutus's thin shade,
Protect if it may from the blaze
At midday, my worried sheep.
Summer is torrid, and the buds swell.
Laurels for Phoebus, but as long
As Phyllis loves hazels they
Chiefly shall make my song.

Thyrsis:

The ash is most beautiful
In the forest, and like the day
In gardens the pine, while the poplar
Is at home beside the river.
But if you come back Lycidas,
Easily you would surpass
Ash, pine, or any tree whatever.

Meliboeus:

I remember all this. Thyrsis
Had sung in vain. From that day on
The only singer was Corydon.

Eclogue VIII

The muse of Damon, shepherd, and
of Alphesiboeus, I sing.
Did not the cattle leave grazing
To hear them, and the lynxes stand
Astonished, and the rivers stop flowing?

But you, whether you are now crossing
The rocks of Timavus, or coast
Hard by Illyris, what I most
Want is to sing your deeds. When may
I, when above all will be the day
I may make known your Sophoclean
Art? Meanwhile I sing –
A little ivy among your laurels.

The shadows of cool night had gone,
The dew was on the grass, when Damon
Sang, leaning upon his staff:

Damon:

Be born, O morning star, before
The day in which I fill with tears.
Nysa sleeps with another. Hear
What you have chosen to ignore
You gods, now, in my dying hour.
 Begin, Arcadian flute, begin.
Mopsus has Nysa. The griffin covers
The mare. You may expect the deer
To drink with hounds without fear.
 Begin, Arcadian flute, begin.
Light torches, Mopsus, for your bride
And bride-groom, throw the nuts. The star
Of evening brings her to your side.
 Begin, Arcadian flute, begin.
Gone to a worthy man, you are
Now one who hates my pipe and goats.
Well enough. Leave an old coat
And do not suppose the gods care.
 Begin, Arcadian flute, begin.
In our garden among the apples

268

I saw you first, the sap
Was new in me. I was twelve
Years old and you a child
Walking with my mother, I tell
Enough to reach the boughs. I saw
You and perished. What wild
Error bore me away?
      Begin, Arcadian flute, begin.
After that day
I knew what love is. The hard
Hills bore him, out beyond the far
Garamantes, Rhodope or Tmarus,
Not of the same race as us.
      Begin, Arcadian flute, begin.
Love taught a mother to find blood
From her own children on her hands.
Which of the two, Love or she, could
Be more heartless? Both in a cruel land.
      Begin, Arcadian flute, begin.
Now let wolves flee the sheep, the oaks
Bear golden apples, alders choke
With blossoms of narcissus, amber
Sweat from tamarisks, the croak
Of frogs pass for the nightingale
Or Tityrus for Orpheus,
Arion with his dolphins fail.
      Begin, Arcadian flute, begin.
Let all become the sea. Good-bye
To woods. I pitch from some high
Crag. And this with my last sigh.
      End now, Arcadian music. So.
That was Damon's song.

Alphesiboeus began before long:

Alphesiboeus:

Bring water now, and round about
The sacred altars hand a fleece.
May I disturb my lover's peace
With burning herbs and magic shout.
      My songs, lead Daphnis from the town.
An incantation may bring down

The moon from heaven. And Ulysses
Was threatened by that song of Circe's.
Snakes split when a musician frowns.

     My songs, bring Daphnis home again.
I pull three threads around you, three
Of different colours, image, see
For heaven is a trinity.

     My songs, bring Daphnis from the town.
And, Amaryllis, tie three knots.
And call them lovers' knots, for what
Are three coloured knots if not that?

     My songs, bring Daphnis home again.
As this clay hardens and this wax
Grows soft in the same fire, Daphnis
The same. I scatter meal, and crackling
Laurel burn. Daphnis the same.

     My songs, bring Daphnis from the town.
So Daphnis shall feel love. As when
A heifer seeking for her bull
Sinks down at last to an amen
Beside a water-course, her full
Heart thinking no more of her home.
So may love hold him. And no pity.

     My songs, bring Daphnis home again.
These things he left me, which we
Valued together, bury
Them now. They are for earth. His debt.

     My songs, bring Daphnis from the town.
The herbs and poisons that you get
From Pontus, Moeris gave to me.
I have seen him in a dark cave
Of forest, become wolf, from graves
Call up dead spirits, seduce seed
Silently from another's field.

     My songs, bring Daphnis home again.
Bring out the ashes, throw them
Over your head into the stream.
And do not look. With them
I will approach Daphnis. He does not care
What god, what singing is in the air.

     My songs, bring Daphnis from the town.
Look, how the ash has broken into

Flame, with its own breath, while I
Hesitate at the door. The dog barks.
Shall I believe? Does this come dreamingly?
    My songs, bring Daphnis home again.

Eclogue IX

          Lycidas:

Which way, Moeris, your foot? To town,
As the path goes?

          Moeris:

O Lycidas,
The day has come when our own
Is no longer so. Alas, with 'These
Are my acres. Go.' We
Evicted, in our grief, deliver
Up our goats to the newcomer.

          Lycidas:

Certainly I had heard, these hills
Down to the water's edge, where beeches
Stand with their broken tops, had been
Saved by Menalcas, or his music.

          Moeris:

So it was said. But who fills
Himself with songs, when Mars
Bellows? They are
The eagle and the dove. Had not
An old raven from the oak told me what
Course to follow, neither I
Nor Menalcas, would be alive.

          Lycidas:

Who falls into such crime? Alas!
And did we nearly lose the solace
Of your songs, Menalcas?

Who would have sung the nymphs? Whose hand
Would have scattered flowers here, and
Induced green shade at the spring?
And the day I found you going
To Amaryllis, with sweet songs,
Who would sing them? 'Along
This way I go, a short one, Tityrus,
Feed my goats till I come, it
Is a small matter, water them, and
Beware the butting horns, till I come.'

Moeris:

Or these he sang to Varos. So:
'Varus, your name, if Mantus
Is spared, the singing swans shall bear
Past all suspicion of despair.'

Lycidas:

Your bees avoid the poisonous yew,
Your cows munch clover and are full.
If you have any song, so sing.
I am a poet too, the tall
Muses have given me songs, calling
Me as the shepherds do. I trust
Little to this. My songs are dust
To those of Varus or Cinna.
Among swans a goose-din.

Moeris:

It is that I am searching
My mind for. It is no mean song.
'Come to me, Galatea. The cold waves
Are not the game for you. Here spring
Scatters her purple. To this cave
Come, there is shadow about it. In this place
The vines also embrace.
Leave therefore the cold shore.'

Lycidas:

What did I hear you sing, alone
Under the night? I half have the tune.

'Daphnis, why do the old stars hold
You? Have you not heard of this?
Caesar's? Dione's? It unfolds
Wonder on wonder. A kiss
Upon fields of corn, the vine
Ripening for subsequent time.
You put in the small shoot;
For your children the fruit.'

Moeris:

Everything goes with age. I once
Had music in the setting sun.
It is forgotten now. Even the voice
Has gone. The wolf has passed this way.
There is no choice in a sad day.
But my songs eat Menalcas' heart.

Lycidas:

You give me your excuse. Now
The sea lies down below the ploughland,
There is no murmur to be heard.
We are half way. Bianor's tomb
Stands where the hedger clears the room.
Here let us sing. Or, if you will,
Sing as we cross the misty hill,
For rain may come. But if you sing
We shall have cheerful journeying.
I will take half your load; so come.

Moeris:

Say no more, boy. I am not dumb
But we shall sing better when he comes.

Eclogue X

A last task, Arethusa. A few
Verses for Gallus, whom none refuse,
But such as, ready by Lycoris, . . .
But begin, Muse,

Fountain, slipping under the waves
To Sicily, unless you would have
Your waters salted by the crushing
Sea. Let us tell of Gallus
And his brow-knitting loves
While the goats nose the bushes.
Deaf, did you say? In the woods doves
Answer. In what groves,
What glades did you live, Naiads,
When Gallus died for love? In what sad
Walks? You were not on Parnassus,
No, nor upon Pindus.
No delay held you by
Aonian Aganippe.
For him the laurels wept. He lay
Groaning under a rock, the day
Parted over Maenalus, its crown
Darkened with tears.
The sheep
Stood around, sulking. Adonis also
Fed sheep beside a stream.
The shepherd comes, and the swineherds,
Slowly forward. A few words
From Menalcas, and from them.
'How is this love, to you?'
Apollo comes: 'Gallus, a true
Servant but a mad lover,
Your Lycoris is discovered
Among the snows, in camps. Another
Has her.' Sylvanus came, fennel
And lilies nodding upon his crown.
Pan god of Arcady, well
Able to ask: 'What way down
From this torment? Love does not care.
Never enough tears.
As soon satisfy
Grass with dew, bees
With clover or he –
Goats with what they need.'
But sadly Gallus: 'Arcadians,
You will sing to your land,
As you are skilled, this matter.

I should be happy in another
Place, my bones rest, if you sang
My affections and the woods rang
With my notes as yours,
Shepherd or dresser of the mature
Vine. Surely either with Phyllis
Or Amyntas, or whoever is
The fury of the moment
(And is Amyntas dark? So are hyacinths.)
I should lie among the willows.
Phillis would pick me flowers, Amyntas
Choose a few songs. Lycoris!
Cool streams and soft meadows.
Enough to lie on. Here I
With you could consume time.
But now another affection, Mars,
Keeps me at the wars.
You too, far from home, far
From me, look at the Alps, hard
As they are, at snows and the cold
Rhine. Oh may the ice
Not cut your feet.
I will go free, and the reed
Accept my song. It is better
Certainly, in the woods, to devise
Marks of love on young trees,
Among wolves. They grow, and for her
My love will grow. Meanwhile to please
Myself with nymphs I will wander
Over Maenalus, or hunt
Wild boars, hounds
Circumventing the glades, though the cold
Bite like their teeth. What has been told
I see already, I am there
Among the rocks and forest, the air
Echoing with dogs. I imagine
Arrows from my Parthian engine.
As if this could do me good, or
That god mitigate sorrow!
Nothing we can do can change him, not if
We drank the Hebrus in mid-winter,
Suffered the Thracian snows, watery

And cold. Not if we,
Under Cancer, when the sun
Withers the bark of the elm, drove
Sheep for the Ethiopian
– We could not resist love.
He conquers, we give way.'
This is enough for one day.
Your poet sits, and his fingers
Weave baskets of the slender
Hibiscus. And for Gallus
These songs shall be enough.
Gallus, for whom my love
Grows hourly, as in spring
New shoots in everything.
Let us go now, the shade
Brings danger to singers.
The juniper is afraid.
Without the sun nothing
Will ripen. Go home,
Full goats. Hesperus comes.

Notes from Georgics I

'What makes for smiling cornfields, under what star
The earth should be turned over, or the vines
Trailed over elm-trees, how to look after cattle
And how to breed them, how much skill is called for
If bees are to be thrifty, these things, Maecenas,
Are now to be my subjects. You brilliant lights,
Sun, moon and stars, which draw the passing year
Across the sky; you, Bacchus and kindly Ceres,
By whose favour the earth, instead of acorns,
Produces now the plumped-up ears of grain
And, in the cup we drink, mixes the grape;
You too, who haunt the country-folk, you Fauns,
Move this way, dancing with your Dryad girls:
What you all give, I sing. And you, who struck
The earth with your great trident so that the stallion

Was uttered from it snorting, you, Neptune;
Inhabitant of the groves, for whom so many
Snow-white bullocks crop Cea's rich thickets;
Yourself, Pan, leaving the woodland pasture
Of your ancestral grove on Lycaeus,
Guardian of sheep, if you care for Arcadia,
Be with me now, Tegean, and be favourable;
Also Minerva, who first found the olive,
And you, the boy who showed the use of ploughs;
Sylvanus, holding a young cypress uprooted;
All gods and goddesses who sustain the fields,
Some giving life to fruits no hand has sown,
Some nurturing the crops by sending rain.'

And then comes Caesar to complete the work,
Because without this last civility,
No work survives for long, and although, with it,
No harvest and no skill remain for ever.

Hactenus arvorum cultus (Georgics II)

Up to now the fields
Have been ploughed and the stars
Sent us home to our cottages
At the end of the day.
There has been the vine,
Even on these hills, and the slow
Growing olive.
Not only the Cotswold shepherd
But I too, with even pace,
Treading where the wind can be heard
Or some horn perhaps. But this is over.
Not even metal ringing
At the smithy, or a voice.
Water sucking the rotting
Piers,
The algae lifted

Tide by tide.
A single gull
Banking, back to the dead sea,
Cries.

Palinurus (Aeneid, V, 835ff)

Ho! Palinurus. Night came
Softly upon your dream.
The sailors lie, wherefore?
Slumped at the oars.
Your dream wakes still.
Not for long, while
Sleep hangs over the sea.
It is you she seeks.
Palinurus, innocent,
In quiet spent.
'Shall I entrust Aeneas to
This monster? Not so.
I have watched the fallacious air.'
Behold, god, the Lethean
Dew-laden branch is shaken
Over the sinking head.
You may call your comrades.
Palinure,
When Aeneas stirs.
'Naked and unknown,
Palinurus, your bones.'

The Descent (Aeneid, VI)

It follows my footsteps over these hills.

Some seek the seeds of flame
Hidden in the veins of flint.
Some crash through the undergrowth, point

278

To new rivers. But the same
Passions do not seize Aeneas.
He climbs where Apollo is.
And the secret parts
Of Sybil, in a dread cave,
Open, having the future.

Cut in the rock, lying huge,
A hundred mouths, you might say,
A hundred voices, Sybil responds.
To ask the Fates,
Time, it is time.
God.
Not one face or colour,
Her hair would not stay, nor colour. Panting,
Her breast like an earthquake,
Her heart swelling.
Not an ordinary voice. There is breathing
That is not her own, nearer to the god's.
'Do not stop praying, Trojan
Aeneas, must you stop? If you do
No gates can open.'

'Do not trust
Verses to the winds, but speak.
Leaves will not hold them.'
There was no prophecy. In such words,
Truth wrapped in darkness, that the utterance
Escaped my patience.
In such words, thus speaking:
'God's blood, Anchises'
Son, and a Trojan.
To descend, yes, through my entrance is easy.
Will you see the light again?
But if your mind is love, go down, cupid
Of the Stygian lakes, twice black Tartarus.
On a dark tree,
Golden, in leaf, the stem bending, a bough
This for Proserpina, a gift,
When it is torn, another and another
In its place, the same bough,
The same metal.

There lies your friend,
A corpse.'

Two doves flew.
They were my mother's birds, and therefore
Indicate.
Discoloured, in dark foliage,
As it were mistletoe,
Luminous on the oak.
Aeneas breaks it off
And carries it away under the roof of the Sybil
While on the shore the Teucrians
Paid to the last dust,
Misenus, your wishes.
The ground rumbled and the ridged
Woodlands dipped.
Through the unstable shadows
The dogs howled.
The goddess was approaching.
Then the vatic: 'Far
From everything, from this grove
Those who do not know love.'
The sword now out of the scabbard.
She entered herself, and Aeneas after.

Gods of the world of spirits, silent shades,
Chaos and Phlegethon lying in night,
Allow me to speak.
They went darkly, through night and shadows.
The whole kingdom was empty.
If there were moon's light, a wood,
A path in the undergrowth.
Night has taken the colours.
On the threshold, but inside,
Where Orcus begins,
Straw laid for Care,
With Sorrow upon her.
There are sick-beds enough. Age,
Fear, Evil Persuaders, Shortage.
They have terrible faces. Death,
Passing us ruthlessly. Sleep,
Also a brother, and the evil

Pleasures which exist only in the mind.
There were others. War
And one coifed with vipers.

A dark elm, huge, with dreams under every leaf.
Aeneas offers his sword to all comers.
I cannot however see the dead
Wailing by the water-side.
Why should they go over? A sordid
Old man, watching the girls.
Let them come to him. Charon,
Do not tip the boat in your excitement.
The dead are not lovers when
They pass your way.

I can hardly move now,
Aeneas, without your wishes.
There are several ghosts
I would wish to see.
And one especially, her hair
Plentiful where they have it,
Weeps from her head,
Too fragrant to be among the dead.
And beyond her,
One whose matted hair
Resembles Charon's.
Of him
Nothing is to be said, except
I came to seek him and
He does not exist.
The mist
Swirls up over Tal-y-maes.
He is gone with it.
An empty hill-side.
Fortune, if you are old.

OVID & PROPERTIUS

From Book One of Ovid's Metamorphoses

My mind inclines me to discourse
Of bodies changed into new shapes.

Breathe on my enterprise, you gods
For these mutations were your work

And so, from the world's origin
Bring me down safely to our time.

Before the sea and land, before
The sky which covers everything

The whole of nature had one face.
This was called chaos, rough, confused,

A mixture of the seeds of things.
No Titan then lit up the world;

There was no Phoebe with her horns;
The earth did not hang in the air

Rocked by its weight, nor the long arms
Of Amphitrite hug the shores.

But where the land was, there was sea
And air as well, unstable land

Unstable sea and the air dark.
Then nothing stayed in its own shape

And everything got in the way.
So, in a single body, heat

Made war on cold, and wet on dry,
The soft on hard, and weightless things

Made war upon the things of weight.
A good and better nature put

An end to that and first cut off
Earth from the sky, and sea from earth

And liquid sky from thicker air.
Then having drawn the elements

From this blind mixture, the god put
Each of them in its proper place

And tied them up again in peace.
The fiery substance of the sky

Having no weight, came out on top.
Air, as the lightest after that

Spread itself neatly underneath.
Earth, with its heavy elements,

Piled itself quickly further down.
The water, flowing round about

Sank, and surrounded all the world.
The god, whoever he might be

Arranged things in this way, and then
Divided matter into parts.

And first the earth: he smoothed it out
And rolled it up into a sphere.

Then sea: he taught it how to spread
And blow itself up with the wind

And wash around the shores of earth.
He added springs and standing pools,

And rivers held by sloping banks
Which, in some places, lose themselves

And elsewhere flow away to sea;
Received in that free water they

Beat upon shores instead of banks.
He ordered plains to spread themselves

And told the valleys to go down,
The woods to dress themselves with leaves

And stony mountains to rise up.
The sky, divided into zones,

Two on the left, two on the right,
With a fifth, hotter, in between.

And underneath it is the same.
The middle country is so hot

Nothing can live there; the extremes
Are covered deep in snow; between

Two temperate regions, where he put
An equal part of hot and cold.

Above this spreads the air, which has
Less weight than water or the land

But more than fire. And here it is
The god set up the mists and clouds

Thunder to frighten human minds
And winds that send the lightning out.

The maker of the world did not
Allow the winds themselves to blow

Across an undisputed air;
And even now, although they live

Each in his country, it is hard
To stop them tearing up the world

The brothers are so quarrelsome.
The East wind drew back to the dawn

Over the Persian mountain-tops;
The West wind hugged the evening star;

The howling north wind Scythia
Kept, and the seven stars by the pole;

The south wind wets the other side.
Above all this the god imposed

The liquid ether, free of weight
And also of impurities.

When he had sorted out the world
The stars, before that covered up,

Blazed suddenly across the sky.
And every region was filled up

With constellations and with gods.
The waters filled with shining fish;

The land had beasts; the sky had birds.
But earth still lacked an animal

Who had a more capacious mind
And could command the other beasts.

The man was born; either the god
Who made the world used his own seed

Or else the earth, so newly dropped
From ether, had some of its own

Or Japetus mixed with a stream
To make a model of the gods.

The other animals look down
But man is ordered to regard

The sky and, beyond that, the stars.
So earth, from having had no shape

Became the habitat of man.
The golden age was first, when none

Set up as champion of the right
Because there was no need of law.

There was no punishment, or fear
Or notices of penalties;

Nobody quailed before a judge;
All lived in trust and all were safe.

No pine was then cut down and launched
To take men into foreign parts

They were content to stay at home.
There were no cities with steep moats

Bugles and trumpets were unknown.
No swords, no helmets; no one fought

The time was passed in idleness.
There were no spades or ploughs, the earth

Gave freely all it had to give.
Men were content with what she gave

And took the fruit the trees prepared,
Wild strawberries or the acorns from

The spreading tree of Jupiter.
Spring was eternal, and the flowers

Sprang of themselves without a seed.
The field where none had worked soon gave

A yellow harvest of thick corn.
Rivers of nectar and of milk

Flowed past the honey-bearing trees.
When Saturn fell to Tartarus

And Jove began to rule, the world
Entered upon the silver age,

Worse than the gold, better than bronze.
Jupiter cut the ancient spring

And winter, summer, autumn came
To make the seasons of the year.

Then, for the first time, the air burned
And water was congealed in ice.

Men first sought shelter, and found caves,
Thick foliage, branches laced round bark.

Corn was first set in furrows and
The oxen first moaned at the plough.

The age of bronze came next, more cruel,
Combative but not criminal.

The iron age came last. All sorts
Of crimes irrupted on the world.

Shame, truth and trust were gone, instead
Came fraud and force, and perfidy,

And the desire of ownership.
The sailor sailed his sail, although

He did not understand the winds.
From the high mountain-tops the barks

Plunged into seas they did not know.
The earth which had been common as

Sunlight and air, was parcelled out
And men were not content to reap

The harvest which her surface gave
But travelled in her entrails and

Dug what was hidden by the Styx,
The riches which would make them mad.

So iron and, worse than iron, gold
Came to the day, and so did war

Whose bloody hand employs them both.
Men live by stealing, and the host

Is safe no longer from his guest
Nor father from his son-in-law.

Brothers are without trust, and wives
And husbands wish each other dead.

Stepmothers mix the poison up;
Sons ask how old their fathers are.

The last immortal, Astraea,
Now leaves the impious, blood-stained earth.

To make the heavens unsafe as earth
The giants pile the mountains up

And try to get to the stars.
Then the Almighty Father broke

Olympus with a thunderbolt.
Pelion was knocked off Ossa. Earth
(unfinished)

Actaeon

So Cadmus founded Thebes: the dragon's teeth
Turned into soldiers who grew tired of killing.
Yet in the midst of this prosperity
Another miracle destroyed Actaeon:
The dogs he followed tore him limb from limb.
The newsmen, happy to observe the blood,

Considered that the story ended well
And were delighted to find how it happened:
The cameramen had not arrived in time,
Unfortunately, for a front-page picture,
And so the tale was left to literature.
Actaeon, hunting innocently enough
– For killing deer was then accepted practice –
Had given up that sport and found another
Not less agreeable to a young man.
He came across a cave in which Diana
Was cleaning up a bit after the chase
– For she liked hunting, too – and, being a goddess,
She had a score of beautiful attendants.
She gave her bow to one, and then the arrows
To the next nearest, then took off her dress
And handed it to a third. The rest were anxious
To show that they could help, and they took pitchers
And filled them from the bubbling, winking spring
To pour over their mistress. In those days
That was the only way to have a shower.
As the first buckets full went over her,
She noticed – she was taller than the rest –
A young man watching her with more than interest.
She blushed – the habit had not quite been lost.
All the attendants, who were also naked,
Crowded around her to obscure the view,
Which still, however, had a certain charm,
Or would have done, had not Diana thrown
A pail of water in Actaeon's face.
Some might have left the episode at that,
But not Diana: she was furious.
'Now go and tell them what you saw,' she said;
She thought Actaeon was a journalist.
He would have answered, but he could not speak.
The goddess, who thought quickly, had already
Affixed a pair of antlers on his head,
Lengthened his neck, made his ears end in points,
Changed his hands into feet, and turned his arms
Into long legs, and covered all his body
With dappled skin which did not look like his.
She changed his character, and made him timid.
He fled at once, and was surprised to find

How fast he went. Then he looked in the river,
And saw there the reflection of a stag.
All he had left was reason, so he groaned;
It was the only voice that he still had.
He hesitated, but his dogs did not.
The quickest of them caught the scent at once.
They bayed, all all the pack came hurtling after,
Down rocks, up vallies, following the young man.
It was not long before one took a bite.
One on his back, another on his shoulder.
Soon there was no square inch for a fresh bite.
He groaned again; and it was not the sound
A stag makes; it was not that of a man.
His knees gave way, and he was suppliant.
His friends called out his name but could not see him;
They were surprised he took so long to come
To see the prey that they had found for him.
He wished he had been absent, but was present
To see the savage exploits of his dogs.
They tore him into shreds, and so his spirit
Escaped at last through all those gaping wounds,
And only thus could he assuage the goddess.

In Allusion to Propertius, I, iii

When I opened the door she was asleep.
It is thus I imagine the scene, after Propertius.

The torches flickered all over the world
My legs staggered but I went to her bed

And let myself down gently beside her.
Her head was propped lightly upon her hands.

I passed one arm under her body
And with my free hand I arranged her hair

Not disturbing her sleep. She was Ariadne
Desolate upon the coast where Theseus had left her,

Andromeda, no longer chained to the rock,
In her first sleep. Or she was Io,

A milk-white heifer browsing upon her dreams,
I Argus, watching her with my hundred eyes.

I took kisses from her and drew my sword.
Then, through the open window the moon looked in:

It was the white rays opened her eyes.
I expected her to reproach me, and she did:

Why had I not come to her bed before?
I explained that I lived in the underworld

Among shadows. She had been in that forest.
Had we not met, she said, in that place?

Hand in hand we wandered among the tree-trunks
And came into the light at the edge of the forest.

Imitated from Ovid

(Tristia ex Ponto, V, x.)

Rivers have frozen and the seas grown hard
How many times, since I have been in Pontus?
How many years since my country left me?
It seems as many as the cat has hairs.
The clocks have stopped, it almost seems, so slowly
Has time gone by, and the year never moves.
The longest day does not make the night shorter:
The darkest night takes nothing from the day.
For me, the only fresh turn nature takes
Is to make all long-drawn-out as my worries.
Or does time move as usual, only I
And my perception of it stand stock still?
I am held by a lying sea which has no tides
And by a land which is in truth ill-omened.

Numberless are the people who surround me;
All that is certain is their ill intent.
Beyond the frontiers nothing is secure,
And what thin walls this island has today!
When you least think it hostile birds fly in
And feed in droves before you see them here.
Often, and in despite of our defences,
The enemy's weapons clutter up the streets.
And in the country-side, who can grow anything,
When we fear arms more than we hope for crops?
It is not wolves that threaten the sheep now,
But men in helmets spray the earth with poison.
We are scarcely safe at home; within our cities
A barbarous mob jostles the crowd we know.
A savage rabble we may not distinguish
Already occupies over half the houses.
Fear them or not, you still may hate the sight of them,
With skins and hair none of our fathers had.
Even those whose forebears were not outlandish
Now ape the dress and manners of the strangers.
They have a common tongue for their exchanges;
I can no longer speak except in signs.
I am the barbarian, understood by nobody,
While they laugh at the language that I use;
They speak ill of me openly, as they may;
Perhaps they jeer at me as a poor exile.
Whether I nod or merely shake my head,
They think, of course, that it is all pretence.
The knives are out at once to prove injustice
And stabbings in the street are commonplace.
Why were my days not shorter, rather than I
Should live to witness this hard turn of fate?
The features of my country and my countrymen
Are lost, and I am here among strange races.
If I deserved this exile from my city
I did not merit such place as this.
What am I saying? I am mad: whoever
Offends the people has no right to live.

HORACE

Odes I, i

Maecenas, your old family of kings
Protects me now, honour and friendship too.
Dust on the race-course is what some admire;
They like the screeching wheels, also the prize.
The masters of the earth have several pleasures.
One finds it is a fortunate election
Which brings him to a row of pleasant jobs.
Another will prefer to make a corner
In some commodity that others want.
You will not tempt a man who likes to scratch
Domestic acres, to the dangerous sea.
Yet there are venturers who like their home
Only until they see money abroad,
Though I can think of men who would prefer
A bottle in the middle of the day
And then an hour or two stretched on their back.
Many like camps and military things,
Although their mothers draw the line at war.
The sportsman with a gun stays out all night
Although he has a wife at home in bed;
His dogs and mares distract him, that is all.
For me it is the ivy on my forehead,
The trick of being a poet: the cold woods
Alive with nymphs and satyrs, keep me out.
I want no people if I have a flute,
A lute, anything musical, a Muse
To hand it to me. For I am a poet.

Odes I, ii

Iam satis terris nivis atque dirae

Already enough snow, hail, thunder and lightning
Our Father has sent us, bloody-handed.
He has thrown down the Capitoline buildings
        And terrified the city,

Terrified the inhabitants, who fear the return
Of the age of Pyrrha, a time of floods and marvels
When Proteus led his monsters up to the hill-tops
            Although they belonged to the sea,

And the whole genus of fishes found its way to the elm-tops
Which were more accustomed to entertaining pigeons
And the tender-eyed deer found themselves permanently
        swimming
            On a limitless ocean.

We saw the yellow ochre of the Tiber
Turned back violently at the mouth by the Etruscan sea,
Flooding over Numa's monument, wrecking also
            The temple of Vesta

When, for the sake of the querulous Ilia
In vengeance he threw himself, spreading
Far over the left bank, in defiance of Jove;
            The stream is uxorious.

He heard the the Romans had been sharpening their knives
To cut up one another – it would have been better to cut up the
        Persians –
Heard also that children had become scarce,
            Their parents being vicious.

Which of the gods is it best for the people to call upon
When the empire is falling? What prayers are best for the Vestals
To use in a time like this, though their goddess
            Pays little attention?

Jupiter has to give someone the task of expiation.
Come, as we pray, your muscular shoulders shining
In a cloak of cloud, you perhaps were the best,
            Far-seeing Apollo,

Or, if you prefer, send us the smiling Venus,
With every delight as usual flying about her
Or, if the neglected race of your progeny
            Deserves that attention,

Father of Romulus, you have seen enough of war,
It has gone on too long, forget the sort of spectacle
You are most at home with, the Moorish foot-soldier
        Desperate against his enemy.

Or, changing your shape, as you come among us on earth,
Son of Maia – she will be kind – assume the appearance
Of this man still in his prime, and well suited to be
        The avenger of Caesar.

Go back late to heaven, and meanwhile
Be among your people, the Quirinals
And I pray only that no fault of theirs may
        Drive you away.

Here rather may you enjoy the triumphs you love,
A prince and our benefactor;
Do not leave even the Medes unpunished
        While you lead us, Caesar.

Odes I, v

What fine young man who stinks of scent
Shoves you, who are so innocent,
Down on a bed of roses in
A handy cave, and you begin

Pyrrha, to do your hair? He too
Of course will have a lot to do,
Complaining of your treachery;
When storms blow up he's all at sea.

Yet now the simpleton believes
That you and he are thick as thieves;
The lad will think it very strange
If after all the wind should change.

Hard luck on those who find the sea
Dazzling, and try it! As for me
I've had my ship-wreck and I find
Old photographs more to my mind.

Odes I, xi

Tu ne quaesieris, scire nefas, quem mihi, quem tibi

You do not ask – useless to ask, Leuconoë –
What end the gods will give, to me, to you.
Consult no augurers. Suffer what comes,
Whether some winters still, or this one only
Which now wears out the sea under the cliffs.
Think, take your wine. You are better off with sleep
And no long hopes. For, while we speak, age falls.
Collect your day, and have it. The next, you may not.

Odes I, xxii

Integer vitae

The man who congratulates himself on his own value
Does not need, say, javelins from Africa
Or a quiver loaded with poisoned arrows,
        None of these things, Fuscus.

It does not matter if he is eddying past the Syrtes
Or finding his way over the bleack Caucasus
Or into those places which the golden Hydaspes
        Fabulously waters.

For as I was wandering in the Sabine forest,
Singing of Lalage, careless, beyond the boundary
Of my own property, I started a wolf and he bolted
        Although I was empty-handed.

Yet this monster was such as the martial Daunia
Hardly hides in the thick of it oaken recesses;
It was such as arid Numidia would not generate,
    Though she nurtures lions.

Put me on the lazy plains where no breeze
Refreshes the summer or disarranges the leaves,
A side of the world where mists and a rainy Jupiter
    Weep more than I can say.

Put me under the wheels of the sun's chariot
Where it rides too close to us and makes a desert.
I shall still continue in love with the laughing Lalage
    Who keeps her charm even though she talks.

Odes I, xxxviii

Persicos odi

I hate all this elaborate stuff,
My boy, you've brought more than enough:
Don't bother now with spending hours
Looking for out-of-season flowers.

That bit of myrtle there will do.
The effort is no good to you
And does nothing for me, who choose
To sit under the vine and booze.

Odes I, xxxi

Quid dedicatum poscit Apollinem

When he makes his petition to Apollo
What does the poet ask for? What, as he pours
New liquor out of the cup? Not rich
Estates in Sardinia, heavy with wheat,

Nor in burning Calabria, with herds
Of cattle. Not ivory and gold from
India. Not even the fields whose edges
The Liris nibbles with her quiet waters.

Those to whom fortune allows it can trim
The vine with Calenian pruning-knives, so that
The well-to-do business man can drain
Wine from golden cups, on the strength of the Syrian trade.

He is dear to the gods themselves, since he sails
In the Atlantic three or four times a year
Without disaster. I feed on olives,
Chicory is my meat, I eat mallow.

Allow me to be content with what I've got,
Latona's son and, I pray, to pass my age
Well and sensible, without disgrace
And not, I beg you, without the Muse.

Odes II, x

Rectius vives, Licini, neque altum

You live more suitably, Licinius, if you're not
Always pressing out to sea or, on the other hand,
In your anxiety to avoid storms, always
Skirting the dangerous rocks.

Whoever is able to choose the half-way house
Is safe, on the one hand, from living in a slum
And with equal discretion avoids the residence
That his neighbours will envy.

It is most often the tall pine that is shaken
By the wind and it is the high towers which go down
With the heaviest crash, while lightning strikes the highest
Mountains for preference.

Hopeful in adversity, fearful when in luck,
The heart is always ready for the opposite
Of what happens. Jupiter brings in the shapeless
Winters but he also

Takes them away. If things are bad now, and have been,
They will not always be so. Sometimes Apollo
Rouses the silent Muse with his lyre; he is not
Always stretching his bow.

When times are difficult put on the appearance
Of courage; but if the wind is too favourable,
As it can be, the judicious thing
Is to trim your sails.

Odes II, xiv

Eheu fugaces, Postume, Postume

The years go by, the years go by you, nameless,
I cannot help it nor does virtue help.
  Wrinkles are there, old age is at your elbow,
  Death on the way, it is indomitable.

Not if you choose, as you will choose, to doctor
Yourself with hope, will you weep out your pain.
  The underworld is waiting. There are monsters
  Such as distended you before you died.

The subterranean flood is there for every-
one who has taken food and drink on earth.
  A light skiff will put out, you will be on it –
  And, win the pools, you still will go aboard.

The blood dried on you and you came home safely
– Useless. You blew out an Atlantic storm.
  – No need to fear the wind, it can do no harm.
  It brings you where you will be brought at last.

The dark, the black and, in the blackness, water,
A winding stream, it will not matter to you.
    The fifty murderesses are there, the toiler,
    Exhaustion beyond hope, condemned to dreams.

Your house, your wife, and the familiar earth,
All will recede, and of the trees you prune
    Only the cypress follow you, ill-omened.
    You were here briefly, you are here no more.

The heir you leave is better than yourself,
What you kept closest he will throw away.
    Your books are on the pavement, and his laughter
    Sounding like broken glass through all the rooms.

Odes II, xv

Iam pauca aratro iugera regiae

There will be nothing soon for the plough
But huge bulks everywhere. On all sides
    Wider than lakes, the city
    Lamp-standards drive out the elms,

Planes, beeches. Once it was fertile here.
Edges of violet circumscribed
    The grove; there was everywhere something for the
    Nostrils, but now there is nothing.

Where there were once forests a region of
Concrete. Until quite recently
    There were meadows at Westminster.
    The salmon leaped where Raleigh was beheaded.

Once there was only nature for ornament.
Then there was ornament and art flourished;
    Now there is only the South Bank
    And, of course, the Arts Council.

It was not laws but a less abstract
Technology made the turf spring.
   The churches in those days, you may
   Remember, were built of stone.

Odes III, xxx

I have completed a memorial
More durable than bronze, and yet more tall
Than pyramids which mark the graves of kings,
No rain can wear it down, no buffetings
Of north winds break it up, or centuries,
Fly as they will, alter its power to please.
I shall not die entirely, much of me
Will have no funeral, but anew will be
Praised and grow greater in the future time.
While Pontifex and silent Vestal climb
The Capitol, it shall be said that I
– Where Aufidus roars and yet the land is dry,
Where Daunus ruled the country people, great
Although he was not born to high estate –
First brought Greek lyricism to our verse.
Melpomene, the honour this deserves
Is yours, and yet the laurel crown which serves
To mark the triumph, properly belongs
To the executive who wrote the songs.

Odes IV, vii

Diffugere nives

The snows have gone; already the grass comes back,
   The trees have their leaves.
The earth is changing once more; down goes the river,
   The water is low on the banks.

There are the Graces, all of them, naked again
As they lead their gang around.
Don't expect it to last, the year says, it may be mild
But that is only today.

Cold cannot stand up to a breeze, spring finds the summer
On top of it, and that won't last,
Autumn bombards it with fruit, soon
Back comes the winter, dead.

As the moons fly past at least they make up their losses:
We, when we go down,
Following Aeneas, a line of prosperous kings,
What are we? Dust and shadow.

Why suppose that the gods will add a single day
To those you have had already?
The greedy hands of the heir will close on nothing:
So look after yourself.

Once you have gone down what is coming to you?
An exalted judgement.
It will take more than your family, Torquatus, or eloquence
Or virtue, to put you right.

When Hippolytus died, in spite of his chastity
Diana could not save him:
The same with Pirithous, dear as he was to Theseus,
Once beyond Lethe, he stayed.

Carmen Saeculare

O sun, and moonlight shining in the woods,
The best things in heaven, always to be worshipped
As long as they give us exactly what we want

Now, at this season when selected girls
And the boys who are about to venture upon them,
Though still in bud, sing what will please London,

As you bring out one day and conceal another
Shine on the arms and legs and make them brown.
May all you see be greater than we are.

The time will come to open thighs in child-birth.
Gently, supervising god, look after the mothers.
Bringing to light is the true meaning of genitals.

Could you bring up these children without laws?
The statute-book is crowded, what wonder therefore
If all that interests them is an obscure kindness?

A hundred and ten years it may easily be
Before songs and games which come as speedily
As these three days, ah, and delicious nights.

You have sung truthfully enough, O fates.
Once it was ordained that everything should be stable
And will be again, but not now, or for ever.

Rich in apples, yes, and seething with cattle,
The succulent earth is dressed in barley whiskers.
And grow plump, embryo, from the natural gifts.

The sun will shine, as long as the boys are suppliant,
That will keep sickness away; and you girls,
Listen, for the moon will hear you if you do.

If you made London, as before it Engelland,
The Jutes coming over in ships, but only to be Romans,
Part of that remnant to join this one

The ways that have led here are multifarious,
Even Brutus from Troy, our ancestors believed,
But whatever they left they found better here.

You cannot credit the wish, that the young should be teachable
And old age quiet. Yet it is these wishes
Spring from the earth at last, when the country flowers.

Might you not even remember the old worship?
I could name ancestors, it is not done any more.
It remains true that, before you are king, you must win.

We have been through it all, victory on land and sea,
These things were necessary for your assurance.
The King of France. Once there was even India.

Can you remember the expression 'Honour'?
There was, at one time, even Modesty.
Nothing is so dead it does not come back.

There is God. There are no Muses without him.
He it is who raises the drug-laden limbs
Which were too heavy until he stood at Saint Martin's.

It is he who holds London from Wapping to Richmond,
May he hold it a little longer, Saint George's flag
Flap strenuously in the wind from the west country.

Have you heard the phrase: 'the only ruler of princes'?
Along the Thames, in the Tower, there is the crown.
I only wish God may hear my children's prayers.

He bends now over Trafalgar Square.
If there should be a whisper he would hear it.
Are not these drifting figures the chorus?

Epodes, II

Happy the man who, free from business
        As Adam was when innocent,
Pretends to farm paternal acres
        And never thinks of the investment.

Nobody send him tiresome papers
        Which leave him utterly at sea;
He is not harried by his brokers
        Or people better off than he.

Oh no! He cultivates his vineyard
        And lets his vines get out of hand;
His cattle graze without regard
        To the condition of the land.

In pruning, he will always sever
    The fruiting branch, and leave the new;
At shearing, finds the sheep so clever
    He likes their wool best where it grew;

Finds honey sticky in the autumn
    And fruit a bit above his head;
He does not pick the pears, they all come
    Bouncing on top of him instead.

His wine is fit for a libation
    Upon the ground, but not to drink;
He much enjoys the preparation
    And he is proud if it is pink.

His private stream meanwhile runs purling,
    The birds sing as they're paid to do;
His fountains never tired of plashing
    And they are soporific too.

But when the proper sporting weather
    Arrives, he has to take a gun
And stir up something in the heather
    As gentlemen have always done,

Or even venture out on horse-back
    And hope a fox will come his way;
How awkward he should lose the pack
    So very early in the day!

With such delights he can forget
    That tiresome girl at the week-end:
He plans to have, but not just yet,
    A wife on whom he can depend

– Children perhaps – some sunburnt lady,
    He'd feel a proper farmer then;
She'd bring in firewood, have tea ready,
    He'd come in tired, not curious when

311

She penned the geese or milked the cows,
    So long as she'd drawn cider and,
From home-grown chicken and potatoes,
    Prepared a meal with her own hands.

No Yarmouth oysters could be sweeter,
    Smoked salmon, turbot, what you please,
Not any delicacy caught here
    Or found, long dead, in the deep freeze.

It's not too bad to dine off pheasant
    But home-grown olives do as well,
And what he finds extremely pleasant
    Is chewing meadow-sweet and sorrel:

Which one of course can supplement
    By hedgerow herbs that taste of tar,
Or better, when such boons are sent
    A lamb run over by a car.

'Amidst such treats as these, how fine
    To see beasts by your own front door,
The latest plough, the latest combine,
    And plan what you will use them for.'

So spoke the city man, and sold
    The lot, preferring stocks and shares.
Too bad that he had not been told
    The full extent of rural cares.

The Poetic Art

A version of the **Ars Poetica**

You may think nothing of zoological marvels
Or mind what a painter does to the human shape.
After Picasso, no one is shocked by distortions,
Yet, even so, there are rules to be observed.
Cork Street is not exempt from all derision
And there are books at least as bad as the pictures
– Flippant images out of a sick man's dream.
The serious work must do more than hang together.
It is no use saying: 'Painters and poets are equal'
– Of course – 'and equally free to use their invention.'   10
Of course. I invent things myself and am not against others.
That does not mean that I tolerate any stupidity
Of blots on canvas or words poured over a page.

Begin a work as if it were going to be serious
And decorate here and there with a modern image
Presenting the utmost secrets of the unconscious
Or else some scene of spectacular sexual interest
Or something putting the white man in his place.
Thank you, but not just now. I see you're enlightened;
But it isn't you we are after at the moment.   20
It's nice sometimes to stick to objective matter.
Funny that someone should start off telling a story
And end up treating us once more to himself.
Whatever you do, no harm in a little coherence.

Most poets – not least those born in a literate family –
Remain on the surface of things. I try to be brief,
The result is clear as mud. I try to be smooth,
The result is nerveless and bears no trace of a mind.
Aim to impress, the effect is merely inflated;
Try to keep out of the wind, you will probably crawl.   30
If you try for varied effects with a simple subject
It is artful enough but nothing to do with art
– You can get into trouble by trying to get it right.

It is not unknown to find an artist in colour
With only the vaguest idea of handling shapes,

So quite unable to put a work together.
As well, if one should happen to be a writer,
Let bits of the story flutter away down the garden
Then staple them up in the order they come to hand.

Writers should go for a subject they can manage   40
And give some thought to the sort of strain they can bear.
We all have limits. If the choice of subject is right,
The words will come of themselves, in a lucid order
– And order is a matter of strength and pleasure.
A word is pleasant and strong when it comes where it should,
Which means not coming at all unless it must
And the sort of affection that knows when it isn't wanted.

A mark of success in this painful discrimination
Is to find that the way you have used a familiar word
Has made it glitter like new. When what you are saying   50
Is so obscure as to need a novel expression,
It will be time enough for brilliant verbal inventions
– And I do not suppose that that will be very often.
But new-made words can flower, if they come from good roots
And are not allowed to run wild. For why should the reader
Allow to Sterne what he will refuse to Joyce?
And why should I not add something, however little,
To the language which Chaucer and Shakespeare made more
        pointed
By noticing something no one had noticed before?
It has always been right and it will always be right   60
To use the word that bears the stamp of the time.
As woodlands lose their leaf at the fall of the year,
The old words go in turn, while the young
Flower and grow strong. For we are promised to death,
And all our things. It may come, sometimes, in a gale
Which bursts inland to give the sea a rest
And a fen that bore nothing except the plashing of oars
May survive to grow good corn for a neighbouring town.
Elsewhere the crops may go and the river pass
To produce more crops after that: for nothing will stand,   70
Certainly not the repute and pleasure of words.
Many words will come back which seemed to be lost
And many now much in use will be lost again
For nothing but use determines the fate of words.

314

The tragedy in blank verse was pulled by Shakespeare
Out of dreary wars and tales of public events,
While ballad metre was used at once for dirges
And popular stories with plenty of murder and love
– And who invented the form is still disputed
By all the scholars, and doesn't matter at all;   80
At least we know it will never be settled now.
The couplet also was used for telling stories
But Dryden gave it snap and used it for satire.
He also used it for plays, because the French did
Or because it made banging verses that reached the gallery.
There were several forms for lyrical inspiration
And they served for pot-house songs and bawdy as well
As adolescent concerns like a broken heart.
If you cannot distinguish these various kinds of work
You should not expect to be taken up as a poet;   90
If you won't find out you will always be a fool.
Comedy cannot borrow a tragic manner,
Nor is it proper to treat as a casual thing
Domestic horrors you ought to worry about.
The subject must choose the style; you are not important.
Not that comedy has to stick to the merely funny;
An angry old man, for example, is more than a joke,
And tragedy sometimes needs the most un-tragic speech.
Disaster often alters a showman's style
And reduces his taste for foot-and-a-half long words.   100
He must puncture his bag of wind if he wants us to listen.

It is not enough for a poem to be beautiful:
It must have something to get at the reader's mind.
The human face is disposed to smile at a smile
And cry at the sight of tears: if you want tears from me
You had better suffer yourself, then your characters might.
But if they are figures of fun with sensational words,
I shall close the book or switch off. There are mournful words
For the face that mourns, and threatening words for the angry,
The idler can say what he likes, but the serious man must   110
    talk sense.
For nature shapes us to every habit of fortune
Before it comes our way: she drives us to anger,
Pleases us, chokes us with grief, and bows us down to the
    ground;

315

Then she translates with the tongue for interpreter.
If words are out of tune with the speaker's fortunes
The audience can only break into helpless laughter.
It matters whether your man's the heroic type,
A seventy-year-old or a burning man in his youth,
An upper-class married woman, her nanny,
A travelling salesman or someone who works on a farm,   120
French or German, Russian or Chinese Jew.

Either follow old tales or else invent something probable.
If you want to write about Moses, you had better not make him
    ridiculous;
To say the least he held down a difficult job.
And because you have forgotten the Ten Commandments
It doesn't mean he was only after power.
Nor were Adam and Eve a pair of nudists.
If you are keen to show your imagination
Remember you may not have as much as you think
And your characters may become inconsequential.   130

You cannot simply decide to be original.
Better to stick to Bible stories than fancy
That what you happen to think of must therefore be new.
There is such a thing as prospecting and staking a claim
But it is not done by hanging around with the mob,
Or translating word for word like a Loeb translator.
No doubt you are happy enough in your preconceptions
But there is such a thing as the law of the work itself.
You are not to begin like an imitation Milton:
'I think of all disobedience as a fruit'   140
– For how, if you start like that, will you keep it up?
That is the way the mountain gave birth to a mouse.
How much better to say, like *Gulliver's Travels*,
'My father and mother had a house in Nottingham;
I was the third of five sons, and went to Cambridge.'
No squibs at first: better a slow unfolding
As if the figure were coming out of a mist;
After that Lilliput, Brobdingnag, even the Houyhnhnms.
Swift does not dig too far in the boring past
To set a scene for the story – it has to begin –   150
But hurries to get to the point, and the whole affair
Is treated as if the reader knew it already.

316

Whatever he cannot make interesting he leaves out;
The thing is so skilful, with mixture of fact and fiction,
The middle part fits the beginning, the end the middle.

Would you like to hear what I and the public expect?
If you want an audience to sit through a play to the end,
Not even be bored when the cast comes back for applause,
You must notice how people behave at different ages
And change the language for different natures and years.   160
The child who has learned to walk and not long learned to run
Likes to play, gets cross, and changes from minute to minute.
The youth, not long out of school will languish for sports cars
And other ways of actively wasting his time
– Attracted to all bad habits, not fond of advice,
Not anxious to earn his living but fond of spending,
High and mighty, lubricious, and quick to leave what he loves.
Soon he has changed his mind, and looks for money and influence
And, as mature men do, sweats in obsequiousness,
Afraid of having done something that he will want to undo.   170
Old age too has its drawbacks. The man who has got what he
      wanted
Is terrified then of the winnings he dares not use,
Or uses them, as he does everything, coldly and timidly,
Putting off hopes in case they should catch him out,
Difficult, querulous, praising the time gone past,
When he was a boy, as a means of impeding his juniors.
The years as they come bring about much that is pleasant;
      receding
They take back as much. So, unless you aim at depicting
Infantile adults and children old for their years,
Put weight on the characteristics related to age.   180

Events may happen on stage or be reported;
What comes in at the ears will always make less impression
Than what a man sees for himself. Yet do not bring on
What should be done off stage; it is perfectly possible
To tell us all we need to know in the course of the dialogue.
It is rather distracting to butcher children in public
And I can't say I care for eating human flesh.
The abnormal on the whole is better avoided;
You can easily cause disbelief as well as disgust.

Although it seems an antiquated opinion, 190
There was something, after all, to be said for five acts
And the other old rules: no improbable interventions,
And never more than three speakers at once on the stage.

The chorus was given a part, the same as an actor;
It hadn't simply to sing between the acts,
The drift of its words was supposed to advance the plot.
It was civilized, didn't take the side of the rascals
But calmed hysteria and spoke as an ordinary friend.
It was on the side of the man of abstemious habits,
And justice and law, not merely in favour of peace. 200
It kept the secrets they told it and prayed to God
To help the unfortunate and not to encourage success.

Flutes, which were formerly made of a simple shin-bone,
Not, as now, brass-bound, with elaborate stops,
Were then a subdued accompaniment to the chorus
And sounded well when the benches were not too full
– You could count the audience, who were not only few
But sober, hard-working people, even chaste.
When cities began to spread and the country grew bloated
And holiday drinking began before the evening, 210
The music grew less controlled and the noise was greater.
What tastes could there be in an incoherent crowd
Just finishing work, and only some of them honest?
So movement and crude display spoiled the original art
And the flute-player walked around in beautiful costumes;
The instruments learned to make all kinds of noises
And words were thrown round in a quite hysterical way.
The stage propounded idiotic opinions
Like fortune-tellers or bawds or pseudo-prophets.

The poet, who once had worked in the simplest conditions, 220
Now filled the stage with a lot of naked Satyrs;
It was thought respectable also to try to be funny.
The audience could only be kept by novel obscenities
– No wonder they liked to be drunk and to spit on the law.
The best you can do is to present these amusing Satyrs,
Whose task is to ridicule anything thought to be serious,
In such a manner that the superior characters
Are neither forced abjectly to follow the rabble

Nor filled with wind through trying to be unlike them.
Tragedy is not a babble of foolish verses;   230
If called to dance in a heap of lecherous Satyrs
She holds herself as a sensible woman would.
I should not confine myself to commonplace language
If I were to take to writing satyric plays,
Nor should I so depart from the tragic manner
As to make the lines sound like mere buffoonery;
A drunken man may sometimes be a philosopher.
I shall make poetry out of known material
– Which looks quite easy to copy, but isn't, of course,
For all depends on sequence and disposition;   240
The commonplace can be given distinction by that.
If Fauns are brought from the woods, then, in my opinion,
They should not talk as if born in a slum or a market;
Or like adolescents, piddle out sensitive verses,
Nor fill the air with their noisy and boring obscenities.
It will not go down with the better part of the audience
Who won't take everything loved by the great consumers
Of coca-cola and ice-cream, or even cigars.

Short syllables followed by long are known as *iambics,*
Or unstressed followed by stressed, and many excesses   250
Have been committed by scholars attempting to classify
The whole of versification by classical canons.
Of course one can recognize something that looks like a spondee,
Bang, bang: and the other classical feet have their parallels
But that is neither the start nor the end of the subject.
You can see at a glance the comparative dullness of Surrey
And Marlowe's slamming line could be called monotonous,
But I wouldn't say that the twentieth century does better
And the history of blank verse is complete in Shakespeare.
Not every critic knows when a verse sounds badly   260
And some of our poets have got away with murder.
Shall I therefore write without care? Or take so much
That no one can ever say I put a foot wrong?
Neither of these courses will get you anywhere.
There is such a thing as paying attention to rhythm
And it does no harm to know what verse has been written.
Your ignorant ancestors thought that Ralph Roister Doister
Was the funniest play in the world: I would say they were
        tolerant,

Gaping at that stuff. But you and I have seen better;
We imagine a difference between a joke and a brawl   270
And tell what rhythms are right with our fingers if not with our
    ears.

I could tell you some doubtful points about the invention of
    tragedy,
How plays were carried round on a waggon at the wine harvest
And the players appeared with the dregs all over their faces.
Aeschylus brought in the mask – they say – as well as long
    garments
And built the first proper stage as well as being the first
To work out the formal movements and tragical language.
Then the Old Comedy came, and that was much applauded,
Perhaps because it went too far and had to be checked by law.
The outcome of that little *fracas*, however, was that the   280
    chorus
Sank into shameful silence and lost its right to abuse.

Poets in our own tongue have left no subject untried,
And they haven't done their worst when they left the exotic
    behind
And found their plots nearer home, whether tragic themes
Or comedies based on familiar manners and ways.
The English could do as well in literature as in cricket
If their poets, one and all, did not have the fatal weakness
Of refusing to polish their work and waiting to see how it looks.
If I cannot make poets of you, at least I can give you advice:
Plenty of rubbing out is a good way to make a poem   290
And after that lots of attention to get all the details right.

However, since inspiration is reckoned better than cleverness,
One naturally doubts the achievements of those who are in their
    right mind,
So many refuse to shave, or even to pare their finger-nails
And hang back in holes and corners rather than go to the baths,
For the most reliable way to acquire some fame as a poet
Is to keep away from the barber a head that is known to be
    cracked.
I really am rather an imbecile to try to keep myself healthy
For otherwise surely no one would make better poems than I
– But it isn't worth it. So I will act as a grindstone   300

320

And allow you poets to sharpen yourselves on me.
I will not write a line myself, but indicate the requirements
– Where to get your ideas, and how to encourage your genius,
What is proper for poets, and how a man can go wrong.

The first rule of writing then, is to know what you're talking
  about.
Wittgenstein's writings will indicate what you should know
And once you have the matter the words will follow.
It may pain you to learn what you owe to your country and
  friends,
How you should treat a parent, a brother, a guest,
What are the duties involved in the public offices,   310
What a senior officer has to do in a war:
You have to know all this, if you want some notion of character.
Yet you cannot draw except from the living model
And the poet must learn to write from the spoken word.
There are times when a bit of sense in the dialogue
And characters something like life, will give more pleasure
– Although the whole story is really rather dreary –
Than verses containing nothing but beautiful noise.

In other countries and times there may well have been writers
Who spoke as they thought and cared for nothing but fame,   320
But the English learn at school to reckon up decimals
And convert into dollars and marks. Now, this education,
Splendid for money-lenders, is bad for poets.
When everything is reduced to a calculation
There is little prospect that there will ever be poems
To take their place on the shelves with forgotten classics.

The poet seeks, either to give you pleasure
Or to say something about the conduct of life,
Possibly both; but precept should always be brief.
What is rapidly said can be held in the mind   330
While useless words trickle away in the sand.
Fictions designed to please should be close to the real;
There are some exaggerations that don't go down
And I have no taste for fairy tales or science fiction.
The older reader dislikes what he thinks is senseless,
The younger ignores whatever he thinks austere;
Of course if you can be pleasant as well as sensible

You might even sell some books, in distant countries,
And at some remote date even be read at home.

There naturally are mistakes that one can pardon;   340
The mind goes blank, the fingers fumble the note;
We often enough sound shrill when we want to be grave
– It's like missing the bull's-eye on a rifle-range.
Where there are many beauties in a poem
I can forgive a few faults from a careless hand;
The writer is also human. But may I say this?
Repeated mistakes are really quite intolerable
Whether in playing an instrument, or writing
And one reaches the point where there are so many errors
That one laughs at the good lines out of sheer surprise.   350
Yet I object when Homer is inattentive
– Though even the best long works are slightly soporific.

Poems are like pictures: with some, the nearer you go,
The better you like them; with others, you must stand back.
One sort is better in light, and the other in shadow,
Yet there must be light if you make a critical judgement;
The test is, not pleasing once, but pleasing ten times.

May I address a word to the cultured family,
Where the gifted father must have a gifted son?
May I make one observation you should remember?   360
There are certain things in which moderation is bad.
There is some use for even a second-rate lawyer,
Even though he has no remarkable eloquence
And has to look up everything in a textbook
– Still, he can do odd jobs. Mediocre poets
Don't look well even in booksellers' windows.
Just as, if you go out to dinner, you can do without music
And complicated hors-d'oeuvre, unless they are brilliant,
And pass the evening with great satisfaction without them,
So nothing is easier than doing without a poem   370
Unless it is positively going to give delight.
If you can't play games to a respectable standard
You had better avoid a public exhibition;
People normally do, unless they can face the laughter.
Yet everyone tries to write poems. Why not, you may ask
    me?

It is the right of everyone with 'O' levels
And what is more harmless than a bit of literature?

You, of course, reader, would never do anything foolish,
You have too much sense. But if ever you should be tempted
To put pen to paper, let some intelligent person   380
– Your father or me – have a look at it, then lock it up again.
Nine years later, you can take it out and admire it,
But what you publish you can no longer tear up.

Primitive man was soothed by his tribal poets
As Orpheus charmed men away from slaughter and cannibalism.
The legend puts it: He tamed the lions and tigers.
The legend says also that Amphion, founder of Thebes,
Managed to move the stones, by playing an instrument,
To arrange themselves as he wished. It was civilization,
As then understood, to make some distinction of property,   390
Even to set some boundaries to fornication,
To build a few cities and have a few stable laws.
It was these conditions, religious as much as social,
Which gave poetry its place. Then you come to Homer
And other poets who set a value on courage
And had some effect: the poet was also an oracle
And what he said had some relation to life,
Whether in politics or as a recreation
After hard physical work. It is not disgraceful,
At least in its nature, this art of perspicuous speaking.   400

The question is often asked whether the genuine poem
Is the product of gifts or of training. It seems to me training
Is little use unless there is something to train.
On the other hand no one should think he can do without
    training.
An athlete who is seriously trying for records
Has started as young as he can, and sweated and shivered,
And kept off women and drink. A good violinist
Has first to learn, and pay some regard to a teacher.
Yet people think nothing of saying: 'I write the most marvellous
    poems.
Everyone says so, which certainly proves I'm an artist.   410
If I had something to learn, I certainly wouldn't admit it.

You should study also commercial considerations.
You will notice that remarkable bargains are struck
By poets well enough placed to excite admiration.
The writer who has an entertainment allowance,
A place on the B.B.C. or a subsidized journal
Is likely to be so happy as not to discover
What people really think of his commonplace verses.
You also had better be careful, and if you should happen
To do someone a good turn, don't show him your poems   420
Just at that moment; he is sure to say they are marvellous.
He may even look as if he read them with pleasure
Or go so far as saying they ought to be published.
Just as, at a funeral, the undertaker's employees
Manage to look more grim than the mourners themselves,
So the best praise is produced by insincerity.
A business man who is thinking of trusting another
May ply him with drinks in order to discover his mind:
But alcohol is too weak in the case of poetry;
It's truth-drugs you need for your friends, if you will   430
    write verse.

But there is such a thing as the friend who notices what you write
And may point out that this or that won't do,
And when you've tried once or twice without success
To improve what you wrote, invites you to tear it up;
Yet if, after all, you decide to stick to your error,
Will waste no words on insisting on what he thinks
But leave you the pleasure at least of self-admiration.
The man who can actually tell when a verse is lifeless
Will know when it doesn't sound right; he will point to
    stragglers,
And equally put his pen through elaborations;   440
He will even force you to give up your favourite obscurities,
Tell you what isn't clear and what has got to be changed,
Like Dr Johnson himself. There will be no nonsense
About it not being worth causing trouble for trifles.
Trifles like that amount in the end to disaster,
Derisory writing and the meaning misunderstood.

Those who have any sense will get out of the way of the poet
Who fancies himself inspired, as they would of a mad fanatic;
They will fear his touch as they would the bubonic plague

324

And leave him to talk with adolescent admirers.   450
He will explain his theories and offer samples
And wander off in a maze like a statistician.
If he is so blind that he walks slap into the traffic
And then yells out, let no one bother to help him!
To anyone offering to intervene and extract him
My comment would be: He probably wants to be run over;
What was it Mr Alvarez said about suicide?
Creative people must have their freedom, you know;
It isn't the first time, I'm sure it won't be the last;
His death, after all, might make him interesting.   460
It isn't clear why he writes, no doubt some early disorder
Has persisted in its irruption upon his reasonable mind.
What is clear is that unless he is under sedation
He will break out over the town like a bear
To the terror of ordinary people and intellectuals.
If he catches a victim, nothing will stop him reading
Nor will he stop when a glaze spreads over his listener's eye.

APPENDICES

Introduction to Du Bellay

The poets of sixteenth century France can hardly be said to have been a significant influence on English poetry in the twentieth. Pound's reading lists skip this period, for reasons which are good in their context; Eliot points to the superiority of Villon or puts in a good word for the seventeenth century, when he is not more concerned with the world of Baudelaire and his successors. The young David Gascoyne looked towards the surrealists, and the older Gascoyne has shown an interest in some later French work. Among later comers, those who have not been so blatantly insular as Philip Larkin have most often had their eyes on more or less contemporary work, in German, Spanish or Italian – or on Villon, who has held his place. The Renaissance in general has hardly been the most influential of periods for writers in the twentieth century, perhaps because the air has been so filled with notions which have their roots in it. Yet the French literature of the sixteenth century, with its remarkable freedom of movement, has much which should be sympathetic.

Among the poets of the period there is none who comes to us with more freshness and intimacy than Joachim Du Bellay. It is not the intimacy of personal confession or boasting, of which so much has been heard since Rousseau and of which the twentieth century should by now have had its bellyful. It is the degree of familiarity which a civilized and frank young man might be expected to display among intelligent friends of like interest. Du Bellay had many such friends, and among them some of the best poets of the age, Ronsard not least. He was born in Anjou, to which he evinces great attachment, in the little town of Liré on the left bank of the Loire, in 1525. There are some indications that his early years were spent in some isolation, though that is to be understood in the relative sense of which it could be true of a gentleman's son living in a family house. He was an orphan at the age of seven, in the guardianship of a brother twenty years older than himself. He went to the little college of Ancenis, near Liré. We know, from what he tells us in *La Deffence et Illustration de la Langue Françoyse*, that he wandered around the countryside talking to workmen of various kinds and learning what they did, what tools they used and what terms they used in their respective trades. He also read Marot, a poet of more ingenuity than genius but no doubt useful to him at this stage. The inevitable initiation came in the form of what appears to have been a profound love affair with a cousin, Olive de Sévigné, who was about his own age. It was for her that the sonnets of his first sequence, *L'Olive*, were written. They are far more than the exercises of a young man playing at verse. They bring to life a passionate companionship in a countryside less loved only than the girl herself, and one gathers that, for a magical space of time, she shared his passion and rewarded it.

> Pareille amour nous avons esprouvée,
> Pareille peine aussi nous souffrons ores:
> Mais plus grande est la beauté qui me tue.

But the sweet half, the 'doulce moitié' who was to be his till death, in fact married one Mathurin du Gué when the poet, and presumably the girl, were seventeen or eighteen and there is evidence, in a poem called *L'Antérotique*, of a fury of suffering and disillusion. There are also sonnets which show the poet finding or attempting to find a Christian consolation in his distress. There can be no doubt of the critical nature of this interlude.

It seems that the disaster brought about by Olive de Sévigné or – more probably, given the customs of the time – by her family, was noticeable even to Joachim's not very attentive elder brother. At any rate the younger poet was sent off to the university of Blois, a sensible decision no doubt, for there he had the company of other students and certainly acquired friends. One of these was Guillaume Aubert who was responsible for the posthumous edition of Du Bellay's works in 1569. Du Bellay was at Blois to study law; he must also have extended his general reading and his knowledge of what was going on in the literary world of his day. About this time, or a little later, he made the acquaintance of Ronsard, whom he met casually at an inn. A friendship seems to have been established at once, and the two were soon afterwards at the college of Coqueret in Paris, of which the immensely learned and perhaps somewhat pedantic Jean Daurat had recently been appointed the master, with the adolescent Jean-Antoine de Baïf among his charges. Both Ronsard, slightly older than Du Bellay and Daurat, older by perhaps fifteen to twenty years, had had connections with court – Ronsard as an accomplished and promising page and Daurat as a tutor. It was with this fashionable college as his headquarters that Du Bellay published his first books, in 1549 – the year of the First Prayer Book of Edward VI. This – as it may appear – rather far-fetched connection is of significance because Du Bellay made his bow ot only with the sonnet sequence, *L'Olive*, and the *Odes lyriques*, but with the *Deffence et Illustration de la Langue Françoyse*, a fighting defence of the literary respectability of the vernacular. Since Daurat, who none the less wrote some – not particularly interesting – French verse composed in his time some fifty thousand lines in Greek and Latin, it is impossible not to suspect a certain negative influence here, which is not to say that Du Bellay did not, like Ronsard, gain enormously from the master of Coqueret's classical attainments and his abilities as a teacher. But the central doctrine of the *Deffence* is that French is not a barbarous tongue; that all languages indeed have the possibility of development; that there is no possibility of writing Greek or Latin as well as the Greeks or Latins did; and that what can be said had better be said in a language 'understanded of the people'. It must be added that it was no anachronistic anti-élitism which drove Du Bellay in this direction. His concern is not with the vain ambition that everyone shall understand all that is said but the more modest one that poets shall write in a language which is intimately theirs. The French language is capable of improvement; it should be improved, and by attention to the classics. Translation of the ancient masterpieces is not enough – though Du Bellay himself has left versions of the fourth and sixth books of the *Aeneid*, the very books most likely to appeal to a modern temperament. Books in other languages are to be raided for thoughts and sentiments, as well as words, which will enrich the vernacular; a measure of imitation of such sources is excellent while – he justly points out – imitation of works in one's own language is to be avoided like the plague. Du Bellay like Ronsard is for the absorption of the ancient literatures so that the vernacular can equal them. This is the ambition which the poets of the Renaissance bequeathed to their successors until, with the Romantic movement, these successors realized that they could look back on classics of their own – when a new problem arose, with an acute stage of which poets of the twentieth century are still having to wrestle. Du Bellay himself, besides translating the two books of the *Aeneid* and numerous passages not only from Virgil but from Lucretius, Lucan, Horace, Ovid and others, left a book of Latin elegies and epigrams of his own.

It was to wake the silence of the swans – 'Pour éveiller le trop long silence des cygnes', in the vivid phrase he uses in the address to the reader preceding his first volume of poems – that Du Bellay had engaged in the polemics of the *Deffence*. He felt that he and his friends stood at the beginning of something, as indeed they did. But if the Pléiade was about to rise, there is some fiction as to the number of stars. A poetic movement is always something of an illusion, a (sometimes legitimate) social affair which serves to launch a poet or two but falls apart as individual performances and non-performances become apparent. The stars of the Pléiade are genuine, but of very different magnitudes. There are Belleau, Jodelle, Thyard, Daurat and Baïf, but the real stars, who stand out as Charles d'Orléans does in the century before (Villon is another matter altogether), are Ronsard and Du Bellay. For Boileau, with the taste of a later age, the true line went from Marot to Malherbe, with Ronsard as a figure too large and unmanageable to be omitted, but surviving largely as a reckless and pedantic example to be avoided. Already Du Bellay has fallen out entirely. Yet for us, free to admire Ronsard without the preconceptions of the Louis-Quatorze classicism, the question is really whether Du Bellay is not a greater poet than Ronsard. I think he is. Du Bellay learned a lot from his slightly older contemporary, particularly in relation to such courtly poems as those in his second collection, published by the command of Marguerite de Navarre, which must have done much to establish his position in the world of his contemporaries. But it is precisely in this sort of thing that Du Bellay is at his least interesting for us. His great achievement, despite the charm and elegance of, in particular, the *Divers Jeux Rustiques* containing the winnower's song which took the fancy of Walter Pater, is in the almost always unaffected and finely balanced language of *Les Regrets*, of which intimations are given here and there in the early and much less sophisticated sonnets of *L'Olive*. It is in these poems that we become acquainted, not with a mere literary performer – though Du Bellay was a skilful one – but with the mind of a man who survives the difference of centuries and speaks to us directly. This is the real test of literature, and the reason why the fashions and reputations of particular ages, including our own, do not count for much. It is almost incredible now, when one turns to Pater's once famous volume, *The Renaissance*, to read the judgements of that ineffable fashion-monger. That Du Bellay is 'a characteristic specimen of the poetical taste of that age, is indeed,' he says, his 'chief interest'. Speaking of that charming winnower's song, *D'un Vanneur de Blé aux Vents*, the don who fell on his knees to present Oscar Wilde with a lily says that it has 'in the highest degree, the qualities, the value, of the whole Pleiad school of poetry, of the whole phase of taste from which that school derives – a certain silvery grace of fancy, nearly all the pleasure of which is in the surprise at the happy and dexterous way in which a thing slight in itself is handled'. What Pater says about that poem is right, and he was right to single it out, but it – and he – are in fact on the fringes of Du Bellay's real work. One might add that the song, slight as it is, would weigh heavy now in a balance against *Marius the Epicurean*.

The *Divers Jeux Rustiques* as a whole are pleasant rather than compulsory reading, but to remain in that category, after four hundred years, implies a degree of poetic excellence high indeed in comparison with that implied in our ordinary tolerance of our contemporaries. The collection is a miscellaneous one, and the title applied properly only to a small part of it. The poet's preliminary letter puts the matter as no doubt Du Bellay saw it: these verses were amusements, with which he had passed spare hours which might otherwise have been given to the usual frivolities, and he invites the reader to divert himself with them accordingly – unless he is one of those who has no use for anything unless it is full of 'doctrine & antique erudition', in which case he should go elsewhere. In addition to the lyrical pieces, there is a long poem giving the story, improving or not as you look at it, of a girl put into the business of prostitution in Rome – the sort of tale which, by the eighteenth century, was being put into prose – and a pleasing hundred lines by way of epitaph on a cat. It was in Rome that these poems were written; they are, therefore, more or less contemporary with the *Antiquitez* and the *Regrets* which were vehicles of his more weightly, if still casually voiced, reflections. Du Bellay went to Rome as intendant in the household of the Cardinal Jean Du Bellay – a family connection – when the latter was sent there by Henry II in 1553 to watch over French interests.

Joachim had, in fact, landed the sort of job which a young man of his talents, education and family might look for: one which would give him a knowledge of the great world and should open up a career in the closely allied royal or ecclesiastical services. It was to the cardinal that Du Bellay had dedicated the *Deffence*. In 1549, which was the year of its publication, the great man had returned from an earlier mission in Rome, and it must be supposed that Joachim became acquainted with him during this break in the cardinal's foreign service. It is of interest to see what terms Joachim uses in his dedication. The cardinal is playing a role 'au spectacle de toute l'Europe, voyre de tout le monde, en ce grand Theatre Romain'; it is an entirely political role, in the service of the French crown, 'au profit de la Patrie', and in all Du

Bellay's writings the Pope and his intimates are regarded as a foreign court, in which French interests have to be safeguarded in the face of corruptions which no reforming Protestant could have regarded with more distaste. For Du Bellay, with his Renaissance passion for the ancient world and its literature, the first impact of Rome was from the ruins of the classical city. The newcomer, he says, will find nothing in Rome of Rome – nothing, that is, of its former grandeur. The tone of the *Antiquitez* is elegiac: see what pride, what ruin! Spenser translated these poems as *Ruines of Rome*, incidentally abandoning the Italian sonnet form in favour of the English:

> Behold what wreake, what ruine, and what wast,
> And how that she, which with her mightie powre
> Tam'd all the world, hath tam'd herselfe at last,
> The pray of time, which all things doth devouwre.

There is a strong element of rhetoric and preconception about the *Antiquitez*, which are not among Du Bellay's best performances. Fortunately he had not come to Rome to look at the ruins, but to work; not to write poems in impressive surroundings but to lose himself in the ordinary business of the day. Glimpses of his preoccupations appear again and again in the *Regrets*. The management of the cardinal's no doubt considerable establishment involved keeping up with the diary, following his master here and there, being civil to innumerable callers and not saying too much, or too little, and above all not the wrong thing, talking plausibly to bankers when money was tight, and generally following the news of the day from the inside. It is a world which, in spite of the great differences of manners, has not changed in its essentials, the like of which are to be seen in any centre of public business. We get glimpses, too, of more relaxed moments, jokes about the work to be done, pulling the legs of friendly colleagues, eyeing some others distrustfully. Du Bellay is in company with people, in his own office and in others, who know how to value the business of the day. There is the endless strain of tact with superiors and with outsiders who are eminent or who think themselves so; there is an agonized concern about the affairs of France and – still more agonized – about his own career, and increasing pessimism about a happy issue. Above or behind all, there is the melancholy of an exile who is none the less fascinated by his surroundings, a longing for his home in Anjou and a sharp observation not only of the courts but of the streets of Rome.

There is no work of Du Bellay's so packed with matter as the *Regrets*, and it is not matter which he has decided is poetical but what hits him, often painfully, in his day-to-day life. It is this which gives the sequence its greatness. Many of the sonnets are addressed to the poet's friends at home – to Ronsard whose successes in his work and at court he treats generously, but also to Baïf, Peletier, Belleau and others, and to Olivier de Magny who was in Rome as secretary to D'Avanson, the official French ambassador. This fits with their easy tone. It has been pointed out that the classical background of the *Regrets* is not only the *Tristia* – the poems in which Ovid lamented his exile *from* Rome – but also and more powerfully the Horace of the *Satires*. There are suggestions, too, of ironic allusions to Petrarchan themes. But this background is merely what came readily to a well-read young man of Du Bellay's time. Nowhere does it obtrude itself; the tone, the manner, the cursiveness of the sequence are entirely the poet's own. This is Du Bellay's most mature work; it is one of the small masterpieces of European poetry.

There are 191 sonnets in *Les Regrets et Autres Oeuvres Poétiques*, as the volume of 1558 is entitled. I have translated 130. It has been suggested, by more than one editor, that the last sixty sonnets do not belong to the sequence proper but are the 'other poetical works' of the title-page. I accept this. These sixty sonnets are of a different character from the others and were apparently written when the poet had arrived back in France and was busy trying to re-establish himself with the best people. It is true that these later sonnets include some which record impressions of cities passed in his overland journey home. These serve merely to reinforce the impression of a break. For sonnet 128 speaks of a return by sea, in images which, says my editor, are 'not realistic, but classic'. In 129 the poet sees himself approaching an improbable coast of France where his friends stand with their arms stretched out to welcome him – there is Ronsard himself, Morel, Daurat, Delehaie and Paschal – an unlikely story. In sonnet 130 he likens his home-coming to that of Ulysses. These three sonnets, I would guess, were written in Rome when he had been told he was to go home and was making his preparations, full of delighted hopes mingled with fears of what he might find. If this is right, what we have, in the first 130 sonnets, despite the variety and some would say the confusion of subject-matter, is the integral text of Du Bellay's Roman *Regrets*.

The text I have chiefly used for this translation is that in the excellent edition of the *Textes littéraires français* (Geneva, Librairie Droz, 1966), edited by J. Joliff and M.A. Screech, while my general text of Du Bellay's *Poésies Françaises et Latines* has been that edited in two volumes by E. Courbet (Paris, Garnier, 1918).

Postscript to Catullus

Catullus quoque elegantissimus poetarum (Aulus Gellius, Noct. Attic. VII, 20). He was born at Verona, 84 BC. The country north of the Po was then a province, Cisalpine Gaul; it was not until a few years after Catullus's death that the inhabitants acquired the full rights of Roman citizenship. Verona had been a Gallic town, but must be supposed to have been more or less completely romanised by the time Catullus knew it.

Catullus's family was well off. They entertained the governor of the province, which was no doubt expensive. It was natural that when Catullus went to Rome, where he settled, he should mix in the best society and consequently feel poor. His life is described in his poems or, if it is not, we know nothing about it. He made at least one long journey out of Italy, to Bythinia, where he joined the staff of Memmius who was propraetor. There are verses to bear witness that he was profoundly touched by the visit to his brother's tomb in the Troad, and by the association with the spot where Europe and Asia met. Of course for him this was the site of the Trojan War. By habit very much a metropolitan Roman, the remoter frontiers of the world were often in his imagination (VII, XLVI, LXIII, LXV, LXVIIIA, CI).

It was the world of Julius Caesar. Caesar, who was perhaps sixteen years his senior, was that governor of Cisalpine Gaul whom his father entertained; Catullus was near enough to the man who was re-making the world to see the man as well as his public actions. By some commentators Catullus is supposed to have had an unaffected admiration for Cicero; I do not read XLIX that way. It would have been surprising if he had been at the feet of that man of so many words, who as well as being an orator was a versifier in a tradition Catullus was in the process of extinguishing.

I am not competent to discuss the nature of the literary revolution Catullus effected. It has been the subject of studies by a contemporary scholar (K.F. Quinn, *The Catullan Revolution*). Catullus was a student of the Alexandrian poets; there are numerous references to Callimachus (Battiades), and LXVI is a translation of a poem of Callimachus of which some fragments remain. The attractions of Alexandrian sophistication, at the point in Roman literary history when Ennius and Plautus were being relegated, are obvious enough. Most significant for us, 'Catullus has evolved a style that appears not just simple and direct, but frequently slangy and at times ostentatiously obscene.' (R.F. Quinn, in *Critical Essays on Roman Literature*, edited by J.P. Sullivan, 1962, p.47.)

The obscenity of Catullus has long been a stumbling-block. There are now perhaps those for whom any obscenity is, *prima facie*, the mark of a good thing. They are far from understanding the mind of Catullus. On the other hand it will not do to talk of 'poems which do not lend themselves to comment in English' and omit them, as C.J. Fordyce does – admittedly in an edition (1961) intended for universities and schools. The poems have produced some comic blushes in grown-up scholars. Nettleship (*Lectures and Essays*, 1885, p.93) says:

> But, as Mr Munro wisely warns us, the kind of charges brought by Catullus against Caesar are in no way to be taken seriously.

– 'in no way' is rather rich –

> It cannot be too often repeated that much of the indecency of the classical poets and orators was purely conventional, and carried no slur on the character either of the writer who uttered it or of the person whom he attacked.

Alexander Guarinus (1521) was probably better placed to understand his author. I have not had access to his commentary, but it was extensively used by Robinson Ellis, of whose work (1876) it is impossible to speak too highly, and who says of him:

> No doubt modern taste is offended by the plainness, not to say grossness of his explanations; which indeed perpetually suggest that he was illustrating the corruptions of Catullus's time by observations drawn from his own.

Reading Catullus one is brought face to face with the Roman world. By Virgil and Horace the blinds were drawn; they tried to make out that the human race was all right, as the *divus Augustus* made out that he had achieved an eternal political settlement. In the world of Julius Caesar the lid was off; and Catullus is, among other things, the poet of that age. His charges (*pace* Nettleship) are to be taken seriously. The legionaries sang:

> Ecce Caesar nunc triumphat, qui subegit Gallias.
> Nicomedes non triumphat, qui subegit Caesarem.

The sexual morals of the ancient world are not those of our own. Two things alone – and there are others – serve to make an absolute difference: the existence of slavery and the fact that Christianity had, if I may so express myself, not yet been invented. The birth of Christ was an event, not to be denied by us who come afterwards, however we squirm.

The poems of Catullus are full of personal allusions. There is no need to insist on those which relate to Lesbia, whether she was Clodia or another like her. There is an even more radical concern with Eros, and one is left wondering what the gods meant to a sophisticated Roman, as they were fading. Obviously LXIII (*The Attis*) is a crucial poem. It has the air of having a high personal import; what that was we cannot exactly know. The worship of the Magna Mater had been introduced into Rome during the Second Punic War (218-202 BC), and Catullus's friend Caecilius wrote a poem on the same subject (XXXV). One may still have the suspicion that the life of Catullus's poem owes something to the breath of the east he must have felt in Bythinia, and something to a more personal experience, there or elsewhere.

The *Ars Poetica* in English Literature

'A vast bibliography now blocks the road to the *Ars Poetica*.' That is what Professor C.O. Brink says, and he has read as much of it as anybody.* He has given a good deal of attention to Horace's sources, for there were 'vast bibliographies' in those days too, although time has, not unmercifully, erased most of them. The point is that the *Ars* was written against the background of a tradition of literary criticism already several centuries old, for Horace (65 BC – 8 BC) did not live at the beginning of time. Indeed the library at Alexandria must have suffered from many of the same disadvantages as those of an American university. Classical scholars properly look among the rubble for indications of the way Horace's thought was formed. For the student of English literature there is another pursuit. This is to trace the influence of the *Ars* on the formation of English literature. The seventeenth and eighteenth centuries are the high points of this influence and, many would say, of our literature. It was in the nineteenth century, as Professor Brink himself observes, that Horace's literary criticism 'suffered an eclipse'. 'The link with the Horatian tradition had snapped.' Before that, poets and literary critics paid attention to what Horace was saying and to the way he said it. He was reckoned a great practitioner and it was thought that his advice might be of practical use. After that, 'both the teaching and the presentation became irrelevant or suspect'. The Romantic and Victorian periods were upon us. Horace became more part of a strange scholastic cult than of the living world of letters. Neither Horace nor Virgil re-emerged in the re-orientation of English verse which followed the work of the Imagists. Pound preferred, quite rightly for the technical purposes then in view, the several directnesses of Ovid and Catullus.

A way back to the two greatest Augustans is now practicable. It is also a way back to a more familiar reading of a good deal in the literature of the seventeenth and eighteenth centuries. For to read the writers of those times as freshly as they can still be read one must at least have some understanding of how the Roman Augustans came to be treated as friends about the house. The key work in this connection is the *Ars Poetica*.

The *Ars Poetica* did not suddenly break upon the modern world

---

* C.O. Brink, *Horace on Poetry*, C.U.P., vol. 1, *Prolegomena to the Literary Epistles*, 1963; vol. II, *The Ars Poetica*, 1971.

at the Renaissance. It seems never to have been entirely lost. This does not mean that its importance was continuously recognized from the Augustan age to the sixteenth century. The perspectives of its occasional readers – mainly, no doubt, in monasteries in southern Europe – did not include a clear view of classical literature. That is an understatement; such books as the *Ars* were usually lost in a jumble, as the masterpieces of modern Europe will perhaps be lost in a jumble in the great technological libraries of the future. All one can say is that there was a relatively large number of copies in circulation whereas Catullus disappeared completely from view and we owe the text of his work to a single manuscript.

There are references to the *Ars Poetica* in a number of medieval writers. Chaucer makes one or two but, although he had a certain interest in the subject-matter, they were probably at second-hand. With the spread of printing, the *Ars* like the rest of Horace became a book in wide circulation and often the subject of learned commentary. It did not make a prominent appearance in the English literature of the sixteenth century; Wyatt and Sidney learned more from contemporary Italy and France than directly from classical Rome. The movement to make use of classical metres in English verse was part of a wider Renaissance movement and owed no special debt to Horace. Perhaps the impact of the *Ars* could not be felt until the achievements of Elizabethan literature had given poets a certain bulk of good contemporary work to reflect upon, and a degree of sophistication which made the sophistication of Horace's own comments more accessible to them.

For in a sense the solemn seeking of a set of rules in the *Ars*, which has gone on intermittently throughout the centuries since it was written, has obscured the nature of this remarkable little work from all but wily readers at certain pitches of civilization. Rules always deceive the pedantic, because they get taken for wilful instructions when they are in fact the laws of the material. Many of the generalizations which can be elicited from the *Ars* are indeed, as commentators have copiously illustrated, less Horace's own than the findings of a tradition. It is only very ignorant people who dream of an absolute originality in such matters. One has to be ill-informed, or like so many people in the modern world to make a living out of pretending to see novelty where there is none, to imagine that individual contributions in any field of thought are really revolutionary. The contribution of

Horace was neither to lay down a set of absolute prescriptions nor to upset the course of Latin literature. Indeed that literature went into decline not long after his day, apparently without benefiting from his advice.

The valuable thing about the *Ars* is the presence of a mind immensely accomplished in the practice of literature, and with a just appreciation of the point it occupied among the performances of the time. Horace's mind was not only equally but – a much rarer thing – simultaneously critical and creative; he had besides, like Swift, an experience of the world which put him beyond the reach of certain sorts of pomposity, even in literary matters. It is pointed out by Ford Madox Ford – and wherever he got it from, it is an excellent point, which has been overlooked by many scholars – that when one reads how Horace threw away his shield at Philippi (*Odes* II. 7) one should remember that it was tactful in the days of Augustus to make out that no one would have wanted to oppose Caesar seriously. Horace had been subjected to all the pressure of great events and if he came out fortunate he was also well able to appreciate his good fortune. It is from a very ripe and wary mind that we have the *Ars Poetica*, and it was Ben Jonson, who was not always drinking at the Mermaid but had been a soldier in the Low Countries and had in London been subjected to the pressures of the religious politics of his time, who first put Horace's little masterpiece firmly at the centre of the literary scene in England. Jonson was thirteen years younger than Shakespeare. Spenser had been dead several years and there was a lot in English poetry to look back on when, in 1604, Jonson made his first version of the *Ars*. He was neither at the beginning nor the end of his own work, but in full production.

Yet though in Jonson the *Ars* had, so to speak, found the right man, it had not altogether found the right moment for its assimilation into English. Jonson's version followed the Latin doggedly and we do not really have the spectacle of the play of his mind upon Horace's – of which we should have seen more, no doubt, if his preface, which was in the promising form of a dialogue with John Donne, had not, most unfortunately, been lost in a fire. Indeed the version has had the misfortune to call out unfavourable comment from the two greatest English critics in historical line after Jonson – Dryden and Samuel Johnson. Dryden, in the preface to the *Translations from Ovid's Epistles* (1680) is severe and, incidentally, more in the spirit of Horace than Jonson himself.

He notes the literal nature of Jonson's version, and comments that "'tis almost impossible to translate verbally, and well, at the same time', and that Latin certainly does not admit of such treatment. He goes on:

> In short, the verbal copier is encumbered with so many difficulties at once, that he can never disentangle himself from all. He is to consider, at the same time, the thought of his author, and his words, and to find out the counterpart to each in another language; and besides this, he is to confine himself to the compass of numbers, and the slavery of rhyme. 'Tis much like dancing on ropes with fettered legs: a man may shun a fall by using caution; but the gracefulness of motion is not to be expected: and when we have made the best of it, 'tis but a foolish task; for no sober man would put himself into a danger for the applause of escaping without breaking his neck. We see Ben Jonson could not escape obscurity in his literal translation of Horace, attempted in the same compass of lines: nay, Horace himself could scarce have done it to a Greek poet.

Dr Johnson was even more merciless; he spoke of the translation as an 'absurd labour of construing into rhyme' (*The Idler*, No. 69). None the less, Ben Jonson did bring the *Ars* before the English literary public in such a way that it could not thereafter be ignored, and he may be said thereby to have opened a literary epoch. Of course it is not only in this translation that the impact of Horace on Jonson is to be seen. It is felt in the *Discoveries*, his posthumous book of prose jottings and indeed much more widely in the temper of his poetical work. It is in his sympathy with the Horatian literary temper, and its singular combination of the inventive and the critical, that the real reach of Jonson's literary influence is felt. For a whole generation, and perhaps more, Jonson exercised in the seventeenth century something like the decisive influence of Ezra Pound in the twentieth. For this reason along, his tips as to what was worth reading, especially something so immediately relevant to the poet's task as the *Ars*, were not likely to be thrown away.

Right at the beginning of its voyage, Jonson's translation of the *Ars* attracted the adherence of a younger contemporary who was one of the most remarkable minds of his age. Lord Herbert of Cherbury, who was not talkative as a poet, wrote these lines 'To his Friend Ben. Johnson, of his Horace made English':

'Twas not enough, *Ben Johnson*, to be thought
Of English Poets best, but to have brought
In greater state, to their acquaintance, one
So equal to himself and thee, that none
Might be thy second, while thy Glory is,
To be the *Horace* of our times and his.

Carew, in a poem which gently reproves Jonson for 'an immodest rage' against his detractors – after all the sign of a certain lack of magnanimity – refers with admiration to the Jonsonian practice, and Horatian precept, of polishing work to produce 'terser poems'. Jonson's great energies, and no doubt the necessity of earning his living, often burst through his own and Horace's doctrines, but it was the widely diffused critical element in Jonson's verse, his aspiration after lucidity and polish, which attracted younger men who might well think that some such elements were needed after the more disorderly splendours of the Elizabethan age had played themselves out – much as Lionel Johnson and his friends might aim at harder and neater work after the explosions of the nineteenth century. Herrick explicitly called on Ben Johnson to help him write:

When I a verse shall make,
Know I have praid thee,
For old *Religions* sake,
Saint *Ben* to aide me.

Neatness is one of the virtues of Herrick, and although that is not a virtue that can stand on its own it is not a negligible one and something that is lacking in our enjoyment of the literature of the seventeenth century if a taste for the more important figures of Herbert, Vaughan and Crashaw should lead us to neglect the *Hesperides*. It was the school of Jonson rather than the school of Donne which had the sense of the direction in which English literature was developing, for better or worse but inevitably, in concert with wider European movements and the development of science, and it is worth while reflecting on the fact that the intellectually more curious Donne now interests us because he looks backwards on the Middle Ages as well as forward to the Age of Science.

It was in the management of the heroic couplet that the new direction of literature was most clearly marked, and the current became so overwhelming that Johnson's *Poets* starts with Cowley and Denham – by what seems to us an extraordinary trick of perspective, the only poets Johnson notices before Milton. Cowley was, as Johnson himself remarks, a follower of Donne rather than of Jonson, but his following was superficial and the temper of the man is better shown in his prose, which has much of the pragmatic quietness of the late seventeenth century about it. Denham wrote some Cavalier songs but his title to fame – which for well over a century was reckoned considerable – was that he put the heroic couplet on a footing which the eighteenth century regarded as proper, that is to say, he used it with more regularity than his predecessors. Denham's own work shows a fairly continuous progress in this direction; as Johnson has it: 'It will afford that pleasure which arises from the observation of a man of judgment naturally right forsaking bad copies by degrees, and advancing towards a better practice, as he gains more confidence in himself.' The new correctness went beyond any practice of Ben Jonson's, but that is a poor reason for denying his influence. It was in fact the main solution which succeeding writers found to the technical problems of the disarray of Elizabethan and Jacobean literature and the development of a simplified, and one might say impoverished, notion of rationality. Horace was to become, in England as in France – with Pope as with Boileau – the key Roman poet of the self-styled reasonable world, and if the development of the heroic couplet could owe nothing to him directly, the spirit in which the movement took place owed a great deal, for Horace, in relation to earlier Latin literature, stood in precisely the position of those who were seeking to make the literature of France and England 'more correct' than it had hitherto been. It could be added that in France, at any rate, the gathering forces of centralization and despotism provided a remarkable social parallel to the Augustan settlement in Rome.

Roscommon and Waller are the two other principal improvers of the heroic couplet before Dryden. 'Waller was smooth' became a critical commonplace of the eighteenth century, and Waller *was* smooth, as everyone knows from his unforgettable song, 'Goe, lovely Rose', which Pound took up again in *Hugh Selwyn Mauberley*. Waller had digested the *Ars*, and the verses he wrote in commendation of Roscommon's translation of it showed that he thought of Horace's work as contributing directly to the movement away from the 'negligence' of the older poets.

Horace will our superfluous branches prune,
Give us new rules, and set our harps in tune.

The whole fifty or so lines of Waller's commendation are replete with indications taken from the *Ars* itself. Roscommon's translation, curiously enough, was not in the now fashionable couplet but in blank verse, and his preface shows that in choosing this medium he had in mind the difficulties which Ben Jonson had encountered and which, he said, made him 'want a comment in many places'. Roscommon's 'chief care' was 'to write intelligibly', for he thought 'Horace must be read seriously, or not at all.' The version is not inspiriting; Roscommon's contribution to criticism in verse was rather in his *Essay on Translated Verse*, which is in heroic couplets and is, incidentally, very much a development of notions to be found in the *Ars*. Such essays are much out of fashion, but, although the content offers no great novelties, it is as interesting as that of many a critical essay warmly recommended to students, and it is at least presented with such elegance that no one's style will be the worse for reading it.

A much more interesting version of the *Ars* was produced, only a few years after Roscommon's, by John Oldham, the satirist whose death at the age of thirty Dryden celebrated in some of his most moving lines and whom he clearly recognized as a momentous loss to English poetry. Oldham felt it necessary to apologize for following so hard on Roscommon's heels – after all, Roscommon was an earl and he was only a schoolmaster – though his real concern was to excuse himself for coming after Ben Jonson, still regarded as so great an authority 'that whatever he did is held as Sacred'. Oldham's justification of his new attempt was 'putting Horace into more modern Dress than hitherto he has appeared in, that is, by making him speak as if he were living and writing now. I therefore resolved,' he says, 'to alter the Scene from Rome to London, and to make use of English Names of Men, Places and Customs, where the Parallel would decently permit, which I conceived would give a kind of new Air to the Poem, and render it more agreeable to the Relish of the Present Age,' He explains that he has not 'been over-nice in keeping the Words of the Original, for that were to transgress a Rule therein contained'. But he insists that he has been strict as to the sense, in such a manner that Horace himself would forgive him. It is interesting that Oldham expresses a special care to retain 'the easie and familiar way of writing which is peculiar to Horace in his Epistles'. This he sees as Horace's 'proper Talent above any of Mankind'. Oldham's eye was as much on the manner as on any set of rules, and in this he shows himself closer to Horace than Jonson was, as indeed the spirit of the age was growing closer to that of Horace's times. True to his scheme, Oldham replaces references to the older Latin poets by the names of Spenser and Chaucer, and Lee and Dryden serve for contemporary references. The whole reads well, and there are outbreaks of the vigour which appears in the *Satyrs upon the Jesuits*. As for the suicidal poets of Horace's closing section:

> Troth, I could be content an Act might pass,
> Such poets should have leave, whene'er they please,
> To die and rid us of our Grievances.
> A God's name let'em hang, or drown, or choose
> What other way they will themselves dispose,
> Why should we Life against their Wills impose?

and a few lines later:

> But certain 'tis, for such a crack-brain'd Race,
> *Bedlam* or *Hogsdon* is the fittest place.

There is not only vigour here, but a freedom of handling which looks forward to Johnson's imitations of Juvenal and a conversational style which is eminently Horatian and looks forward to Pope.

One could hold it against Oldham – it is difficult to think of any other charge – that the existence of his version perhaps prevented Dryden making one. Dryden, like Oldham, had a trenchancy which is not altogether Horatian, but he was the greatest practitioner of poetry in the new tradition. He has claims also to be the greatest English translator in verse, or the second, with Chaucer in the first place – 'Grant translateur, noble Geffroy Chaucier,' in the words of his contemporary, Eustache Deschamps. Dryden did versions of Ovid, Juvenal, Persius, Horace, Lucretius and others, including Chaucer himself, for whom he had practically a veneration, and his great masterpiece was the complete works of Virgil, with an *Aeneid* which rivals that of Gavin Douglas himself. It would have been interesting to see what he would have made of the *Ars*. It was a book in his mind, as appears here and there in the prose works, but Dryden in his maturity probably thought, with reason, that he knew too much about writing plays to take much notice of the distinguished Augustan who merely advised from the wings. In the world of Dryden, and still more in that of

Pope and Swift, we are indeed among people who feel so much at home with the Augustans that they treat them on a footing of equality. There is a touch of social tone about this, though perhaps only Swift, of the three, managed – at some cost – to maintain that stance in the society about him. And Swift liked to treat Dryden a little *de haut en bas*. He was, anyhow, too much a Tory and a High Churchman to be over-impressed by anyone's theories. 'Get scraps of *Horace* from your friends' he advised in *On Poetry: A Rhapsody*

> And have them at your Fingers Ends.
> Learn Aristotle's Rules by Rote,
> And at all Hazards boldly quote:
> Judicious *Rymer* oft review:
> Wise Dennis, and profound Bossu.
> Read all the *Prefaces* of *Dryden*,
> For these our Criticks much confide in,
> (Though merely writ at first for filling
> To raise the Volume's Price, a Shilling.)

Although Dryden did not translate the *Ars*, he did translate Boileau's *Art Poétique*, a work which would certainly not have been written if the *Ars* had not existed.

By the time we get to Pope the Horatian tradition had been so completely absorbed that it was natural that he should write his own *Essay on Criticism*, not translating but as it were starting afresh from a contemporary but entirely Horatian point of view. After that, and although poets like other moderately educated persons in the eighteenth century, continue to know their Horace, it is to Pope rather than to Horace that they look as the source of critical guidance. The eighteenth century are and slept Pope, and one knows to what depths that obsession in the end took them, though the climb out of them, with Smart and Cowper as well as with Blake and Wordsworth, began earlier than is sometimes credited. What is still less credited, but is worth reflection and some exploratory reading, is that all is not servility in the verse of the mid-eighteenth century, and that there were minor figures who played even in the shadow of Pope. Robert Lloyd is one of them. His elegance has all the easiness of the eighteenth century and none of the pedantry. He may be said to have learned from Horace by way of Swift. If writing well and pleasantly were accounted a virtue, he would still be read. After the turn of the century there is only a rearguard action. Byron's *Hints from Horace*, written in 1811 before he had found his true vein in *Don Juan*, is in this class. Landor resuscitates Horace to talk with Virgil, but merely as a figure in a literary dialogue, not as a critical force. Horace had been taken into English literature so completely as to cease to be noticeable. The nineteenth century, like the twentieth so far, did without the *Ars*.

The case for pushing this famous little work out once more into the stream of contemporary literature is the extraordinary relevance of much that Horace has to say, in our situation, and the remedial wholesomeness of his tone. There is no point in arguing the case. It is made, by implication, in the version itself and in the notes.

Notes to the *Ars Poetica*

The *Ars Poetica* is in the form of a letter to the Pisos – a father and two sons. Nobody knows who they were. The poem itself points to their being a family who dabbled in literature. No doubt they were well-to-do.

The Pisos wanted to write poetic plays. There can have been little prospect of their succeeding. They could look back on the classical Greek drama, and on Plautus and Terence, but the Augustan age had no plays to speak of. When Horace says he will give advice but not write himself (1.302) he means he won't write plays.

It can be assumed that Horace did not think that his advice would make poets of his correspondents. The irony of this situation has sometimes been missed. The *Ars* is not a set of rules but a series of observations by a poet on his art and on those who professed to practise it. It may be compared with *A Stray Document* reprinted in Ezra Pound's volume of essays, *Make It New*.

1-13. A literary work, like a painting, must be all of a piece. Horace thinks of figures in a painting rather than of the picture as a whole, perhaps because of the predominance of sculpture in the ancient world and certainly because he takes for granted the Graeco-Roman tradition of the well-proportioned male or female body as the key to aesthetics. Nothing could be more grotesque, he says, than a human head on the neck of a horse, or the top of a woman joined to the tail of a fish. The heraldic beasts had not yet grown, as they were to do in the course of centuries, out of the lions and birds on Roman tombs. It would be to lose Horace's point, so far as writing is concerned, to insist on the comparison with the already decadent visual art of his day. It remains true that the literary work must be harmonious, as the human body is harmonious, in the relationships between its parts.

Cork Street, London W.1., is one of the centres of the trade in modern paintings.

14-24.   Because a book must be a whole, there is no place in it for 'purple patches' – beautiful descriptions of beautiful things put in for their own sake. They will get in the way of the development of the story or the argument or the main drift of the poem. It is because 'the grove and altar of Diana' is an attractive and moving spectacle that its introduction should be treated with suspicion. So it is with the popular and exciting themes of our own day. It is easy to excite a momentary interest with the commonplaces of sex or politics. Only the writer should not imagine that because his reader responds to such things that he is responding to a *poem*; or indeed that he has written a poem at all.

25-33.   The Pisos could easily try too hard to get it right. Avoiding faults is also a matter of art, and therefore for those who have learned already. A discouraging the realistic doctrine.

34-9.   Horace speaks here of a craftsman who must have undertaken sub-contracts for sculpture. He made marvellous fingernails but was no good at producing a work as a whole. The point, however, is simply that the artist or poet has to keep the whole work in mind, not just a particular element. That is what art is about.

40-7.   These lines contain the essential directions for the poet or indeed any writer. Find what you can write about and you have solved your problem. Of course the aspiring writer has to face the possibility that the answer may be, Nothing. At any rate the beginning, as the continuation, of literary capacity involves a certain self-knowledge. Nothing is further from it, than the intoxications of publicity and reputation.

48-74.   Whether or not the poet can be said to keep the language alive, the language is alive in the poem and a language which has virtually ceased to live ceases to produce poets, though it may be prolific in the writers and explainers of verse. The question here is what the individual writer can do for the life of the language. If one has not a certain confidence or at any rate hope that he can do something, one has no business with poetry at all. To make the old word new one has only to use it properly. A word not only carries meaning but derives significations from the context in which it is put. The full meaning of a word in a poem is the product of its history, including the current usage, and its location. How far one can increase the charge on a word by deliberate placing is questionable. Horace is very precise in what he says on this subject. 'You will have said well' is how he puts it – *dixeris egregie* – if it turns out that the way you have placed the word in fact renews it. The novel impression is a critical test you can apply when you have written your poem rather than a trick which can be recommended to anyone wanting to turn out a good one. Wilfully or ambitiously putting in clever meanings is likely to offend against the over-all effect which Horace has already characterized as the essential of a work of art.

Horace is as far as he could be from any plea for a special and slightly antiquarian literary language. You may even invent terms if necessary, as the older writers did. The older writers Horace mentions are Caecilius, of whose plays there are only fragmentary remains, and Plautus. The contemporaries he mentions are Virgil and Varius, the latter presumably the Varius Rufus whose only surviving distinction is to have been the friend of both Horace and Virgil, though he was well known as a poet in his day. The liberty of inventing new terms is to be used sparingly, and with a proper sense of the root meanings. What is implied, therefore, is not the heedless seizing of any terms which happen to be flying around or come into the writer's head, but the liberty of what by the standards of the twentieth century must be considered a learned or at any rate well instructed man, who habitually has in mind historical usages and derivations. Might one say that much current writing, here hardly less than in America, exhibits a thinness which is evidence of the lack of such preoccupations? The causes of these deficiencies go deeper than academic syllabuses, but there is a connection with the fading of Latin from the educated mind or, some would say simply, the fading of the educated mind in our technological barbarism. One may recommend the use of Johnson's dictionary, as an ordinary working tool, to the apprentice writer – an expression which includes all writers worth their salt.

75-101. In this section Horace rather briskly goes over some of the traditional classifications of ancient literature – epic, elegiac, lyric, tragic and comic. He is conveying information well known to those he is addressing, and to be found in any textbook. But he makes two critical points. The first is that anyone who aspires to be a poet had better understand thoroughly these classic distinctions of genre. The second is that, in the last resort, they are not to be taken too seriously – or at any rate the academic classification cannot determine what the poet writes; only the requirements of the subject can do that.

The English verse forms of blank verse, ballad metre, heroic couplets and so on do not correspond with the classical forms Horace speaks of. Moreover their separate uses are somewhat lost sight of in contemporary literature. It remains true that an understanding of the use made of these various forms is an essential part of the poet's education.

102-21. When people believed in philosophy they used to argue about aesthetics. What was the nature of the beautiful? As this tradition declined, it was possible to have a prolonged success with any sufficiently tarty expression. Clive Bell, admittedly with the initial advantage of being a family member of the Bloomsbury circle, did well for years with 'significant form'. This was promulgated in a book called simply *Art*; there was another from the same hand called *Civilisation* so that really one hadn't to look any further for one's education. However unsatisfactory the formulas of aesthetics and its derivatives might have been, there remains an invincible passion for generalizations about what makes a poem work. The negatives are the best bet, and Horace is an early winner with the dictum, *non satis est pulchra esse poemata*: it is not enough for poems to be beautiful. In one sense it is nonsense, for if a poem succeeds it is reasonable to call it beautiful. No doubt Horace's habitual irony is not far from the scene: what *you* call beautiful is not enough – smooth, polished verse, without flaws and without anything else of interest. There is always a good deal of beauty of that sort to be found in the successful writers of any era; it fades soon enough. What Horace is saying is that a poem will not move us except through the natural sympathy between one human being and another, as one smiles when smiled at. Moreover, he says, in dramatic representations the words must answer to the movements of the mind and to the quirks of social tone. No doubt this does not take us very far, but if one must talk in terms of aesthetics, it points to a humane basis for that science.

122-30. The predominance of traditional themes in ancient literature seems odd to us. We set great store by 'originality' even if we do not get much of it. To accept a traditional theme is to admit the humane basis of poetry to which Horace draws attention in lines 102-21. The traditional theme is one of permanent or at any rate enduring interest, common not only to all people living in a particular place at a particular time but to successive generations in a particular civilization. It represents stores of common mind which go beyond the 'I smile, you smile' of line 104. The loss of these stores is a characteristic of the modern world, deplored or welcomed according to taste. It is the inevitable product of the rapid mixing of cultures, itself the inevitable product of improved transport. One advantage of the use of traditional themes is that it removes at any rate some of the ground for bogus claims to originality; any novelty has to be in the handling. The invention of 'new' characters and situations anyhow by no means keeps up with the gabble of new names. Most characters in plays or novels are faint indications of well-known types.

131-55. In the twentieth century the most thorough discussion of plot has been in relation to the novel, and the discussion to be found *passim* in the works of Ford Madox Ford has an interest which extends beyond the novel, as Horace's discussion here has relevance beyond the dramatic poem. Work in every genre has to be arranged, and plot is only arrangement.

156-80. The importance of this reminder that dramatic characters must be differentiated according to age is not lessened by the too exhilarating geriatrics which insists upon the youthfulness of age, nor by excessive hopefulness about the maturity of youth.

181-89. The forbearance which kept violent and revolting incidents off stage, and made them instead the subject of narratives spoken by the characters, is far from the customs of the modern stage, as indeed from the general spirit of contemporary literature, which is favourable to the widest possible display not only of the violent but of the erotic. The question is how much distraction the work of art can bear. Given that a work of art must be some sort of unity, any disproportionate effect of any part will tend to destroy it. Television has gone some way towards reinstating the popular pleasure in violent spectacles of which the public was deprived by the abolition of public hangings. The arts need not therefore feel any duty to compete in this branch of therapy. The case of public displays of fornication, and its approximations, is different and there are perhaps those who hold that such spectacles should be made so widespread that they are as ordinary as lighting a cigarette – though perhaps that would be evidence of a certain biological lassitude. Meanwhile erotic movements, like acts of violence, tend to produce disproportionate effects and to destroy the coherence of the work of art. The limits of classic propriety in this matter are perhaps represented by Wycherley's play, *The Country Wife*, where the lady is carried off stage to the next room with deliberately inadequate protestations.

It may be added that the humane reciprocity (the 'I smile, you smile' of line 104) is at least threatened by violent or erotic display on the stage. The stage narrative, as part of a dialogue or triologue, on the other hand puts the most intractable subjects back into the field of universal social reactions. There is a further possibility, rarely achieved except in the context of a settled tradition, of such formalization, with the help of dance or otherwise, that the action ceases to be an imitation and becomes a symbol.

190-93. The classic five acts have long given way to three, which is certainly a no less eligible vehicle for the movement of the play, though it can be argued that it gives less room for development and for the static qualities which are also a feature of the classic drama.

194-202. The attitudes here recommended to the chorus are the opposite of those exhibited by the popular media, which prefer to stir up anger and praise luxury.

203-19. Horace notes the habitual bad taste of the mixed urban audience, the only one now subsisting.

220-48. This passage deals with the satyric drama, which was historically connected with tragedy and was, according to one authority (Müller, quoted in Macleane's edition of Horace) 'not a comedy, but a playful tragedy. Its subjects were taken from the same class of adventures of Bacchus and the heroes as tragedy; but they were so treated in connection with rude objects of outward nature that the presence and participation of rustic petulant satyrs seemed quite appropriate.'

249-71. How important is the theory of metre? The 'rules' of metre are the practice of poets, who learn from the practice of other poets and sometimes contribute their own inventions. The dependence of Latin literature on the Greek for so many of its forms, as well no doubt as the pullulation of critics and grammarians as Greek literature declined, made the Romans somewhat selfconscious on this subject. The 'Augustan' age in which Horace wrote was, as compared with the earlier literature, one in which technical progress was in the direction of propriety and polish, as it was in the ages of Dryden and Pope – which does not mean that the 'Augustan' writers, either in Rome or in England, were better poets than their predecessors. Horace was, in any case, a great master of versification, but his comments in this section are mere stuff derived from the grammarians and do not let us into the secrets of his invention. One might wonder, indeed, from the practice of almost all poets in all languages, whether there is a form of technical discourse which would do this. Certainly metrical analysis is no more than an abstraction from the performance which makes a poet's work of interest to us, and a laborious versifier could produce verses which contained any number of metrical wonders and were none the less insipid. It remains a fact that the theory of metre is of intermittent but persistent interest to poets. The prestige of Greek and Latin literature has naturally given rise to many attempts to force modern languages into the straitjackets of what were believed to be their rules. The most intelligent discussion of English verse in the light of the Latin rules is that of Thomas Campion, *Observations in the Art of English Poesie*, 1602. Campion started from his experience as a poet who set his own songs to music, or perhaps invented words and music simultaneously. 'In joining of words to harmony there is nothing more offensive to the ear than to place a long syllable with a short note, or a short syllable with a long note.' His discussion of quantitive verse – the length and shortness of syllables and their arrangement – goes on from there.

Campion's own poems – which are among the most accomplished in the language – for the most part use rhyme and stress, in spite of his theories, for their predominant structure, but his ear was never dead to the length of syllables. And indeed, it is only by abstraction that we can talk of English verse as being 'stressed' or 'rhymed and stressed' as if this excluded all other elements. Historically, one can distinguish at least three elements: *stress*, derived from the Anglo-Saxon element and continued in such medieval works as *Piers Plowman; number of syllables*, to which French influences in the work of Chaucer and others gave a high importance; and *quantity*, which is little more than a *post hoc* observation based on classical models, the contribution of the Renaissance. But the effect of these elements is modified and supported by rhyme, assonance and alliteration, used with varying degrees of regularity and irregularity, as well as by the interplay of stanza-form, syntax, and over-all meaning. If one does schematic analyses of poems it should, therefore, only be in order to forget them again.

272-81. Greek tragedy originated in the dithyrambic songs at the Bacchic festivals. An actor independent of the chorus was at some stage introduced and took various parts under a mask. The shows on a waggon at the wine-harvest probably had more to do with the origin of comedy.

282-91. It cannot be said that Horace has hit on a plausible explanation why Latin literature was not up to the standard of the Greek. If a little more toil and tedium would have done the trick, later Latin writers certainly made up for it, as the substance of what they had to say diminished to nothingness.

292-304. No doubt the practical point behind the advice in lines 286-91 was an attempt to get it into the heads of those whom it might concern that they could not become poets merely by opening their big mouths. Horace now goes on to say that the need for inspiration is not to be taken as an excuse for imbecility or idleness. He concludes with a heavy joke about his own role as a theoretical guide.

305-18. It is a sobering reflection, which was probably not absent from Horace's mind, that Socrates prided himself on knowing *nothing*. Poets might well know that. The general drift of the passage, which continues the didacticism of line 282 onwards, is once more that the poet should use his head before he opens his mouth. Being wise does not mean being born that way, as many claim to be, but applying oneself to the works of the philosophers and others to find out what better men have thought. Nor should the poet imagine that he is exonerated from knowing as much as other people about the world he lives in, political and military matters and the like. He is not to acquire this knowledge in order to be able to point out that everybody else is wrong, but in order to know how people in fact behave and what strings pull them. It is no less a recommended part of knowledge to know what one's own duties are and what loyalties one owes.

319-26.   Horace makes his point here by reproducing the sort of dialogue that went on between master and pupil in a Roman school. Here at least our experience is greater than Horace's and everyone could supply examples of the insane regard paid to number in our own day, forgetting that its place in reality is not more than that of *quantity* in verse. (249-71 above.)

327-39.   The poet should not only give pleasure but say something sensible.

340-52.   *Pas de perfection dans les arts* could be either a statement of fact or an injunction. While Horace has earlier insisted on the importance of revision, he here admits that even the best works have faults. He might have said, ought to have faults, for nothing is more likely to kill a work that trying to make it a treasury of individual beauties or smart phrases. Even in a writer of genius, the determination to 'load every rift with ore' – Keats's phrase – impedes that movement as a whole which is the mark of the successful work, as Keats himself discovered.

353-57.   The important critical comment here is in the last line. The test of any work of art is not to please once but to go on pleasing. It is the nearest thing to an objective test which is available in this field. Edward Fitzgerald says: 'I believe in the Vox Populi of two hundred years: still more, of two thousand.'

358-77.   Poets are always a little harsh about other people writing poems; they want attention to be reserved for the best, which would include their own. Horace says ironically that it is the right of every free and freeborn man, at a certain level of social responsibility, to write poems. We should have to give the franchise a little more widely. Innocent though the pastime of making verses may in fact be, we should beware of too much facility in claiming to write poems, for whatever claims may be made at a particular moment, fifty years later no one doubts that the number was exceedingly small. It not only begs the question, but complicates it with politics and metaphysics, to speak as if the writing of poems were part of an inalienable human right to free expression. Perhaps children should be taught to be slow to believe they have this talent.

378-83. The advice to keep a poem locked up for nine years before publishing it is one of those rules of good conduct which nobody expects will be obeyed. No doubt Horace was just seeing how far he could bully his young victims. There is no reason to suppose that revision after as long as seven or eight years is particularly fruitful, and a good deal of evidence – in Wordsworth, for example – that such tampering will merely fasify the original. That does not mean that it is not salutary to keep a poem for a decent interval in order to see what can be cut out, or whether indeed it can all be dispensed with.

384-400. The point of this somewhat *fantaisiste* account of the origins of poetry is that poetry has a role in the development of civilization and has its connections with all our most profound concerns. It is the fact of this connection which has given such currency – and such durability – to Horace's own work; and in our own day it has been the doctrine of so un-Horatian a group as the surrealists.

401-11. What training should the poet give himself? The question is worth considering, even though it is too complicated to admit of a satisfactory answer. The training of an athlete is, after all, only the final polish on a life well-endowed and hitherto well-spent, so far as fitness for a particular range of movements is concerned. What constitutes the 'well-spent', as far as the poet is concerned, is more than anyone can say. It may include the encounter with and solution of infantile and adolescent problems which everyone would avoid if he could. Poetry is so comprehensive in its subject-matter, and its wells are so deep in the psyche, that there is no reason to suppose that the 'well-spent', in the case of the poet, is in general any different from that of the rest of the world. Certainly anyone who seeks to justify particular lines of conduct on the ground that he is a poet is suspect, if for no other reason than that he will certainly not *know* that what he does will produce better poetic results than the line of conduct that he rejects. The claim by artists to particular indulgences is no better founded than that of other groups who seek to indulge themselves. The only sensible discussion about the training of the poet can be on the more or less conscious polish which corresponds to the training an athlete takes under the guidance of a trainer. Here again, many of the things the poet does must be the same as would be done by any intelligent person who seeks to be literate. For Horace the programme was simpler. It meant above all a close acquaintance with the best Greek literature. An acquaintance with the surviving corpus is still desirable, though inaccessible to most including the author of these notes. Horace does not speak very respectfully of Latin literature, though he clearly knew the older literature well. He was perhaps jealous of Catullus, to whom his one reference (in *Satires* I. 10) is slighting – though one nineteenth-century editor maintains that it is not, on the grounds that Horace refers to him much as one might refer to Tom Moore! Clearly for us some acquaintance with Latin literature is desirable, both for its own merits and because it flows through the literature of modern Europe. It is part of our mind, whether we like it or not, as, on a profounder level, Christianity is in the make of our minds whether or not we choose to think it is of any contemporary importance. In both cases any claim to even a rudimentary literacy must involve some effort to recover for oneself traces at least of the authentic image under the overlay of distorted impressions one collects casually from the world around one. As to which Latin authors it is most important for the contemporary poet to dip into, one can probably not better Pound's choice of Catullus and the Ovid of the *Metamorphoses*, with Golding's version of the latter as a good entrée to the matter and some of the manner in English. Virgil and Horace are in varying degrees unfashionable but one has in the end to try to approach them. The point is that the intelligent reader, *a fortiori* the incipient poet, can get a great deal that is of value from even limited incursions. This is the case also with recommended models in other languages, such as Dante. No doubt a facile eclecticism is one of the vices of the time, but one has to look around one and some foray into one or more other European literatures is almost indispensable for a critical sharpening of one's appreciation of work in one's own language. The 'almost' before indispensable is a saving for the exceptional case; but the fact that some intelligent people have done without this degree of instruction by comparison does not mean that it would not have been profitable for them. None the less it should be clear that no range of eclecticism can excuse or comepnsate for a lack of solid knowledge of the

359

literature of the tongue to which one was born – an initial fatality to which every writer is subject. This is hardly the place for an English syllabus, and there are properly many approaches to the high and deep points of our literature. It is part of a natural process to begin with authors you afterwards reject. To that extent one's models are negative. In so far as one looks for positive indicators, it should be in the direction of the more astringent (Swift, Dryden), the more removed from the yap of contemporary chatter (Vaughan, Herbert), the more ruminatively considered (Hooker, Burton). For technical instruction, Shakespeare is so omnicompetent as to be confusing, and there are no limits to the programme which should at least not exclude Chaucer, the ballads, Wyatt, Marlowe, Ben Jonson, Donne, Marvell, Rochester, Collins, Clough and Christina Rossetti – which is not to say that these are the ten best English writers or that they are all equally important. One's immediate starting techniques as a poet will in any case be learnt from one's somewhat older contemporaries who may not be very good and whom one will learn to discard and – properly – date one's real start as a poet from the date of that discarding.

412-30.   This is social rather than literary criticism and in spite of changed circumstances remains valid as a guide to behaviour. The risks to taste in our own day are less from wealthy individuals than from institutions ostensibly set up to promote or purvey the arts but in reality to serve other political or financial purposes. The position of men occupying posts as editors, subeditors, administrators of artistically beneficent institutions and broadcasting nuclei, provides uninterrupted comedy in our time.

431-46.   There is such a thing as the man who will give an honest and instructed critical opinion, and the poet who has one such among his friends is fortunate. It is not merely a matter of goodwill; as Horace says in line 260, 'not every critic knows when a verse sounds badly.' Horace was speaking from experience in this matter. The Quintilius he mentions was a neighbour and friend of Virgil, and that is probably how Horace got to know him.

447-67.   The comedy of the final section shows how little the manners of the marginal literary world have changed. This is social rather than literary criticism, yet not unconnected with

Horace's main theses. For if the pleasures of literature, even if not enjoyed by everyone, have a common humane basis – as is Horace's contention – the quirks and aberrations of poets deserve just the same degree of indulgence, neither more nor less, than those of the rest of the world.

For what Mr Alvarez said, see A. Alvarez, *The Savage God: A Study of Suicide*, Weidenfeld & Nicolson, 1971; Penguin, 1974.